THE REDEMPTION OF LOVE

# THE REDEMPTION OF LOVE

Rescuing Marriage and Sexuality
from the
Economics of a Fallen World

## CARRIE A. MILES

**BrazosPress**
Grand Rapids, Michigan

© 2006 by Carrie A. Miles

Published by Brazos Press
a division of Baker Publishing Group
P.O. Box 6287, Grand Rapids, MI 49516-6287
www.brazospress.com

Printed in the United States of America

Library of Congress Cataloging-in-Publication Data
Miles, Carrie A.
    The redemption of love : rescuing marriage and sexuality from the economics of a fallen world / Carrie A. Miles.
        p.      cm.
    Includes bibliographical references.
    ISBN 1-58743-150-5 (pbk.)
    1. Marriage—Religious aspects—Christianity. 2. Sex—Religious aspects—Christianity. 3. Sex role—Religious aspects—Christianity. 4. Family—Religious aspects—Christianity. I. Title.
BV835.M533  2006
261.8′35—dc22                                                                2005024050

For Nicole and for the future

# Contents

# Introduction

Sex is a difficult word. In the early 1960s, my teacher introduced it to my fifth-grade class as referring to "male" or "female." Jokingly, she warned us to be careful about using the word around our parents, to whom it meant something else, about which she did not tell us. We knew what that something was, of course, although we didn't know much.

A few decades later, *sex* and its derivatives mean many things, and even very young children know a lot about them. In rap music, the multipurpose noun has even become a verb. Moreover, in this more complicated world, my teacher's simple definition of sex as referring to male versus female is considered incomplete, even controversial. Now we make a linguistic distinction between *sex* and *gender—sex* referring to whether one has the physical organs of a man or a woman, *gender* to one's social behavior—but an ongoing controversy over whether sex/gender differences are innate or learned implies that they might be the same thing after all. Then there are additional categories that *sex* modifies, categories to which my fifth-grade teacher paid little attention, assuming that she had even heard of them: sexual politics, sexual prerogatives, sexual identity, sexual preference, and all their subgroups: transsexual, bisexual, homosexual, heterosexual, etc.

Fortunately for me as writer and for you as reader, I am not going to drag you through a linguistic analysis. The problems of the meaning of *sex* today are not linguistic but social and spiritual. These problems of meaning now expand to include definitions of *family*, *marriage*, and *morality* as well. Moreover, these controversies contain in them the implicit redefinition of yet another word, one that is even more important than the others—*love*.

The past one hundred years have brought massive change in the hard-to-define but vital human institutions of love, sex, marriage, and family, particularly in the developed Western world. Some of these changes have been positive, but many others are proving destructive of marriage, the well-being of children, and the happiness of individuals. "Love" as caring concern for another person is being swamped by more self-centered attachments. Although early Christianity effectively reformed ancient marriage and household patterns, the contemporary church has not yet found a way to stave off the decadence of today.

As an organizational psychologist, I work as a consultant to troubled workplaces. I have found that when confronted with a problem, clients are eager to rush in with solutions. Unfortunately, often they lack a clear understanding of what the problems really are, and so their solutions prove to be worthless or to make matters worse. My most important task is often not to provide solutions but to help my clients slow down and accurately define the problem and its causes. Once they have a clear grasp of those, the correct solutions are often obvious.

In an analogous way, our culture is full of problem solvers who have jumped too soon to solutions to dilemmas that fall under the general category of love: sex, relationships, marriage, gender norms, and family, including women's employment outside the home and questions of how to balance parenting with career. On the liberal side, these solutions almost always prescribe more freedom for some categories of people, often at the expense of the freedom of other kinds of people. On the conservative side the solutions include attempts to shore up the old sexual morality and gender norms. Such solutions have done little to slow the tide of change, and some have made the problems worse while damaging the credibility and authority of those proposing them. As normative institutions, churches face the greatest loss of credibility and authority—and frustratingly so, since social change puts them in a classic double bind: liberal churches lose authority because they accommodate social change, and conservative churches lose credibility because they resist it.

This book takes a novel approach: looking to the Bible not just for solutions to today's problems but, first, for a clear understanding of their causes. Looking for these causes, I apply to scripture the relatively new tools of socioeconomics or economic sociology—an interdisciplinary approach that has been hailed as "the new paradigm" for the social-scientific study of religion. By *economics* I do not mean things like stock prices, interest rates, or inflation. Rather, the insights and tools of the academic field of economics—defined as the study of how we "allocate scarce resources among competing ends"—can be applied to broader material constraints and incentives, recognizing that these forces influence our behavior not just in the marketplace but also in the home, church, and society. Extending an economic-type analysis to aspects of life usually considered the province of psychology or sociology enables us to understand the trade-offs people make in spending not just their money, but also their time, effort, and energy; why they behave as they do and how often; why they believe and value the things they do; how they interact with other people around these values; and how these choices shape identity. Only when we understand these material forces influencing our behaviors, beliefs, and identities can we rid ourselves, our families, and our churches of those that are worldly and destructive.

A socioeconomic analysis of what the Bible says about marriage, gender, and family works because its central story of creation, fall, and redemption asks whether we as individuals and as a society will live only by bread (materially) or by the Word of God (spiritually). Human love and relationships are inextricably woven throughout that story. Significantly, the Bible tells us that God originally intended that decisions about how to "allocate scare resources among competing ends" should have nothing to say about human love and our interactions with each other. Bountifully provided for, man and woman in creation know nothing about scarcity. One flesh, man and woman had no competing agendas. God intended that his human creation should always share this abundance in unity and joy.

In eventually choosing to turn away from God, however, man and woman suffered the physical consequences of living outside of God's abundant provision. After the fall, these tough decisions became the driving force of human life, a force that corrupted sexuality and destroyed the oneness for which man and woman were created. Socially, the fall resulted in patriarchy—the subordination of women, children, and most men to the service of the powerful few. Although contemporary critics charge religion with being the source and supporter of patriarchy, the Bible teaches exactly the opposite: patriarchy and its abuses, including the alienation of woman and man from each other, resulted from the material demands of life outside of the Creator's abundance, a state God never intended human beings to experience in the first place.

God's intent to redeem us and return us to abundance is seen in the teachings of Jesus and Paul, both of whom challenged the economic and patriarchal order of the fall. As the Christian movement transformed the economically based family, it eventually reined in the practices of polygamy, slavery, and sexual decadence and elevated the status of women. Although the "traditional" family that resulted—defined as a married couple with an employed, dominant father, a homemaking mother, and their obedient children—was strongly decried by activists in the 1960s and 1970s as patriarchal, it was a far cry from either traditional or patriarchal when contrasted with the pre-Christian family.[1]

By the late twentieth century, however, marriage and family faced a different set of challenges. As William J. Bennett writes, "Promiscuity, adultery, cohabitation, divorce and out-of-wedlock births have severely damaged the institution of marriage."[2] Peter Spring of the Family Research Council similarly notes:

> The divorce revolution has undermined the concept that marriage is a life-long commitment. As a result, there's been an epidemic of broken homes and broken families. The sexual revolution has undermined the concept that sexual relations should be confined to marriage. As a result, there's been an epidemic of cohabitation, sexually transmitted diseases, abortions, and broken hearts.
>
> The concept that childbearing should be confined to marriage has been undermined. As a result, there's been an epidemic of out-of-wedlock births, single parenthood, and fatherless children.[3]

I agree that the institutions of marriage and family have been badly damaged in the last century. But here is where the commonly accepted definition of the problem—that "revolutions," corrupt values, grand ideas, or different ways of thinking have undermined the family—fails. The error is slight and subtle: this explanation simply has cause and effect reversed. The sexual revolution, rising rates of divorce, promiscuity, and out-of-wedlock births are the results, not the cause, of the breakdown of the family. Family institutions as we once knew them were based on the economic need of farmers for labor, a need most efficiently met by having many children. In preindustrial societies, families were the original "social safety net"—indeed, there was little other available—providing all of the goods and services needed to live, from food and clothing to health care to support in old age. Often the larger the family the better, as even very young children provided important labor, and the services of older children were indispensable. Over the last two hundred years, however, technological advances eliminated the economic imperative for family. Consequently, while the average American woman in 1800 bore over seven children, by the year 2000 she would bear fewer than two. In many European countries, the number of children born is getting close to one per woman. As the material incentives and constraints that necessitated bearing children have evaporated, the institutions of family, marriage, and traditional sexual morality have all collapsed. The "problem"—the confusion, dissent, unhappiness and bad outcomes for both children and adults—that we witness today encompasses attempts to rebuild a new base to support the love, human connectedness, and concern for each other that we still crave.

This redefined statement of the problem with family today tells us that the moral institutions that we have lost were only loosely based on Christian principles in the first place. People before the divorce and sexual revolutions were not really more virtuous than we are today. Rather, they married, stayed married, and refrained from having sex or children outside of marriage partly because this is what the church taught, but even more so because these virtues were the material requirements of survival under the economic conditions that prevailed then. Understanding how these material requirements shaped the family before the twentieth century and how they have changed to produce a completely different set of sexual patterns in the twentieth and twenty-first is critical to rediscovering, and recovering, the Christian basis for marriage and family.

This understanding will make it apparent that the solution attempted by some conservative groups—reaffirming the gender-role traditionalism of preindustrial family relations—becomes at best a non sequitur in a world in which people have sex and children without a relationship at all. Defining today's worldwide problems with family, marriage, and sexuality as wives' failure to submit or fathers' irresponsibility misses the terrifyingly large scope of these problems, and for some people only makes matters worse.[4] A more accurate problem definition equips Christians to undertake the tough task of sorting the chaff of economic material imperatives from the wheat of the true underlying spiritual principles for marriage and family, and to determine which parts of Christian belief are nonbiblical and culturally relative and which are eternal truths, applicable to every person in every culture at every point in time.

My observations and analysis of *modern* issues of family, marriage, and sexuality (found in chapters 5, 7, and 8) are relevant mostly in wealthy nations like the United States and those of Western Europe. In these modern economies, the radical decline in the economic usefulness of children has spawned massive social change. One bit of evidence that the new way of thinking about the problems of sexuality is more accurate than the old one, however, is that it applies equally well to the different problems of poor and developing economics. Marriage counselor Dr. James Koch, who ministered extensively in eastern Europe after the dissolution of communist control there, has observed that the traumas of poverty and repression leave men and women at odds with and unable to comfort each other. The conservative message that family and marital problems stem from a breakdown in "traditional" family structure or gender norms is not useful (or perhaps even sensible) under such conditions. In fact, insisting on the correctness of male authority over women (as do many religious leaders, Christian and Muslim) in countries where the status of women is already appallingly low only reinforces a situation that is miserable enough as it is. Many believe that in Africa, the low status of women contributes to the high rates of HIV/AIDS.[5] Unfortunately, economies such as these fit the model of patriarchy described in chapter 2 only too well.

Fortunately, the biblical solutions to the dilemmas of male/female relations apply both in poverty and in wealth. Many pastors and counselors who help couples prepare for marriage or to survive difficult times in their relationships might wonder whether someone can get a whole book out of what the Bible has to say about marriage and family. Gathered together, statements on these topics account for just a few of the Bible's thousands of pages. Further, the contents of these few pages do not seem at all applicable to today. Some biblical injunctions, such as the admonition that wives submit to their husbands, make many women (and men) cringe. Others, like the Old Testament practice of polygamy, appear little short of barbaric. The author of a book subtitled *What Christians Believe about Marriage* dismisses biblical marriage as concerned mainly about economics and property rights over women. He states, "Most Christians who want answers to difficult questions turn first to the Bible. . . . What I found is that it doesn't teach us as much as we would like. . . . It's important to see that the Bible contains very few guidelines or instructions about marriage. . . . Considering how important marriage is to most Christian people, that's surprising."[6]

Approaching the Bible with a new way of looking at the problem, however, reveals that it has much more to say about marriage than is commonly realized—and that what it has to offer is surprisingly affirming, comprehensible, joyful, *and attainable*. According to Jesus, God created marriage to be a blessing for humankind. He meant for us to want romance, committed love, and even sex. The biblically ideal marriage includes harmony and compatibility, passion and compassion, self-fulfillment as well as self-sacrifice, and equality as a necessary stepping-stone to unity. Moreover, the Bible provides a model for regaining that ideal even outside of Eden.

Within this framework of creation ideal, fall, and redemption, even the apostle Paul must be read in a different light. The fear-driven need for control in the fallen world leads to the tendency to see all human interactions in terms of power. Prejudiced biblical interpretation results. Read in search of hints about such a hierarchy, even a wonderful statement such as "Woman is the glory of man" (1 Cor. 11:7) somehow ends up interpreted as proof of female inferiority. Biased translations have rendered Paul's liberating message nearly inaccessible, and today he is assumed to be antimarriage, antisex, antiwoman, and proslavery, the ultimate Male Chauvinist Pig. Approaching Paul's statements with Jesus's teachings about the appropriate use of power in mind, however, it becomes clear that Paul's views on submission and "headship" have nothing to do with hierarchy or family structure. In Pauline writings, the head does not rule the body but facilitates unity with it. For Paul (and in the Song of Songs) marriage is a beautiful paradox in which each partner is both the fullness of and the thing that fills the other. What redeemed lovers want is not authority over each other but to be of one heart and mind.

This book, then, attempts a biblical theology of marriage. In looking at what the Bible says about marriage, I found a consistency of purpose and attitude that is astonishing for a document that was written by dozens of people over thousands of years. The consistencies between what the Bible says about marriage in Genesis and then marriage as it is portrayed in the Song of Songs—two pieces written hundreds of years apart—are themselves staggering. Then, after a few hundred more years have passed, Jesus used the same themes and allusions in the Sermon on the Mount. The texts that explain woman's alienation from man also explain the problem of evil, and the same forces that redeem individuals from evil take us a long way toward restoring the wholeness between man and woman. God's promise for marriage begins in Genesis and ties up neatly in Paul's eschatological vision for the entire human race.

And amazingly, understanding this promise will deepen your relationship with Christ as much as it will improve your marriage. Not for nothing does the traditional wedding ceremony end with the blessing "[May God] fill you with all spiritual benediction and grace; that you may faithfully live together in this life, and in the age to come have life everlasting."

# Love and Sex as God Created Them

According to the Gospels of Matthew and Mark, a group of Pharisees came to Jesus one day with the question "Is it lawful to divorce one's wife for any cause?" (Matt. 19:3; Mark 10:2). Jesus answered them with a question of his own:

> "Haven't you read," he replied, "that at the beginning the Creator made them male and female, and said, 'For this reason a man will leave his father and mother and be united to his wife, and the two will become one flesh'? So they are no longer two, but one. Therefore what God has joined together, let no one separate." (Matt. 19:4–6)

When the Creator made humankind as male and female, Jesus said, he intended marriage to be the melding of two individuals into one. Anything less was not part of the plan. This answer, however, did not satisfy his questioners.

"Why then," they asked, "did Moses command that a man give his wife a certificate of divorce and send her away?"

Jesus replied, "Moses permitted you to divorce your wives because your hearts were hard. But it was not this way from the beginning." (vv. 7–8)

The Pharisees disappear from the account at this point. Perhaps Jesus's reply left them too outraged to continue. But Jesus's response took his own disciples by surprise, too, and they continued the discussion, saying: "If this is the situation between a husband and wife, it is better [expedient or profitable] not to marry" (v. 10).

Today, to say that husband and wife were meant to be "one flesh" may not seem that surprising, but people in Jesus's day held very different expectations about marriage and family life. For much of human history, including the first century, nearly all marriages were arranged by parents, in large part to satisfy the economic concerns of the families and often with little consideration for the feelings of the bride or groom.[1] New Testament historian S. Scott Bartchy says that people in this kind of economically motivated marriage did not expect to have close emotional ties with their spouse. If someone wanted an intimate confidant, he or she was more likely to turn to a brother or sister, not a mate.[2] Further, men and women in those days were brought up to be very different from each other. Working largely within the household, women were unlikely to be educated or to have much interest in the things that concerned men. The wife did her job, the husband did his; and if each did it well, what more could they ask of each other? Fortunate people got along well with their spouse, might even learn to appreciate and love them—but to become "one" with them? And to *stay* one with them for life? If marriage was to be that unreasonable, the disciples objected, then it was simply "not profitable"[3] to marry. Like the Pharisees' hearts, the goal of oneness was too hard, too much trouble, too out of keeping with common sense, and perhaps not even possible.

Jesus agreed that it is hard to be one with another person. "Not everyone can accept this word," he said.[4] For, he went on, there are many reasons that people remain unmarried—some even to better serve the kingdom of heaven. But "the one who can accept this should accept it" (v. 12).

By quoting a hard-to-grasp word from Genesis, Jesus (and later Paul) points men and women back to "the beginning," before hearts became hardened, and so to a different kind of relationship between them—a union governed not by expediency or material constraints or custom or law, but by God's intent in creation.[5] Remarkably, this ancient account will get us on the path to understanding what God meant us to be to each other when he made us male and female.

## What We Were Created to Be

The beginning of the creation account, Genesis 1, recounts that God, as his crowning act, created humankind. Creating them as sexual beings, God created marriage at the same time.

> Then God said, "Let us make human beings in our image, in our likeness, so that they may rule over the fish of the sea and the birds of the sky, over the livestock and all the wild animals, and over all the creatures that move along the ground."
> So God created human beings in his own image, in the image of God he created them; male and female he created them. (Gen. 1:26–27)

Immediately, this account challenged longstanding notions about male-female relationships. Marriage as Jesus's disciples knew it required that men and women play complementary, but very different, roles. These roles, which persist to the present day, define men as the task leaders of the family and women as the guardians of the family's social and emotional needs. Women care for children and men fight tigers (whether high- or low-tech) to protect them. Men, these beliefs tell us, are dominant, aggressive, and concerned about power; women are submissive and nurturing. In the 1950s television show *I Love Lucy*, which parodied this kind of marriage, Ricky had the career while Lucy stayed home to care for little Ricky. Of course, certain personality characteristics go with these complements: Ricky was the one who gave orders, Lucy the one who schemed and manipulated to elude them and get her own way. Many people believe that these differences are innate, that people are born with such definitions of masculinity or femininity built into them. Genesis 1, however, fails to mention any such roles in creation. Rather, the Bible says that God made both man and woman in his own image and gave them both the same injunctions: "God blessed them and said to them, 'Be fruitful and increase in number; fill the earth and subdue it. Rule over the fish in the sea and the birds in the air and over every living creature that moves along the ground'" (Gen. 1:28).

No gender-specific responsibilities are given in creation, nor does the text in any way imply that one sex will take a role different from the other. God did not make woman nurturing and man dominant. Man as well as woman was to provide care and nurture to children ("be fruitful and increase in number"), just as woman as well as man was to rule the earth ("fill the earth and subdue it").

Moreover, the imperatives in verse 28 are not commandments as often thought but gifts or *blessings*. The wording is like that used by the Vulcans in *Star Trek:* "Live long and prosper!" "God *blessed* them and said to them, 'Be fruitful and increase in number . . .'" Then, as a final gift, God gave both man and woman the abundance of the earth: "Then God said, 'I give you [plural] every seed-bearing plant on the face of the whole earth and every tree that has fruit with seed in it. They will be yours for food'" (Gen. 1:29).

Genesis 1 portrays man and woman as the beneficiaries of God's great munificence. The Creator himself planted and watered the garden, creating the humans to dress and keep it beautiful, not to labor painfully over it. Everything on earth was a gift to them, intended for their happiness. Even sexuality itself—humankind as male and female—was one of the blessings of creation.

## The Creation of Sex

While Genesis 1 presents the big picture of creation, the next narrative, Genesis 2, spirals in to give more detail on the creation of sexuality.[6] Ancient Hebrew literature often used such altered repetition of key stories or passages, with each version providing a richer understanding of the point being made. Elaborating on the themes established in Genesis 1, Genesis 2 explains the meaning of the one difference God created in making humankind as male and female, introducing it thus:

> These are the generations of the heavens and the earth when they were created.
>
> In the day that the Lord God made the earth and the heavens, when no plant of the field was yet in the earth and no herb of the field had yet sprung up—for the Lord God had not caused it to rain upon the earth, and there was no one to till [cultivate, dress, or work] the ground, . . . then the Lord God formed man from the dust of the ground, and breathed into his nostrils the breath of life; and the man became a living being. . . .
>
> The Lord God took the man and put him in the garden of Eden to till [cultivate, work, or dress] it and keep [guard] it. And the Lord God commanded the man, "You may freely eat of every tree of the garden; but of the tree of the knowledge of good and evil you shall not eat, for in the day that you eat of it you shall die."
>
> Then the Lord God said, "It is not good that the man should be alone; I will make him a helper as his partner." (Gen. 2:4–7, 15–18 NRSV)

Genesis 2 opens the story of humanity's creation as sexual beings by asserting that God initially made only one creature. The word for this being—*ha'adam*—is used throughout both chapters to refer to both the singular and the plural creation. Although English translations call this first being "Adam" or "man," the word is not a proper name, nor does it mean "male." Rather, *ha'adam* is a title derived from the Hebrew word for the earth from which the first human was made. *Ha'adam* is not "Adam" at this point but an undifferentiated "the human," or, more literally, "the earthling" or "the earth creature."[7]

Following each act of creation detailed in Genesis 1, God had pronounced his creation "good." After the Genesis 2 creation of the single earth creature, however, God reverses this pattern for the first time:

> Then the Lord God said, "It is *not good* that [*ha'adam*] should be alone. I will make him a helper fit for him." (v. 18, RSV)

Genesis 1 told of God's making us male and female. Genesis 2 tells why: creation was not complete with a single being. *Ha'adam* was lonely; it needed a companion.

Science today testifies to the full truth of Genesis' statement that it is not good for human beings to be alone. Although people have always known that loneliness can be unpleasant, we are now learning that it can be fatal. Infants who are fed and kept warm and dry but who do not receive social stimulation—a caregiver who holds them, looks them in the eye, talks to them—fail to develop properly and in some cases die.[8] Children who receive minimal physical care but are otherwise left alone later exhibit problems like uncontrollable rage, indifference to other living beings, and learning disabilities. Human beings cannot thrive alone. They need someone else to activate their human soul, to make them truly human. Significantly, God made this statement about the creature's loneliness even though the human already had God as a companion. *Ha'adam* needed not another god but someone else who was human.

God called this someone else that the earth creature needed an *'ezer kenegdo*. Most modern translations of the Bible render these words as a "helper fit" for *ha'adam*. Unfortunately, this particular choice of words loses the rich and beautiful meaning intended in the original Hebrew. Ironically, this misunderstanding springs from modern ignorance about the meaning of a word used in the first popular English translation of the Bible, the King James Version. In this translation, the Hebrew words were translated "help meet," which is actually a very good translation. Unfortunately, contemporary English speakers have difficulties understanding the language of the now four-hundred-year-old King James translation. In common use, its "help meet" was corrupted into "helpmate," a nonsensical term that gives the impression that *ha'adam*'s companion would be merely an assistant or a subordinate, "the little woman," a kind of junior partner rather than a full one. These words have been used historically to argue that woman was a secondary creation, made to be less than man and only for his sake, and therefore subordinate to him.

Modern translations of the Bible do not call the *'ezer kenegdo* a helpmate, of course, but they manage to maintain the diminutive by expanding the word "help" into "helper." While not as condescending as "helpmate," "helper" still carries connotations of inferiority. A "helper" is someone we get to do what we do not want to do ourselves (dig holes, wash dishes) or who works under direction. There are four words in Hebrew for such a subordinate helper—but none of these are the word used in Genesis 2.[9] An inferior helper is not at all what was intended by the Creator's use of the words *'ezer kenegdo* to describe what he intended the female to be relative to the male.

The first of these two words, *'ezer*, refers to a help who will "succor another, e.g. . . . help them or aid them."[10] It is used twenty-one times in the Old Testament and refers not to a subordinate or inferior helper but "to help which comes from one who is superior. In most cases, the 'help' is God Himself."[11] Consider, for example, the *'ezer* in Psalm 121: "I lift up my eyes to the mountains—where does my help come from? My help comes from the LORD, the Maker of heaven and earth." Or Psalm 46: "God is our refuge and strength, an ever-present help in trouble." In the few Old Testament cases where *'ezer* does not refer to God, it refers to powerful equals, such as a king coming to another king's aid.

An *'ezer* is someone who is strong enough to render real assistance. And it is this, not an inferior helper or a junior partner, that God said the solitary earth creature needed. The modifying word, *kenegdo*, further clarifies the status of the help. This word, which was translated "meet" in the King James Version, means, "corresponding to him" or "like him"—"meet" as in "suitable" or "fitting." This word emphasizes "the common nature and essence of the two beings."[12] The human did not need an inferior helper, or even another god, but a help suitable for or like him. Taken together, this means, as Semitic language scholar David Freedman writes, "When God creates Eve from Adam's rib, His intent is that she will be . . . 'a power (or strength) equal to him.'"[13] Old Testament scholar Phyllis Trible says, "According to Yahweh God, what the earth creature needs is a companion, one who is neither subordinate nor superior; one who alleviates isolation through identity."[14] God said that it was not good that his creation be alone. The earth creature needed a partner, someone who was of the same nature as he, someone who could fully meet the first human's human need for companionship.

What happens next in the creation account is curious but also informative. Searching for a mate for the man, God brings to him the *animals:*

> Now the LORD God had formed out of the ground all the wild animals and all the birds in the sky. He brought them to the man to see what he would name them; and whatever the man called each living creature, that was its name. So the man gave names to all the livestock, the birds in the sky and all the wild animals.
>
> But for Adam no suitable help[er] ['ezer kenegdo] was found.

The seemingly odd passage creates a contrast between the man and the rest of creation, revealing a great deal about both the nature of humanity and how we are to relate to each other. Long after these verses were written, the philosopher Aristotle argued that women were more like animals than they were like men. Learned men would debate whether woman really had a soul. Feminist historians claim that at the time the Old Testament was written, the world was firmly in the grip of "the Patriarchy," bent on opposing and enslaving women. But taken in its own context, the Bible betrays no such attitude. For the 'ezer kenegdo was not to be found among the animals but instead would be part of the unique creation of humanity.

This passage opens up the discussion of the contemporary Christian problem of separation of the animal or "natural" from the spiritual. *Parade* magazine has a regular feature in which a columnist interviews teenagers on various subjects. A few years ago, she asked an eighteen-year-old girl if she expected fidelity when she married. Her answer was "I don't know. Is it natural to be with the same person all your life—or is it against our animal instincts to be with just one person for 50 years?"[15] This is really the same question with which Jesus was confronted in Matthew 19: "Is it okay to divorce my wife when she no longer pleases me?" The prevailing philosophy and science of the past one hundred years hold that human beings are animals, biological organisms driven by genetically programmed desires, and nothing more. The little side trip through the animals in Genesis 2, however, provides a different picture of the earth creature's true nature. Looking for his 'ezer kenegdo among the animals, the human learned that none of them was a "strength equal" to him. None of them were like him, because although biologically the earth creature was an animal, made from the dust of the earth as were they, spiritually he was not. Spiritually, he was made in God's image and told that he was to have dominion over the animals, not be dominated by them. Although humans are perfectly capable of behaving like animals, Genesis 2's juxtaposition of animal nature with the earth creature's in his search for the 'ezer kenegdo suggests that, especially in relation with each other, human beings must be more than what their animal nature tells them to be.

Human mating, then, was meant to be more than animal—meant to be motivated by more than animal lust or the animal drive for procreation. There must be something of God's image as well in the human act of sex. And indeed, although today's media preach that uncommitted sex is great fun and good for everyone, human beings ultimately yearn for more than this. Even the teenager quoted above eventually admitted that fidelity is indeed what she wanted; she just didn't know if she would get it. "Maybe my ideal—two people love each other, get married, have kids and stay faithful to each other—isn't realistic," she said. Maybe not; but the earth creature's search through the animals for a mate shows that God created humankind for something more than expediency.

Often, it is only by looking at the alternatives that people can figure out what it is they really want. Originally driven by simple feelings of loneliness, the search through the animals taught the earth creature what he longed for—someone like himself. Only a being like the earth creature could meet the earth creature's need. Only a being made in God's image could be a suitable help for the human.

So now that the human understood, God, in response, completed creation: "So the LORD God caused [ha'adam] to fall into a deep sleep; and while he was sleeping, he took part of [ha'adam's] side and then closed up the place with flesh. Then the LORD God made a woman from the part he had taken out of the man, and he brought her to the man" (vv. 21–22 TNIV).

Woman is made out of man's very being (and more than just a rib), a fact that the man recognizes when he sees her for the first time:

> Then the man said,
> "This at last is bone of my bones
>     and flesh of my flesh;
> this one shall be called Woman,
>     for out of Man this one was taken." (NRSV)

The man's joy in finally finding the *'ezer kenegdo* and the depth of his longing is apparent in the manner in which he greets the woman. In Joy Elasky Fleming's more literal translation of this passage, on seeing his mate for the first time, *ha'adam* says,

> "This [one] at last!
> Bone from my bone!
> Flesh from my flesh!"

This one at last! The earth creature found she for whom he yearned. He wanted for himself what God wanted for him—not a servant, not a beast of burden, not a pet, not even another god. And when he found her, he exclaimed, "Here at last is someone like me!" For, as he recognized, woman not only was made of the same substance as man, she was made from *his* substance. This one at last was his perfect match.

Interestingly, modern research into marriage has found that successful relationships are those in which the partners are most alike. Similarity in intelligence, education, religion, social background, attitudes, innumerable personality characteristics, and even level of attractiveness makes for the best and most stable marriages. Matchmakers in cultures that practice arranged marriage are well aware of this fact and try to match potential couples on as many dimensions as possible.

With God as his matchmaker, the first human found (at last!) the one who shared his essence. She was a true "soul mate," a match literally made in heaven. And isn't this what we all want today?

The last part of the man's greeting is also significant. Theologians at least as far back as Martin Luther have argued that when the man called this new creation "woman" in verse 23, it meant that he had been given power to name her and hence held dominion over her.[16] But *woman* was no more a name then than it is now. *Woman* (*'ishshah*) is just a feminine form of *man* (*'ish*). All the human had done was to take the word for what he was and add a feminine ending, like making Eric into Erica, or Daniel into Danielle. In calling her *'ishshah*, the man was again marveling at her similarity to him. They were the same creation, in male and female, and they shared their name as well as everything else.

In fact, except for the use of the masculine pronouns (and Hebrew had no gender-neutral pronoun that could be applied to a person), the text does not give the sense that gender and sexuality were meaningful categories before the creation of the woman. Only after the creation of woman was the earth creature designated male—'ish. In creating the female, God created sex. Connecting back into the narrative of Genesis 1:

> So God created humankind (ha'adam) in his image, in the image of God he created them; male and female he created them.
>
> God blessed them, and God said to them, "Be fruitful and multiply, and fill the earth and subdue it . . ." (Gen. 1:27–28 NRSV)

In calling the new creation 'ishshah, taken from 'ish, Genesis 2 only elaborates on Genesis 1. Genesis 1 states that God made humankind male and female: Genesis 2 demonstrates how and why. This repetition-with-variation is typical for Hebrew poetry, which rhymed ideas rather than sounds in order to make its point. When the two accounts are considered together, like two stanzas of the same poem, they recount how the blessings of Genesis 1 required the solitary earth creature to have an 'ezer kenegdo, a help that was like him (Gen. 2). This help could not be an animal, because although made from the dust of the earth (Gen. 2), ha'adam was also made in God's image (Gen. 1). So to solve this problem, God made the 'ezer kenegdo out of the earth creature's own being—in effect, divided one into two (Gen. 2). The two new categories into which humanity falls are simply 'ish and 'ishshah—the male and the female version of the same thing (Gen. 1 and 2).[17]

In creation God brought into being the aspects of the world that preceded the earth creature—the heavens, the earth, the plants, and the animals—and pronounced them all *good*. The creation of the earthling as a solitary creature was *not good*. But humankind made male and female completed creation. And this God pronounced *very good* (Gen. 1:31).

## One Flesh

After Adam joyfully greets his mate in Genesis 2:23 comes the critical passage, the one quoted by Jesus and later by Paul. In fact,

Matthew 19:4 says that Jesus attributed these words, which are simply part of the narrative in Genesis 2, to God himself: "The *Creator* made them male and female, and *said:* 'For this reason a man will leave his father and mother and be united to his wife, and the two will become one flesh.'"

Genesis 2's account of the creation of humankind begins with one creature; it ends with two, but in that division lies the source of true oneness; in two bodies, *ha'adam* is now complete, fully human, and no longer lonely. For the difference God created in dividing *ha'adam* into male and female, sexuality, is not a divisive one but a difference that unites. In creating sexuality, God divided one being into two in order for them to come back together again as one.

This "oneness" goes beyond physical, sexual union. Physical union alone does not make two people "one." When God created sexuality, he intended it to be more than what passes for intimacy on television. As we will see in the Song of Songs, a "one flesh" union includes the physical but also goes far beyond it.

For two things to be "one" has several meanings, and according to the creation account, man and woman are meant to be one in all these ways:

- "One" can mean "complete" or "whole." Man and woman are complete together. The human by himself, even with God as a companion, was not enough. After all, God himself said, "It is not good for the man to be alone."

- "One" can mean "equal to" or equivalent. Woman in Genesis 2 is not an animal or a lesser creation, nor is she an alternative to God (as the man might have thought if God had not modified *'ezer* with *kenegdo*, "corresponding to him")[18] but is on the same level as man. This oneness means that, contrary to the teachings of the theologians who used creation to argue for male dominion or a chain of command (and the complaints of feminist critics who believe that the Bible does support sexual hierarchy), there is nothing in Genesis 2 that contradicts the egalitarianism of Genesis 1. There is no mandate given for hierarchy in marriage or justification for male authority over the female.

Unlike the recently "hot" school of philosophy, postmodernism, which analyzes or deconstructs all human relationships in terms of power, the biblical teachings about women and men are not about power and authority at all. Failing to support hierarchy does not make the creation accounts feminist, at least not as secular feminists would recognize feminism. The reason given in Genesis 2 for woman's existence in no way implies her inferiority, but neither does it support the notion that she is complete in herself. Woman is not creation's all in all any more than the man is. Eden did not sport bumper stickers reading "Woman needs man like a fish needs a bicycle." Rather, sexuality in creation belongs not to the individual but to the relationship. Female and male exist only for the sake of the other. Power has nothing to do with it.

- "One" can mean "identity" or "sameness." In Genesis 1, man and woman were alike, both created in God's image. In Genesis 2, woman was created out of man's own flesh. And when Adam saw her, his first thought was *Here at last is someone like me!* The first two chapters of the Bible are not interested in the differences between man and woman but in their similarities and their mutual uniqueness in relation to the rest of creation—their partaking in God's image. Woman was created, and delighted in, because she was like the man.

- Finally, "one" can mean "united." In Genesis 2:24, man and woman are united: "A man will leave his father and mother and be united to his wife." The man was to leave his father and mother for his wife. She was to be his primary allegiance and help. To further this end, the one difference that God does create—sex and sexual desire—is not a difference that divides the man and the woman but one that draws them together.

Genesis 2 answers the question of why God made us male and female: to meet the yearning for someone who is like us and yet different in just the right way, a way that unifies us even more. That "just right" difference, however, is not the same as either old-fashioned or contemporary popular notions of masculinity and femininity. As we will see in chapter 6, sex as God created it is pure romance and companionship. Sexuality in creation was intended for consumption, not production. Like man and woman in the garden, it exists to nurture. It has no unpleasant work to do. Sex is *le difference*—that which, as Plato wrote, makes "woman a woman and man a man"[19]—without division.

There is one verse left in Genesis 2. Following God's pronouncement that "for this reason a man will leave his father and mother and be united to his wife, and the two will become one flesh," the passage concludes:

And the man and his wife were both naked, and they felt no shame.

# The Economics of the Fall and the Subordination of Women

One flesh, naked and unashamed. Jesus said this was God's intent for humanity when he made us male and female.

Man and woman were certainly physically naked in the garden. Eden had been made just for them, and so the humans needed no screens or defenses against anything in it. Shame, however, is a social rather than physical state: the text's addition of "and they felt no shame" suggests that man and woman not only were without clothing but were emotionally naked as well. To be naked and unashamed in relationship is to be honest, open, spontaneous, without pretense or defense, with no striving for advantage over the other person. Made for each other as much as the garden was made for them, the first man and woman had no need for any such shields, defenses, or advantage over each other. This, Genesis tells us, is how we were created and, Jesus tells us, how we will yet be.

Sadly, however, the structure of the text reveals that this beautiful statement, "The man and his wife were both naked, and they felt no shame," introduces only a brief idyll before the ugly tragedy soon to follow in Genesis 3:

> Now the serpent was more crafty than any of the wild animals the LORD God had made. He said to the woman, "Did God really say, 'You must not eat from any tree in the garden'?"
>
> The woman said to the serpent, "We may eat fruit from the trees in the garden, but God did say, 'You must not eat fruit from the tree that is in the middle of the garden, and you must not touch it, or you will die.'"
>
> "You will not surely die," the serpent said to the woman. "For God knows that when you eat of it your eyes will be opened, and you will be like God, knowing good and evil."
>
> When the woman saw that the fruit of the tree was good for food and pleasing to the eye, and also desirable for gaining wisdom, she took some and ate it. She also gave some to her husband, who was with her, and he ate it. Then the eyes of both of them were opened, and they realized they were naked; so they sewed fig leaves together and made coverings for themselves.
>
> Then the man and his wife heard the sound of the LORD God as he was walking in the garden in the cool of the day, and they hid from the LORD God among the trees of the garden. But the LORD God called to the man, "Where are you?"
>
> He answered, "I heard you in the garden, and I was afraid because I was naked; so I hid."
>
> And he said, "Who told you that you were naked? Have you eaten from the tree that I commanded you not to eat from?"
>
> The man said, "The woman you put here with me—she gave me some fruit from the tree, and I ate it." (Gen. 3:1–12)

With this, humankind fell from paradise and their unique walk with God. Like all satans (tempters), the serpent did not offer the man and woman some exotic inducement but only the hidden desire of their hearts—to be like God. Trying to hide their nakedness, the couple betrayed their knowledge of the enormity of their act, but they stood by their choice: nowhere does the text record any attempt to be reconciled to God before or after he confronted them with their disobedience. The first and most elemental sin, capital *S* Sin, was not a simple eating of a forbidden fruit but a purposeful and willful choice to separate from God, to usurp his role in guiding their lives.

Moreover, sin broke the humans' relationship not only with God but also with each other. "The man and his wife were both naked . . . and felt no shame" is a poetic beginning, parallel to a sorrowful conclusion, "Then the eyes of both of them were opened, and they realized they were naked; so they sewed fig leaves together and made coverings for themselves." Humankind's wholeness in creation was covered over in shame and fearfulness.

God next describes just what their new alienation will mean (vv. 14–19):

So the LORD God said to the serpent, "Because you have done this,

> Cursed are you above all livestock
> > and all wild animals!
> You will crawl on your belly
> > and you will eat dust
> > all the days of your life.
> And I will put enmity
> > between you and the woman,
> > and between your offspring and hers;
> he will crush your head,
> > and you will strike his heel." (TNIV)

Unto the woman he said, "I will greatly multiply [your] sorrow [could be translated 'painful or sorrowful toil'] and [your] conceptions; In sorrow [pain or toil] [you] shalt bring forth children; and [your] desire [or turning] *shall be* to [your] husband, and he shall rule over [you]." (KJV)

To Adam he said, "Because you listened to your wife, and ate from the tree about which I commanded you, 'You must not eat of it,'

> Cursed is the ground because of you;
> > through painful toil you will eat of it
> > all the days of your life.
> It will produce thorns and thistles for you,
> > and you will eat the plants of the field.
> By the sweat of your brow
> > you will eat your food
> until you return to the ground,

> since from it you were taken;
> for dust you are
> and to dust you will return." (TNIV)

## Commandment or Curse?

The life described in Genesis 3:14–19 differs dramatically from the life God created. Instead of being at one with God, their physical surroundings, the animals, and each other, man and women faced alienation on all fronts. No one debates the deadly accuracy of God's prediction for the relationship between man and woman as it would be after the fall—in their "sorrowful toil," man and woman will lose their oneness. For hundreds of years, however, there has been disagreement on the meaning of this prediction, especially regarding the statements addressed to the woman. Most salient has been the argument that Genesis 3:16, "Your desire will be for your husband, and he will rule over you," expresses God's will that wives be subordinate to their husbands. The contrast between Genesis 3 and the creation account, however, makes it clear that this passage cannot be a commandment. The sufferings listed in Genesis 3—painful toil, sorrow in childbearing, woman's subordination to man, man's anxieties about wrestling a livelihood from the hostile earth, their eventual deaths—stand out as the exact opposites of what God created. The beauty of creation had been destroyed, but not by God's command: man and woman were already covered up, shamed and fearful, before God said a word to them (vv. 7–10).

More careful theologians have therefore argued that Genesis 3:14–19 is not a commandment but a punishment, a "curse" placed on humankind for disobedience.[1] They acknowledge that these new roles do not reflect God's intent in creation, but argue that humankind still should not seek to escape them. Thus pain in childbirth was once widely regarded as a punishment that should not be relieved with painkillers.[2] Similarly, theologians have argued that woman was not to be relieved of an obligation to obey man. Curiously, the analogous argument, that to pay for his sin man should continue at hard labor until he dies, has rarely been made.

Both interpretations of Genesis 3:14–19—commandment or curse—deny that man and woman will ever reclaim the unity of the relationship for which they were intended, at least not until reaching heaven. However, both Joy Elasky Fleming and Phyllis Trible point out that the text in Genesis 3 actually records curses on the serpent and on the ground but not on the people.[3] This subtle point may appear to be only a detail, but to quote Mies van der Rohe, "God is in the details." The cursing of the ground changed nothing about the basic nature of man and woman or about how God wanted them to live, but it dramatically changed the way they *would* live.

Before the fall, the academic field of economics could not have provided much insight about human life in Eden. Economics is defined as the study of how scarce resources are allocated among competing ends, including not just things like the stock market and interest rates but the other, more personal trade-offs that people make on a daily basis. Living in abundance in the Garden of Eden, the human beings had no trade-offs to make. Their environment was so benign that they could go about naked. Hence they did not need the one thing God had withheld from them, the knowledge of good and evil. Any choices they had to make—which do I eat today, this fruit or that one?—were trivial. The curse on the ground and its consequent production of thorns destroyed that freedom from worry. In a world of thorns, man and woman needed all the knowledge possible to go with their newfound privilege of making decisions. Their harsh new environment required a constant eye to managing scarcity. The questions with which they now struggled were no longer choices among abundant alternatives but more frightening issues like who eats today, my children, my mate, or me?

What is remarkable about Genesis 3 is how accurately it describes the economic and in turn the social, emotional, and spiritual consequences of living in a world in which the ground is cursed. An economic analysis of the effect of scarcity on male-female behavior predicts exactly the same results as those described in Genesis 3:14–19: masculine drive for power and control, feminine subordination, and a hardening of hearts between them. Applied to Genesis 3, economic theory explains the source of many of the old and new questions, problems, and disputes between the sexes, including the difficulty of regaining the creation ideal of marriage, the emergence and nature of gender differences, and women's historic subordination to men.[4]

## The Economics of the Fall

Immediately, and significantly only after God described what would be required in this new world of thorns, the man—now properly called Adam—gave his wife a name separate from his own: "Adam named his wife Eve, because she would become the mother of all the living" (Gen. 3:20). This new name, mother of all living, emphasized not the couple's unity ("Bone of my bone! Flesh of my flesh!") but the demands of their new environment. God's gifts in Genesis 1—dominion over the earth and children—were no longer simple blessings but problematic necessities, and the imperatives of achieving them corrupted sexuality itself. Sexuality would become utilitarian, reproductivity in service of productivity, and put to hard work. For after the fall, what Adam needed from his wife was not their mutual pleasure and companionship but the tool her difference from him gave him in his struggle against the hostile world—her ability to bear children.

Children were and are critically important resources in traditional rural economies, the kind of life that Adam and Eve faced after their expulsion from the garden. Before the industrial revolution (which began around 1790) and still today in many unindustrialized parts of the world, nearly all the necessities of life were produced at home. Even the wealthy were farmers, and their grand estates were ultimately just farms. Households had to produce for themselves nearly everything they consumed. As recently as nineteenth-century America, for instance, households would purchase metal implements and salt, which generally could not be produced at home, but grew or made everything else.[5] The demands of being self-sustaining meant that a household required many members. A young couple might start off alone, but they acquired servants and laborers as soon as they could possibly afford them.

A better source of labor than servants, however, was children. The loyalty of servants was always in doubt: even the wealthy were considered to be putting their lives at risk if they had no one to care for them in illness but servants.[6] Children, in contrast, were much more likely to be devoted to their family's welfare, if for no other reason than that their family's welfare was also their own. Moreover, children didn't have to be paid, and they could be produced at home. The great economist Adam Smith estimated that in colonial America, a child's labor contributed one hundred (English) pounds sterling to his family before he left home, a substantial sum of money in those days.[7]

The difference in fertility rates between an industrialized nation, where the average woman bears fewer than two children, and an agricultural nation like Kenya, where until a few years ago the average woman bore ten, reflects not so much a greater love for children (or even the relative unavailability of birth control) as a greater need for farming help. In addition, in the absence of social security, pensions, or even the possibility of accumulating more food than was necessary to survive the winter, children were the only source of support for those parents lucky enough to survive to old age. "Children are a heritage from the LORD," says the psalmist. "Blessed is the man whose quiver is full of them" (Ps. 127:3, 5). Blessed indeed. From biblical times until the beginning of the twentieth century, and still today in much of the world, infertility was more than a personal heartbreak—it was an economic disaster.

Between the need for large families and the fact that throughout most of history child mortality has been extremely high (so much so that even wealthy families were lucky to raise a couple of children to adulthood),[8] women were under a constant obligation to bear children. American fertility figures from the early part of the 1800s indicate that more than one-quarter of the women between the ages of fifteen and forty-four gave birth each year.

Thus, after the fall, Eve is mentioned again only in the role of mother, giving birth to Cain, Abel (not coincidentally, both farmers), and Seth. Adam was no longer a leisurely keeper of a garden but a subsistence farmer eating his bread by the sweat of his brow, and he needed children to help in the endless struggle with the ground.

## Sorrowful Toil and Women's Work

In the preindustrial world, childrearing was woman's most important task. However, woman's many conceptions did not free her from other sorrowful or painful toil (Gen. 3:16). Modern translations tend to lose the work dimensions of Genesis 3:16 by confounding Eve's painful toil with pain in childbirth. The New International Version, for example, translates the first part of verse 16 as "I will greatly increase your pains in childbearing," but the Hebrew reads, "Multiplying, I will multiply your painful (or sorrowful) toil and your *conceptions*"[9] (emphasis added; note that it is conceptions or pregnancies that are multiplied, not "pain in childbirth"). This "painful toil" is the same word that is applied to the man in verse 17 ("through painful toil you will eat . . . all the days of your life"). This biblical observation is historically accurate, for the rigors of subsistence farming made as heavy a demand on women's labors as on men's.

Few women in farming economies have had the luxury of "just" raising their children; most had to work as much as the men to produce enough to survive. Economist Gary S. Becker, who won the Nobel Prize for his work extending economic tools to understanding "nonmarket" behavior such as fertility, divorce, discrimination, and crime, traces traditional family structure and what economists call "the sexual division of labor" (the patterns of men and women's performing different tasks) to this continuing demand on a mother's time.[10] The need for many children combined with the fact that there was no substitute for human breast milk (infants who did not have a human nurse died) limited the kinds of work that women could sensibly do. Heavy labor was an invitation to miscarriage. Families quickly learned to distribute work so that women did the tasks that were compatible with pregnancy and lactation. Spinning, for example, was the consummate female task, as it was easy to put down when a child needed to be picked up. The next steps in clothing construction—weaving and sewing—were similarly compatible with childcare.[11] Cooking was a time-consuming task in the absence of preprocessed foodstuffs. Mothers, already housebound, were the logical persons to supervise the rising of the leaven and baking bread, to ensure that the beans didn't boil dry, and to remove the meat from the fire before it burned. Women grew vegetables for household use and in some places and times, particularly where plows were not used, participated in farm labor as well.[12] Women nursed the sick and the aged, gathered or cultivated and processed herbs to use as medicines, and supervised family hygiene—important and often time-consuming tasks in a world that was rife with deadly infections.

Women might be directly active in household businesses: in the United States, farm women often kept the financial accounts. Wives supervised the work of slaves involved in commercial production in ancient Greek and Roman households, and less wealthy women kept the shops where such family produce was sold. Proverbs 31:13–27 describes the work of such a "good wife":

> She seeks wool and flax,
>> and works with willing hands.
> She is like the ships of the merchant,
>> she brings her food from afar.
> She rises while it is yet night
>> and provides food for her household
>> and tasks for her maidens.
> She considers a field and buys it;
>> with the fruit of her hands she plants a vineyard.
> She girds her loins with strength
>> and makes her arms strong.
> She perceives that her merchandise is profitable.
>> Her lamp does not go out at night.
> She puts her hands to the distaff,
>> and her hands hold the spindle.
> She opens her hand to the poor,
>> and reaches out her hands to the needy.
> She is not afraid of snow for her household,
>> for all her household are clothed in scarlet.
> She makes herself coverings;
>> her clothing is fine linen and purple.
> Her husband is known in the gates,
>> where he sits among the elders of the land.
> She makes linen garments and sells them;
>> she delivers girdles to the merchant.
> Strength and dignity are her clothing,
>> and she laughs at the time to come.
> She opens her mouth with wisdom,
>> and the teaching of kindness is on her tongue.
> She looks well to the way of her household,
>> and does not eat the bread of idleness. (RSV)

This Good Wife, the author tells us, even in such an obviously wealthy household, is "far more precious than jewels" (Prov. 31:10).

In the 1960s and 1970s, when women struggled to get out of the home and into the marketplace, we nascent Christian egalitarians thought that Proverbs 31 was a wonderful passage. Here was clear biblical precedent for women having careers! But the Good Wife was not an ancient liberated woman. Women simply did all of these things in the ancient world.[13] Tellingly, while the Good Wife's work is for her husband's sake, the poem does not mention anything about companionship or love. As praiseworthy as she may be, the Good Wife is a far cry from the carefree 'ezer kenegdo of Eden.

As a result of the accommodations made for childbearing, women's labor bound them to the home in a way that men's did not. Men's work was determined by what was left over after the women did what they could with children present.[14] Women typically did not get involved in the activities that gave men power over each other and over women—war, long-distance trade, finance, politics—simply because domestic labor gave them no time, training, or interest in these things. Historically, men rather than women were the hunters, blacksmiths, long-distance traders, sailors, and warriors. After all, one could not go to war, to sea, or to Parliament, work a forge, or plow a field with a nursing infant in arms and young children in tow.

The constraints on women's activities caused by childbearing greatly restricted the kinds of careers in which women could readily participate. The English wool trade provides an excellent example of the limitations of woman's domestic specialization. As long as wool production and trade were domestically based, the wool trade was "women's work" (as it was for Proverbs' "Good Wife"). When in the eighteenth century the trade expanded across the channel into continental Europe, however, women were unable to leave their families in order to follow it. As a result, the wool business was eventually taken over by men.[15]

Even off the farm, family life until the modern era required much household production. The increasingly city-dwelling Victorians (as the advocates of the dominant social forces in Europe and the United States in the late 1800s are called), whose doctrines of "separate spheres" between home life (women's sphere) and market activities and employment (men's sphere) provided fodder for critical feminist analysis, can be considered sexist and repressive only in light of contemporary sensibilities. In the context of the demanding world of which they were a part, Victorian efforts to shelter women from the demands of earning a living outside the home were perfectly sensible. With prepared foods largely unavailable, laundry still an onerous task, and children routinely suffering from numerous serious illnesses that were neither treatable nor preventable, the late 1800s was no time to abandon the sexual division of labor. Even as late as 1922 in the United States, "when 'mother worked,' there were children who had no one to nurse them through illnesses, meals that were hastily thrown together from whatever could be found ready-made in the markets, poor teeth, clothing that did not fit, dirty floors, skin rashes, and bad breath."[16] Historian Ruth Schwartz Cowan writes, "Whether she actually did the work or whether she directed the work that was to be done, the presence of a full-time wife and mother meant careful supervision of the family's health, a well-appointed living room, white stockings, ironed hair ribbons, regular church attendance, Sunday dinners, birthday parties."[17] Infant mortality rates among the children of working mothers too exhausted to produce breast milk were horrific. Moreover, working outside the home was a serious threat to a woman's own health. Studies of the U.S. Census showed that the mortality rate of married women mill workers in the early twentieth century was four times higher than for married women who did not work in mills.[18] Small wonder that in this period women sought paid employment only out of dire necessity and that a working-class husband felt great pride when he did well enough that his wife no longer had to work outside the home.

Although many academic theories of gender claim that men became dominant over women because of man's superior size, strength, and aggression, historical differences in the power and occupations of men and women—what social scientists call the sexual division of labor—are better understood when they are seen to be based on a unique *feminine* characteristic: woman's ability to bear children. As the only ones who could bear and feed children, women would still have ended up specialized for the home even if they had been bigger and stronger than men.[19] Becker suggests that even in the 1980s, when a mother did not produce the family's food and clothing and bore only a few children, when there were young children in the home the value of a mother's time, although unpaid, was probably greater than that of her wage-producing husband.[20]

Given the kind of world where children are necessary, most women no doubt accepted their domestic specialization freely. It is likely, however, that prior to the twentieth century even women who had other skills or interests had no real choices as to their roles in life. To see why, suppose that a young woman—call her Eva—in some preindustrial society decides to be something other than a wife and mother. Maybe she has some extraordinary talent that drives her to seek a career. A woman might do well in trade, law, music, art, education, or a skilled craft despite being smaller than the average man. Even in subsistence economies there have always been jobs that do not depend on brute strength alone, and in many cultures women worked as merchants or in professions. Suppose also that Eva acquires the necessary training and has financial backing. Let's make it even easier for her and assume that she does not have to deal with discrimination, sexual harassment, or fear of assault either. Under these optimal circumstances, is Eva better off with a career than she would be in a domestic role?

Probably not. A man in similar circumstances, even a man with significantly less valuable skills than our nontraditional woman, can have children and a wife, and these are significant forms of wealth. Becker notes that a person who has no domestic responsibilities enjoys an obvious advantage in his work over people who have to work both in and outside of the home.[21] But Eva, a woman, cannot have a wife and so has no one to provide for her the things that women produced. She could marry to acquire a partner, although it would be hard for her to compete for a husband against more domestic women, but she would find that men were not trained for work in the home and so could not perform important wifely tasks.

Perhaps our independent woman could live with her mother or hire servants. Unfortunately, neither of these solutions provides her with other valuable resources available to the men with whom she is competing, such as an emotional and sexual relationship. For the nontraditional woman can enjoy a romantic relationship only if she finds a mate who is willing to forgo sex as well as children. Without reliable birth control, sex leads to children, and once Eva has children, she will not be able to carry on her career activities, as she will be tied down at home. A married man or a housewife had the benefits of marriage, children, domestic complementarity/companionship, sex, and at least the possibility of romance. A career woman, even under the best of circumstances, gave up all of these things.

Men's competitive edge against women in the workplace, then, came not from their greater physical strength but from their ability to marry women. Although the explanation traditionally given pre-1960 for women's lack of careers was often "women are bad at . . ." rational thought/mathematics/hunting bears/upper body strength or whatever, it has never been that women didn't have the native ability to compete with men in most modern endeavors or that their objective performance in whatever craft or trade they chose was inferior.[22] It was simply that in a preindustrial world a potential career woman couldn't compete with her own alternative of wife and mother. Abandoning domestic life required women to give up too much personally. In economic terms, a career for a woman offered few benefits and many costs in the form of forgone opportunities. Prior to the industrial revolution, the women who did have a career were largely those who did not have women's usual resources available to them, either because they had never married or because their husbands were disabled or absent—dead, at war, in jail, or traveling on trade.

## Childbearing and Chastity

Another consequence of the need for children is the restrictions patriarchal cultures place on women because of concerns about their chastity. Becker observes that virtually every society has developed some form of the marriage contract to protect woman in her child-bearing, domestically specialized role.[23] By extension, the requirement that a man bind himself in exchange for women's services led to the male insistence on precautions to ensure that the children a woman bore were actually his and not another man's. Restrictions were applied to both married women and pubescent girls and might range from relatively mild measures such as curfews, veiling, rules on who may speak to whom, restrictions on interactions between unrelated females and males (for example, that they always be held in public; that they never be held in public; that they always be chaperoned;

that they never take place at all), to extreme measures such as genital mutilation and the complete segregation of women from men to whom they were not related.

## He Will Rule over You

While becoming a wife and mother was the best thing that could happen to a woman in a world of scarce resources—indeed, it was the state for which all women, including those too poor to marry, strove—at the same time women became defined and trapped by their biological functions. In such an environment, it did not really matter what a woman's natural inclinations were. She afforded greater value to both herself and others in the domestic role than in any other career available to her. Moreover, even if her own interests and talents would take her in a different direction, a young girl growing up in the traditional world would not have had the education necessary to allow her any other choice. Education was scarce and expensive in preindustrial society, particularly so when children were needed to work. Unless they were wealthy, families provided most of the training that children got, and that tended to be "on the job."[24] What extrafamilial training there was went to the sons, whose employment outside of the household made their education a better investment. Self-sufficiency also required too many different skills for any one person to learn them all. Once again, training was allocated by sex: responsible parents trained their daughters to fulfill the role they were most likely to play, that of wife and mother.

For most women, this was not a problem. Few men had a choice about what they would do in life either—after all, for most of history 90 percent of the population, male and female, was employed in agriculture—and aside from childbearing, men got stuck with the most nasty and dangerous work. Ultimately, however, the constraints of scarcity and the resulting need for woman to bear children allowed man to "rule over" her. Economists tell us that the very thing that made a woman valuable—her unique ability to bear children—also made her dependent relative to her husband.[25] The things that a wife and mother produced may have been essential to her family's survival, but she produced them for one particular household and one particular set of people, her own family. A woman's most valuable product, children, were of most worth to their father. In a sense, this made a woman's husband and household her employers, and she could change employment only at the price of a major and risky disruption in her life. She could certainly work in someone else's household, but there she would be a servant, not mistress of the house. Women who left their marriage left all of what they had produced in the first household, including, most likely, their children, who were usually considered to belong to their father. Those who did keep their children put them at risk when they remarried (switched "employers"), as stepparents were notoriously more concerned about their own welfare than about children who owed them no fealty (hence all the evil stepparents in fairy tales).

The husband's skills were more flexible. Less tied to and less invested in the household, he could change employers far more easily than a wife could. When women are domestically specialized, the broader base of demand for men's labor makes husbands less dependent in the marital relationship.

The sexual division of labor explains the historic subordination of women to men in other ways. Woman's domestic, family-centered roles meant that she would have less impact in the community than a man. This was true not so much because she was home bound— women were not necessarily less visible in rural or small-town life than were men—but because many of the government and business issues that determine civic power were of little concern to her. Politics usually did not affect home life directly and so were literally none of women's business. Why would women care who was prime minister or what his policies were on war in India? What busy housewife had time for such concerns? Indeed, Jewish law, recognizing the value of a mother's time, excused women from many of the religious obligations placed on men. The expense of education referred to earlier compounded women's indifference. Few women knew enough about political issues to begin to think of holding office or even of voting. And for a woman to have a working knowledge of war and the military, historically important components of political power, was unthinkable. Analogously, women had no interest in long-distance trading or in manufacturing outside of the home. Although a woman probably held considerable power within her domestic areas of concern, she had little decision-making authority or ability outside it. Thus the fallen world's poverty and resultant demand for the labor of children resulted in the economic realities of separate spheres for men and women and in women's subordination to men in family, society, government, and the church.

## By the Sweat of Your Brow

In Genesis 3, God warns Adam that men will also bear burdens as a result of their alienation from God and God's abundant provision: "By the sweat of your brow you will eat your food, until you return to the ground." While women in the world of thorns became specialized to domestic tasks, men bore the brunt of the heavy, dirty, and dangerous jobs. They were the ones who hunted and fought wild animals. They provided the meat and the field crops. They were the ones who dealt face to face with uncertainty. Scarcity, risk, danger: confronted with these conditions, men responded by trying to gain control over the physical environment.

One man alone could not achieve enough control over the hostile physical world or the other people in it, a fact that required men to organize themselves somehow. A noncoercive system like democracy requires widespread education and wealth in order to function. Historically, instead of democracy, men were governed in patriarchy or some variation on it. While our current use of that term focuses on women as the subjects of men's rule, such a narrow definition misses the main subjects of patriarchy: other men. For patriarchy is not simply the rule of men over women but the rule of a few men over everyone else, male and female.[26] In ancient history, there were only a few patriarchs but a great many slaves (an unpleasant fact that I will return to in chapter 4 to make sense of the writings of Paul).

So for a man, life in the world of thorns came down to questions of whether he would eat or be eaten, whether he would be master or slave, the boss or the grunt, the conqueror or the conquered. It comes as no surprise, then, that men responded by seeking whatever control they could muster. The hostile, competitive environment required aggression and dominance from the man who would be successful. If his circumstances or abilities dictated that a man could not wield power himself, he should at least limit how much other people controlled him. In such a world, male preoccupation with competition and aggression, war and games of war, politics and power, money and trade, and analysis and logic was as natural a product of the fallen world as was female skill with the spindle.

Even when men do not literally sweat at work, they are still subject to the psychological effects of earning their bread by the sweat of their brow. Required by economic imperatives to "fight the tiger," reared to be the best, and specialized away from tasks that call for care and nurturing, men often find it difficult to set aside the need for power and its accompanying anxieties and stress, even when there are no tigers left to fight. It is too dangerous on too many levels to display emotions that might signal vulnerability and detract from one's competitive edge. Perhaps this is why many men have a difficult time disengaging from the pressures of the workplace. They know only too well that to relax and give up their anxieties might mean to give up their chances of getting what they want.

Too defensive to be open with others, many men today as well as in the past do not readily take advice, counsel, comfort, or direction from anyone, be they wife, best friend, or pastor. Indeed, some atheists' and agnostics' decisions against belief stem from their Adam-like resistance to letting anyone or anything else control their life, even God. This alienation—capital S Sin—not only cuts the individual off from God but also deprives him of many other sources of help. Further, in the face of their perceived need to control themselves and their environment, some men cannot resist grabbing whatever power society hands them, even if that power is only control over those they love. After all, the world of thorns told men that they were unmanly and not entitled to the respect of their family if they did not take charge. At the extremes, this mandate that men control those around them results externally in violence, war, and abuse and internally in despair, self-loathing, substance abuse, and heart attacks.

## Your Desire Shall Be for Your Husband

Despite the fall from unity to hierarchy, from peace to anxiety, Genesis 3 warns women that they will continue to desire their husband. Just as the world of thorns requires men to behave in certain ways, it requires women to accept these behaviors.

A woman may not enjoy living with a competitive, emotionally insensitive man, but in many ways it is to her advantage to have such a man as her husband. Ambitious, aggressive men have an advantage over other men, and the wife of a dominant man shares his privileged social standing as well. Men today are routinely criticized for their aggressive tendencies, but at the same time women find "bad boys" desirable. Thus a husband's "rule over" his wife (Gen. 3:16) is partially a product of the feminine demand for a husband who is dominant and ambitious—a "real man."

## Beauty

The importance placed on feminine beauty also reflects woman's "desire" for or "turning to" her husband. Traditionally men *needed* women for what they produced domestically, but then and now they *desire* women based on their physical attractiveness. This is not to say that women don't desire men based on their looks, too. It is just that even moderately wealthy men or men with potential for wealth or power were able to choose their mates on the basis of what pleased them. Women rarely had this luxury.

This disparity between the sexes again stems from the economics of the world of thorns. In traditional roles, the amount of power and material goods that a man can acquire or produce varies a great deal from individual to individual.[27] A male might be a penniless beggar or a captain of industry. A female, on the other hand, doesn't vary much from other females in her childbearing capacity. A woman might have no children or she might have twenty, but this range of variation isn't nearly as great as the variation among men in their ability to produce wealth. If woman's main job in marriage is producing children, one healthy young girl is no different from any other healthy young girl. This disparity means that successful men can pick and choose their mate based on what pleases them, and that, thousands of years of experience has shown, turns out to be good looks.[28] Thus beauty and charm became key dimensions on which girls are judged. A pretty girl, like a wealthy man, will have more and better choices than a plain girl. And because wealthy men can afford sexually attractive wives, people assume that a man with a good-looking wife must be wealthy. Thus a beautiful wife boosts a man's social status, and her beauty becomes just another part of the competition.[29]

## A Naturally Occurring Experiment

A fascinating study of Israeli kibbutzim by anthropologist Melford Spiro shows how quickly the demands of childbearing amidst scarcity can elicit the historic sexual division of labor among even the most unlikely group of people.[30] The Israeli kibbutz movement began around the turn of the twentieth century with young radicals, mostly from Russia, who were strongly committed to building a socialist Zion. One of their goals in founding their utopian agricultural communes was the "total emancipation of women from the 'shackles'—sexual, social, economic, and intellectual—imposed on them by traditional society." The kibbutzim recognized that it was childbearing—which they called "the biological tragedy of women"—that tied them to the "yoke of domestic service." In order to break this pattern, they determined that kibbutz women were to work the land equally with men. Eschewing traditional femininity, the early female pioneers dressed the same as the men and used no cosmetics, perfume, jewelry, or feminine hairstyles. Further, all domestic services—childcare, cooking, laundry, and the like—were handled communally in order to free women's time from monopolization by domestic labor.

Despite this determined and systemic effort to break women's "shackles," the sexual division of labor reappeared with amazing rapidity. The pioneer women were determined to work as hard as, if not harder than, the men in the high-status agricultural jobs, but it quickly became apparent that such heavy labor resulted in a high incidence of miscarriage. If a woman wanted to bear her baby—and the kibbutz was very prochild—she had to avoid this overexertion. Further, the movement strongly encouraged breastfeeding, but this also limited a mother's mobility. Field labor took her too far away from her infant. Within a short period of time, most of the women had transferred from the high-status but arduous agricultural work to lower-status horticultural labor, working in the vegetable gardens, vineyards, and fruit orchards, or to the very low-status service sector—childcare, laundry, and cooking. The pioneers maintained their ardently feminist ideology, but the women themselves had difficulty in putting it into practice.

By the 1950s, the children of the pioneers didn't hold on to even the ideology. They not only practiced different gender roles but regarded them as "innate." "Women," they say, "are most fulfilled by working with and helping other people, while men are most fulfilled when working with machinery and on tasks which give them a sense of power and domination." This attitude was perhaps not surprising given that this statement was made in the 1950s. However, Spiro's next follow-up in 1975 found that the kibbutz women had become even more "traditional." In the rest of the world, the 1970s was a decade that saw the birthrate plunging, women flocking into the marketplace, marriages failing, and marriage itself increasingly dismissed as "irrelevant." On the kibbutz, it had become "impossible to be a bachelor," and a "tragedy" for a girl not to marry. The age of marriage dropped, fertility rose (in the 1950s, no family had more than two children, while in the 1970s three or four were typical and five and six were not unusual), and divorce had become extremely rare. Men saw women primarily as mothers and wives and themselves as workers. Kibbutz women wore feminine clothes and hairstyles and scored as more feminine on attitudes scales than other Israeli women—more tender, more submissive, more likely to prefer feminine occupations and hobbies and to reject masculine tasks. Spiro called this the "counterrevolution" and noted that it occurred not just at one kibbutz but in all of them. And the conditions that prevailed on the kibbutzim matched exactly the conditions of Genesis 3: heavy agricultural labor ("through painful toil . . . you will eat the plants of the field") and the need for children ("in sorrow you will bring forth children"), resulting in willing feminine submission and male dominance ("your desire will be for your husband, and he will rule over you").

### Gender and Personality

A sociopsychological extension of Becker's economic model of the sexual division of labor, combined with the Genesis accounts, explains a surprising number of the observed differences between men and women in personality, behavior, and achievement. The parents of a boy born in a preindustrial society, past or present, know that when he grows up he will have to compete with other men. His comfort, even survival, will be the comfort of the woman he eventually marries and their children, and (since the parents will count on the boy in their old age) their own comfort and survival also depends on how well he does in that competition. Such parents want their sons to be

- strong
- ambitious
- intelligent
- competitive
- independent
- aggressive

It is apparent to everyone, then and now, that the boys who "succeed" are those who strive for power, who have the drive to subdue and master, the will to conquer and to be the best. Ironically, while it is best to be top dog, when he can't be, the successful boy accepts his place in the social hierarchy and becomes a good "team player." Boys will have a competitive edge over their opponents if they are self-centered, task oriented, insensitive to emotion but sensitive to status issues, and tough.

On the other hand, in these same preindustrial cultures, parents know that their daughters are competing not for the best careers but for the best domestic jobs, that is, the best husbands. Parents hope that their daughters can make advantageous marriages to men with family wealth, connections, or valuable market skills—husbands who can bring resources into the family. This is an entirely different kind of competition from the one that boys face. Instead of hoping that their daughters will be strong and intelligent, parents hope that their girls will be

- physically attractive
- nurturing
- a good manager
- accommodating
- emotionally sensitive

- patient
- interested in children

Thus, in the world of thorns, girls and boys are valued and trained for very different things, even though their innate temperament, talents, and abilities may be identical. The lucky family is one in which the children's tastes and talents conform to their roles in life. The unlucky family is one in which there is some kind of mismatch. A child's interest in an activity outside of the prescribed role can be disastrous, distracting him or her from learning the more appropriate skill or branding the child—and the whole family by association—as a social misfit. In a world of scarce resources, whatever gifts or talents the child is born with must be judged and coded "boy," "girl," "appropriate," "inappropriate," and the child must be brought to conform to these judgments.[31]

## Spiritual Impact of Gender Norms

Eve was told that she would bring forth children in sorrow—sorrow because they would be valued not for their individuality or for their relationship with God but for what they could produce. In a sexually divided world, children's potential for wholeness or for simply being themselves must be diverted into role-playing. They cannot be simply male or female: in a fallen world, we can only guess at what God intended the real differences between the sexes to be. Instead, masculinity and femininity is subverted into rigid and socially approved models.

The demands that individuals meet societal standards for how they should behave and what kind of person they must be immediately affect the marital relationship, hampering our ability to be "naked and unashamed" with each other. Economist Deirdre McCloskey notes that the problem with calling the differing expectations for men and women "gender roles" is that these words make the expected behaviors sound optional.[32] A role, after all, is a part to be played, something that can be laid aside with the script and the costumes. Gender norms, on the other hand, are imbued in every aspect of our personality. In the face of such restrictions, no one could be completely honest. It just isn't expedient. If their individual interests, talents, and gifting conflict with their productive gender-typed "role," they will not be allowed to pursue them. In the world of thorns, men and women are not allowed to simply be themselves—and often cannot be what God intends them to be either.

This extended economic explanation for the sexual division of labor maps with uncanny acuity onto the Creator's warnings of the impact of human beings turning away from him, as summarized in Table 1:

| Genesis 3 | Reality of the Fallen World |
|---|---|
| Curse on ground, thorns | • Scarcity, deprivation<br>• Decision-making is based on economics —"the allocation of scarce goods among competing ends"—rather than on faith<br>• Family as a tool of survival |
| Man will face sorrowful toil | • Men must work hard to survive |
| Man eats by the sweat of his brow | • Anxiety, concern about competition, pressure to be the best, to show no weakness |
| Woman brings forth children in sorrow | • Woman's value is in childbearing<br>• Children are valued as resources, not as individuals |
| Woman will face sorrowful toil | • Woman must work hard to survive<br>• Sexual division of labor, woman "domestically specialized" |
| Woman will "turn" to her husband | • Mothers are financially dependent<br>• Girls raised to be dependent on and concerned about attracting men with all of the "feminine charms"<br>• Women want to marry dominant men |
| Husband will rule over wife | • Male dominance of social institutions<br>• Husbands have more power in the marital relationship<br>• Subordination of women to men |
| Will return to the dust | • Mortality, death |

## The Subordination of Women and God's Will

In the late-twentieth-century debates about sexual equality, the "universal subordination of women"—that is, the fact that woman had less power and fewer achievements than man in every known culture—was taken as evidence that women were "naturally" inferior to men. From a theoretical point of view, this historic subordination *is* natural, because it follows from the one absolute difference between men and women: women's ability to bear children. But it is not *innate*, being instead shaped by the material, economic demands of living in an agrarian world of scarce resources.

As I will discuss in chapter 5, the industrial revolution, which began roughly around 1800, changed the way virtually everything in society was produced in Europe and the United States. Technological development made unnecessary the mundane tasks that once occupied vast numbers of people, such as carrying water, chopping wood, growing corn, and grinding meal. With these tasks taken care of by machinery, individuals no longer needed large numbers of children to have a comfortable life; in fact, increasingly it appears that they do not need children or even marriage at all, not in the same sense that they used to. Accordingly, in the United States the number of children born to the average woman has dropped dramatically in the last two hundred years, from over seven at the beginning of the industrial revolution to fewer than two today. Births per woman are even lower in much of Europe. No longer tied to the household, women are far less dependent on men and suddenly not so subordinate anymore. Social change has thus made it apparent that there was nothing innate about women's once limited role in society, church, and family.

While secular debate often focused on whether women's inferior status was innate or the result of oppression, within conservative religious communities the more pressing issue concerned divining God's will. I suggest that this has been a difficult problem for religious institutions because patterns of behavior that are strongly reinforced by the physical demands of survival cannot help but become institutionalized in patterns of belief. What *must be* comes to be considered as what *should be* and is enforced in a culture's moral, ethical, and religious codes. As a result, it can be very difficult for us to sort out God's will from the material imperatives in which we are embedded. The fact that the new forces shaping family and sexual relationships have gone too far to the other side of "liberation," as I will outline in chapter 5, makes this task all the more urgent, how-

ever. As Christians, we can hardly just "go along with" all aspects
of the new norms. The curse on the ground no longer has a literal
reality in the daily lives of many people, but the decadent state of
today's family and sexual norms suggests clearly that spiritually the
world is still full of thorns.[33] How do Christians keep a balanced
understanding of God's will in the face of these urgent but mutable
material demands and incentives?

In pointing us back to the Creator's intent in creating us male and
female, Jesus gave us the key to finding this balance. Genesis 1–3
shows that man and woman's enslavement to the earth was never
God's will. A primary image of the creation account is fruitfulness:
creation teaches that God's intent is that *both* man and woman should
hold dominion over and enjoy the fruitful earth and that they *together*
be fruitful, nurturing children to replenish the earth's abundance.
After the fall, however, these twin blessings became separated and
exaggerated. Care for either becomes no longer the imperative of
blessing but that of necessity, a sorrowful toil. In the fallen world,
man *must* control the earth; woman *must* bear children. The constraints of wrestling a living from the thorny ground push men from
their gentle labors of dominion and nurturing into the aggressive
drive for power. Woman likewise is forced from her God-given role
of responsible stewardship and becomes instead defined and constrained by her biology. Sexuality is no longer primarily a gift to
bless their relationship but a tool of production. Taken together,
the first three chapters of Genesis show that the sexual division of
labor is not God's will for the family, to be salvaged at all costs, but
exactly the opposite.

While the ideal of creation cannot be completely regained in
this fallen world, reconciliation to God through Christ allows us
to relinquish many of the anxieties and fears that accompanied
the fall and hence move toward a reconciliation with each other.
Even more directly, however, as we will see in the next chapter,
when the Gospels are read with this understanding of creation in
mind, it becomes apparent that many of Jesus's teachings were
also designed to combat specific social practices that limit us as
gendered beings. The ethic he introduced, which is elaborated on
by the apostle Paul, provides man and woman with the tools to
transcend, at least in part, the material forces that make the "one

flesh" union seem impossible. Although Jesus's teachings were directed to the correction of the misunderstandings in a way of life far removed from our own, the greater freedoms afforded by our technologically advanced age make his words come alive even more vividly today.

# 3

# Jesus, Power, and Marriage

We are all supposed to be obedient to that love, but we forget love whenever we want power over someone else. We human beings mess it up, over and over again, but God comes into our lives to help us overcome our stiff-neckedness. Indeed, God so loved the world that he sent his only-begotten Son to live with us and teach us how to be the fully human creatures our Maker has always planned for us to be.

—Madeleine L'Engle

In Old Testament times, men in desperate financial straits would sell family land, and sometimes even their families, in order to survive.[1] The Old Testament law allowed this practice, but in order to prevent the permanent alienation of people and land, it provided the role of the redeemer—someone who could buy lands and people back from slavery and alienation. Christianity proclaims that with the whole world enslaved to the effects of sin, God sent a redeemer in the form of his own Son to restore humanity to its proper relationship with him. As shown in the story with which this book began, Jesus taught that God's intent for humankind lies in how he created them (Matt. 19:4–8). Jesus's mission was to accomplish the return, in every way, of man and woman to the abundance and peace of Eden.

Not the least of the things in need of restoration was the relationship between men and women. Although humans were created as sexual beings, the better to enjoy God's munificence, outside of the garden their sexuality became a tool of production instead, humbling itself to the demands of scarcity at the expense of individuality and love.

While the Gospels record only two statements that Jesus made about marriage specifically, many of his teachings nonetheless bear directly on the relationship between men and women. Jesus undid the effects of the curse on the ground, but even more important, he attacked humankind's enduring allegiance to the reason for that curse, our first and universal sin. The applications of his teachings against this compelling human drive for power and control over other people go a long way toward redeeming the relationship between man and woman.

## The Nature of Marriage

In addition to the incident in Matthew 19 with which this book starts, the other statement made by Jesus directly about marriage actually speaks to marriage's negation: adultery and divorce. His declarations about divorce, however, in a significant way broadened his culture's assumptions about marriage. As discussed earlier, Jesus believed that marriage is the union of two into one and that "what God has joined together" human beings are not to put apart (Matt. 19:6; Mark 10:9). The only valid excuse for a man to reject his wife was her unchastity (Matt. 19:9), he noted, but then added a surprising twist. Ancient cultures saw adultery basically as a crime against *men*, and indeed in most of these legal systems it was not possible for a man to commit adultery. Men in the larger Greco-Roman society in which the Judaism of Jesus's day was embedded were not expected to restrict their sexual relations to their wives,[2] and unless the female participant was married, a man's relations outside of marriage were not considered to be adulterous. Although Jewish sexual norms did not allow the kind of license that Greek and Roman men expected, in their thinking it was still the adulteress's husband, and not the adulterer's wife, against whom the sin was committed.

Jesus's definition of marriage as a "one flesh" relationship, in contrast, implicitly recast adultery not as a property crime against men but as a shattering of an essential union created by God. In his revised ideal, adultery is a concern not because it violates a man's exclusive right to his wife's sexuality but because it introduces a third party into the "two become one" relationship. This view of marriage made a husband's unfaithfulness a sin against his *wife*, and the fact that they had obtained a writ of divorce did not change things: "Anyone who divorces his wife and marries another woman commits adultery against her" (Mark 10:11; Matt. 19:9). Further, a man who divorces his wife "causes her to become an adulteress" (presumably because economic circumstances would require her to remarry), and "anyone who marries the divorced woman commits adultery" (Matt. 5:32). While this teaching causes difficulty for divorced people who want to remarry,[3] it reflects a high view of marriage and sexuality, one in which marriage is more than just a material concern. Jesus's rejection of the double standard was an important step in recognizing women as full partners in marriage and in reaffirming the importance of sexuality as a tool of the relationship rather than as simply a physical resource.

## Jesus and Women

### *More than breasts and a womb*

From the fall up until mid-twentieth century, the vast majority of women lived lives circumscribed entirely by their sexual, biological roles of wife and mother. Marriage was the norm for all girls.[4] Childbearing was a woman's most important function, and women who could not bear children—and their husbands—were greatly to be pitied.

Throughout Jesus's ministry, however, he steadfastly affirmed that the value of an individual woman extended beyond her biological functions.

The Gospel of Luke records an incident when "a woman in the crowd raised her voice and said to him, 'Blessed is the womb that bore you and the breasts that nursed you!'" (Luke 11:27). In an age in which women were judged by their sons' accomplishments, this woman was trying to pay Jesus a compliment by praising his mother: "Your mother was really lucky to have a son like you!" But the woman framed his mother's blessedness in terms of her biology.[5] As her praise points out, in her culture's reckoning, the mother of Jesus was not much more than a fortunate womb and breasts.

Jesus turned the compliment around: "But he said, 'Blessed rather are those who hear the word of God and obey it!'" (Luke 11:28). What was important about an individual woman or man is not a biological attribute but that she hears the word of God and obeys it. Although the woman in the crowd could not have known it, this applied especially strongly in the case of Jesus's own mother. Luke began his Gospel with her story: An angel appeared to a young girl named Mary and told her that she would bear a child by the Holy Spirit. Mary knew that according to Old Testament law she could be stoned to death if she were found to be pregnant by someone other than her fiancé. But she accepted the risk in faith and so brought the Christ into the world. Jesus said that what was truly admirable about his mother, or anyone, was such obedience and faith.

### More than a domestic goddess

Preindustrial families' need for children led women to become tied to the house and domestic tasks in a way that men were not. In the well-known story of Mary and Martha, Jesus once again helped his hearers distinguish between what is valued by the world and what is valued in the kingdom of heaven:

> As Jesus and his disciples were on their way, he came to a village where a woman named Martha opened her home to him. She had a sister called Mary, who sat at the Lord's feet listening to what he said. But Martha was distracted by all the preparations that had to be made. She came to him and asked, "Lord, don't you care that my sister has left me to do the work by myself? Tell her to help me!"
>
> "Martha, Martha," the Lord answered, "you are worried and upset ['anxious and troubled' in the RSV] about many things, but few things are needed—or indeed only one. Mary has chosen what is better, and it will not be taken away from her." (Luke 10:38–41)

The expression "to sit at the feet" of a rabbi meant that one was his student or disciple.[6] At this point in history, women did not sit at the feet of rabbis: in a world of scarce resources, what little a family could spare for education went to sons, not daughters. Jesus, however, made no comment at all about Mary's being out of place but accepted her freely as a disciple. Instead, Jesus corrected Martha's anxiety, and no doubt pride, about honorably fulfilling her job as a woman. It was not a question of leaving guests to go hungry: Jesus had turned water into wine and could feed a multitude with a few loaves of bread. "Only one thing is needed," he told Martha, and Mary had chosen that one thing. Like bearing children, hearing and obeying the word of God was more blessed than even the most perfect fulfillment of the housewifely role.

### Ritual limitations

Jesus's challenge to Jewish rules on ritual cleanliness also made possible women's participation in discipleship. Although they involved washings and dietary restrictions, the Old Testament requirements of ritual purity had little to do with health or physical cleanliness. Rather, ritual purity involved avoiding certain foods and behaviors and following certain rites in order to assure one's cultic, or even social, purity or worthiness.[7] Individuals who were not in a state of ritual cleanliness could not participate in religious ceremonies, and because the touch of someone who was not pure contaminated any person or object he touched, the requirements of ritual purity restricted movement within the community and family as well. Among other things, these laws specified that a person was "unclean" when he or she had a bodily discharge. Purity laws applied to men as well as women, but because a woman's menstrual period occurred regularly, ritual cleanliness laws had a disproportionate impact on them. These rules effectively cut women out of an active role in religious life: "The Jewish woman was the mistress of the home, but was . . . exempt from fulfilling religious duties that had to be performed at stated times (because her first duties were to her children and the home and she might not be in the required state of ritual purity)."[8]

Mark 5:25–34 tells the story of the bitter price the requirements of ritual cleanliness could incur:

A woman was there who had been subject to bleeding for twelve years. She had suffered a great deal under the care of many doctors and had spent all she had, yet instead of getting better she grew worse. When she heard about Jesus, she came up behind him in the crowd and touched his cloak, because she thought, "If I just touch his clothes, I will be healed." Immediately her bleeding stopped and she felt in her body that she was freed from her suffering.

At once Jesus realized that power had gone out from him. He turned around in the crowd and asked, "Who touched my clothes?"

"You see the people crowding against you," his disciples answered, "and yet you can ask, 'Who touched me?'"

But Jesus kept looking around to see who had done it. Then the woman, knowing what had happened to her, came and fell at his feet and, trembling with fear, told him the whole truth. He said to her, "Daughter, your faith has healed you. Go in peace and be freed from your suffering."

For twelve years, this woman had been not only ill but ritually unclean as well. Morally obligated to warn people that she was a source of contamination, she lived a lonely life in which no one would touch her, and some would not even willingly be in her presence. Knowing that no rabbi would bother with her, she touched Jesus by stealth. But Jesus insisted on her identifying herself and her disgrace. Then instead of castigating her for making him unclean, he praised her for her faith. Jesus's public denial of the social significance of the woman's affliction not only fully cured this one woman but henceforth freed all his followers from these restrictions.[9]

### Seeing beyond the sexual

In addition to the requirements of ritual purity and expectations about what women *should* do, women were greatly limited by fears about what they *might* do. Many of the limitations imposed on women in traditional cultures arose from concerns about maintaining their chastity. Interestingly, until around the nineteenth century, women were regarded as the more carnal of the two sexes.[10] As a man's honor depended on the chastity of the women of his household, he had to do whatever he could to control their behavior and their reputations. Many cultures still insist on extreme measures to police women's virtue, segregating them from men, chaperoning them in public, or requiring them to veil. In the New Testament era, a Jewish man could divorce his wife for speaking to a man on the street or for going outside with her hair uncovered. In order to avoid any appearance of impropriety, some men would ignore their own wives and daughters in public. Making a show of their virtue, one group of rabbis went so far as to vow never even to look at a woman other than their wives. Their righteously averted eyes sometimes resulted in accidents, earning them the nickname of the "bruised and bleeding rabbis."

Jesus always treated sexual immorality as sin, but he recognized that baseless suspicions greatly limited women's potential discipleship. He refused to allow these cultural fears to limit his ministry to anyone. Just the opposite of the "bruised and bleeding rabbis," he made a point of welcoming women regardless of their reputations:

> One of the Pharisees asked him to eat with him, and he went into the Pharisee's house, and took his place at table. And behold, a woman of the city, who was a sinner, when she learned that he was at table in the Pharisee's house, brought an alabaster flask of ointment, and standing behind him at his feet, weeping, she began to wet his feet with her tears, and wiped them with the hair of her head, and kissed his feet, and anointed them with the ointment. Now when the Pharisee who had invited him saw it, he said to himself, "If this man were a prophet, he would have known who and what sort of woman this is who is touching him, for she is a sinner." . . . Then turning toward the woman he [Jesus] said to Simon, "Do you see this woman? I entered your house, you gave me no water for my feet, but she has wet my feet with her tears and wiped them with her hair. You gave me no kiss, but from the time I came in she has not ceased to kiss my feet. You did not anoint my head with oil, but she has anointed my feet with ointment. Therefore I tell you, her sins, which are many, are forgiven, for she loved much; but he who is forgiven little, loves little." And he said to her, "Your sins are forgiven." (Luke 7:36–48 RSV)

Note that in this incident, it was not the woman's behavior to which Jesus's host objected as much as it was Jesus's. He believed that it was so wrong for a righteous man to allow himself to be touched by a sinful woman that God would intervene. Jesus denied that belief, pointing out that the woman's repentance, gratitude, and love were more important than her sexual past. Unlike those around him, Jesus treated sinful women as though the past could be forgiven and the woman redeemed.

A similar incident took place beside a well in Samaria:

> [Jesus] left Judea and went back once more to Galilee.
>
> Now he had to go through Samaria. . . . Jesus, tired as he was from the journey, sat down beside the well. . . .
>
> When a woman of Samaria came to draw water, Jesus said to her, "Will you give me a drink?" (His disciples had gone into the town to buy food.)
>
> The Samaritan woman said to him, "You are a Jew and I am a woman of Samaria. How can you ask me for a drink?" (For Jews do not associate with Samaritans.) (John 4:3, 6, 7–9)

Jesus held an extended theological discussion with the woman, then abruptly said,

> "Go, call your husband, and come back."
>
> "I have no husband," she replied.
>
> Jesus said to her, "You are right when you say you have no husband. The fact is, you have had five husbands, and the man you now have is not your husband. What you have just said is quite true." (vv. 16–18)

After more discussion, Jesus revealed to the woman that he was the Christ. At this point,

> his disciples returned and were surprised to find him talking with a woman. But no one asked, "What do you want?" or "Why are you talking with her?"
>
> Then, leaving her water jar, the woman went back to the town and said to the people, "Come, see a man who told me everything I ever did. Could this be the Messiah?" . . .
>
> Many Samaritans from the city believed in him because of the woman's testimony. . . (vv. 27–29, 39)

Both the woman and Jesus's followers were astonished that he should speak to a woman in public. The facts that she was a Samaritan woman, whom Jews considered always to be ritually unclean,[11] and had had a checkered sexual history (which Jesus made a point of bringing up) should have made her complete anathema to any righteous man, let alone a rabbi. None of these factors stopped Jesus from talking with her, however, or from revealing to her that he was the Messiah. As a result, the Samaritan woman returned to her village and became his first witness.

In both of these incidents, Jesus was explicitly reminded of the fears that were expected to limit his interactions with women. He just as pointedly defied these limitations, going so far as to tell men that considering women only as sexual objects was as much of a sin as actually committing the act they so feared: "You have heard that it was said, 'You shall not commit adultery.' But I say to you that anyone who looks at a woman lustfully has already committed adultery with her in his heart" (Matt. 5:27–28).

Being the focus of lust or sexual speculation, regardless of their own behavior, greatly limited women's freedom in the ancient world, and it still does today. Although women in the world of thorns often use men's lust to their advantage, the twentieth-century women's movement correctly identified the sexual "objectification" of women as a serious limitation on their freedoms. Jesus opened the door not only to female discipleship but to the possibility of men and women interacting without reference to sex. Further, in shifting the blame for lust from the woman to the man, Jesus removed the assumption of sinfulness that adhered to women's very existence as female.

### Jesus's transcendence of material gender roles

To Jesus, women were more than sources of impurity, temptresses, wombs, servants, hostesses, or whores. He explicitly denied that an individual's demographics—biological, ethnic, or social status—had any relevance at all to her spiritual standing. In fact, whenever Jesus interacted with women, he told those who were caught up in concern over their prescribed social roles, "Choose the best part, and don't worry about the rest." It did not matter how beautifully her house was kept, how delicious was the food she served, how many sons she bore or how prestigious their occupations, how successfully she hid herself from view, or how well she had married. Women are judged on these dimensions in the world of thorns, but these are not God's criteria for participation in the kingdom of heaven. In the kingdom, women do not contaminate men simply by existing or speaking. Rather, women can be entrusted to receive the revelation that Jesus is the Christ and to spread that good news. They were the equals of the wealthy and righteous Simon the Pharisee. Their virtue was assumed, so they could be spoken to in public. They were competent to "hear the word of God and obey it," so they were worthy to be disciples. They were part of God's creation, *individuals* who could choose "the better part" as well as men could, and against whom Jesus would allow no obstacles to be placed.

## Jesus and Men

Just as the material demands of the world system swamp women's individuality, men are trapped by expectations of what they should be. Jesus's ministry to men was also intended to free them from their share of the curse on the ground.

### Man the babe-hound

Jesus's comment about "adultery in the heart," discussed earlier for its liberating effect on women, freed men as well: "You have heard that it was said, 'You shall not commit adultery.' But I say to you that anyone who looks at a woman lustfully has already committed adultery with her in his heart" (Matt. 5:27–28). The crowds hearing this statement knew very well that adultery was a bad thing. Jesus went beyond condemning adultery and urged men to stop looking at women as sexual objects.

Women, of course, would gain a great deal if all men followed this admonition. Fear of men's lust greatly curtails women's freedom. But this passage also addresses the social pressure on men to prove their manhood by making sexual conquests or by being seen with women that other men find attractive. Fears and concerns about sexuality play a dominant, and unpleasant, part in men's lives. "Aggressiveness, virility [and] sexual prowess" were important parts of a man's claim to honor in the Greco-Roman world.[12] Men today often feel the same way, defining sexuality as a contest in which their "manhood" is judged. For example, social commentator Naomi Wolf noted the panic that some men felt when a 1993 "study of male sexual habits found that many respondents claimed to be having sex ten times a week, data which raised the sexual pressure."[13]

In the 1970s, men blamed their inability to perform at such levels on the aggressiveness of the newly liberated woman. In the 1980s, Wolf blamed it on the unrealistic images in *Playboy* magazine, with which real women couldn't compete. But the blame for sexual anxieties might be most appropriately laid on a macho culture in which one is expected to have satisfying sexual relations with an unlimited number of people about whom one does not care and who do not care in return. Ultimately unsatisfying, the pressure to behave promiscuously offers another example of the corruption of sexuality after the fall. Jesus's redefinition of manhood offers redemption from these pressures, placing sexuality back into context as a tool of relationship, not a marker of personal worth or achievement.

### Leaving the dead

The story of Martha portrays a woman who nearly missed the call to discipleship because of her concerns about fulfilling her socially expected roles. Several other incidents in Jesus's ministry tell of men whose adherence to social expectations may have kept them from their calls:

> [Jesus] said to another man, "Follow me."
> But he replied, "Lord, first let me go and bury my father."
> Jesus said to him, "Let the dead bury their own dead, but you go and proclaim the kingdom of God."
> Still another said, "I will follow you, Lord; but first let me go back and say good-by to my family."
> Jesus replied, "No one who puts his hand to the plow and looks back is fit for service in the kingdom of God." (Luke 9:59–62)

In these two cases, Jesus responded harshly to what seem like reasonable requests. His statements sound so harsh, in fact, that New Testament historian S. Scott Bartchy suggests the men were not simply asking permission to attend a funeral or visit their family. Although an individual's choice to follow Jesus could cause dissension within his or her family, Jesus's followers continued to honor family connections and responsibilities. These men's hesitation to follow was not for their family's sakes. Rather, they were reluctant to let go of the prerogatives to which their family position entitled them.

Bartchy suggests that, in all likelihood, the first man could not bury his father quickly enough to join Jesus's retinue because his father was not dead. This man wanted to go home, serve his father until he died, bury him, and then—most important—succeed him. In patriarchal societies, the father held all the power in the family, and everyone else—wife, children, and servants—were expected to bow to his will. If the man defied his father's control by leaving him to follow Jesus, he would lose his inheritance and his chance to be the patriarch. No doubt, like Michael Corleone in *The Godfather*, the man thought he could use his power for good and escape becoming what his father was in the end. Jesus's blunt statement told the man that the world to which he was clinging was the world of the dead, a world thick with thorns. There was no life in it, and he must leave those who already partook of it to serve themselves.[14]

Matthew 19:16–26 recounts the story of a rich young man who also turned down a call to discipleship because he couldn't leave his worldly wealth.

> Then someone came to him and said, "Teacher, what good deed must I do to have eternal life?" And he said to him, "Why do you ask me about what is good? There is only one who is good. If you wish to enter into life, keep the commandments." He said to him, "Which ones?" And Jesus said, "You shall not murder; You shall not commit adultery; You shall not steal; You shall not bear false witness; Honor your father and mother; also, You shall love your neighbor as yourself." The young man said to him, "I have kept all these; what do I still lack?" Jesus said to him, "If you wish to be perfect, go, sell your possessions, and give the money to the poor, and you will have treasure in heaven; then come, follow me." When the young man heard this word, he went away grieving, for he had many possessions.
>
> Then Jesus said to his disciples, "Truly I tell you, it will be hard for a rich person to enter the kingdom of heaven. Again I tell you, it is easier for a camel to go through the eye of a needle than for someone who is

rich to enter the kingdom of God." When the disciples heard this, they were greatly astounded and said, "Then who can be saved?" But Jesus looked at them and said, "For mortals it is impossible, but for God all things are possible." (Matt. 19:16–26 NRSV)

The rich young man had it all—great wealth, many possessions, and the respect of his community. Even his queries about eternal life betrayed the magnitude of his bounty: when Jesus recounted the commandments necessary for salvation, the young man had already fulfilled them.

After this interview, Jesus astonished his disciples by saying that it is hard for the rich to enter the kingdom of heaven. In his day, this was an absurd notion. Everyone believed that the wealthy got to be wealthy because God had blessed them.[15] The rich supported the temple, the heart of Jewish religious life, and only the wealthy could easily afford the expensive rules and rituals that defined "righteousness."[16] So if the rich couldn't enter the kingdom, "then who can be saved?"

Perhaps it is difficult for the rich to enter the kingdom of God because they cannot acknowledge that they need a kingdom other than the one in which they rule. They have all abundance, and in their own right, too. Bartchy points out that Jesus wasn't inviting the rich young man into poverty.[17] Jesus and the disciples were not in want. They had enough that they themselves gave to the poor.[18] But Jesus *was* asking the young man to trust God to provide abundance, and this he simply could not do. The rich young man went away sorrowful, not because Jesus required him to give up his wealth but because the kingdom of God required him to give up control.

The men in these incidents, as well as the man preparing to "eat, drink, and be merry" in his wealth only to die that night instead (Luke 12:17–20), all made the same mistake. "Looking back" like Lot's wife, none of them wanted to let go of the privileges afforded those at the top of the worldly heap. They had, or would soon have, control of their own abundance, and they couldn't let it go, not even at the price of eternal life.

The first man and woman wanted to control their own lives too, to have everything in their own right and not be dependent on God. But as God had warned them, when they took control for themselves, "you will certainly die" (Gen. 2:17). This is original sin, and all human beings suffer from it. Jesus called those who cling to the prerogatives of sin already dead, unworthy of the kingdom of heaven.

### Honor and shame

Jesus directly challenged other aspects of traditional manhood in the Sermon on the Mount:

> You have heard that it was said, "Eye for eye, and tooth for tooth." But I tell you, do not resist an evil person. If someone slaps you on the right cheek, turn to them the other cheek also. And if anyone wants to sue you and take your shirt, hand over your coat as well. If anyone forces you to go one mile, go with them two miles. (Matt. 5:38–41)

In the time of Christ (and still today), the Mediterranean world was an honor/shame culture in which maintaining one's pride and honor (public reputation) was of paramount importance.[19] Any insult or slight must be avenged. This was a man's job, and he was responsible for defending not only his own honor but that of his entire family. In this kind of culture, vendettas and feuds are commonplace. A modern example of such a vendetta occurred over Locherbee, Scotland in 1988, when terrorists blew up an American airplane to avenge the accidental downing of an Iranian airbus by the United States. The problem with the honor/shame cycle is that there is no end to it. Vendettas never end: your opponent won't let you win, accepting loss is unbearably shameful, and there is no "getting even." Every blow, every insult, every slight requires retaliation.

Jesus's comments weren't meant to refuse Christians the ability to resist violent attack. The incidents he cites—a slap on the face, a lawsuit over an item of clothing, and being treated like a servant—are not lethal physical threats but insults to honor. Jesus told men that they must give up their macho concern with honor and shame. If you are insulted, Jesus said, stop the fight right there. Turn the other cheek, give your opponent your cloak as well, and serve cheerfully.[20]

Another aspect of the contest to acquire honor and avoid shame manifests itself in pressure to control other people, or at least not to be controlled. An incident early in Jesus's ministry illustrates the pervasiveness of this drive:

> Jesus and his disciples went on to the villages around Caesarea Philippi. On the way he asked them, "Who do people say I am?"
>
> They replied, "Some say John the Baptist; others say Elijah; and still others, one of the prophets."
>
> "But what about you?" he asked. "Who do you say I am?"
>
> Peter answered, "You are the Messiah."
>
> Jesus warned them not to tell anyone about him.
>
> He then began to teach them that the Son of Man must suffer many things and be rejected by the elders, the chief priests and the teachers of the law, and that he must be killed and after three days rise again. He spoke plainly about this, and Peter took him aside and began to rebuke him.
>
> But when Jesus turned and looked at his disciples, he rebuked Peter. "Get behind me, Satan!" he said. "You do not have in mind the things of God, but merely human concerns." (Mark 8:27–33)

The Jews of Jesus's day were waiting eagerly for the Messiah, the Anointed One who would be a leader like David or Solomon, a holy king who would redeem Israel from the oppression of Rome and restore them to righteousness. Peter and the others expected that Jesus would become the king of a liberated Israel—and that they would be right there beside him in the glory and the power. Having cast their lot with Jesus, surely his disciples would share his glory by becoming rulers in this restored, righteous, but earthly kingdom.

When Jesus acknowledged that he was the Messiah, his companions must have been exuberant. But then he began to explain what this really meant: suffering and death. Peter was astonished by the news that the man he expected to be his ticket to glory thought that being the Messiah meant rejection and self-sacrifice. As the text tells us, Peter "took him aside and began to rebuke him."

Peter was the most vocal of the disciples, but Jesus knew that he was not the only one who did not understand. He turned back to his other disciples and said, "Get behind me, Satan!" (In Matthew's version, Jesus adds, "You are a stumbling block to me" [16:23].) In the Bible, a "satan" is a tempter, a spirit like the serpent in Genesis 3, who knows a person's deepest desires and uses them to lure her or him into sin.[21] Jesus's use of this particular phrase is an allusion back to the temptations:

> The devil took him to a very high mountain and showed him all the kingdoms of the world and their splendor. "All this I will give you," he said, "if you will bow down and worship me."
> But Jesus said, "Away from me, Satan! For it is written: 'Worship the Lord your God, and serve him only.'" (Matt. 4:8–10)

No doubt Jesus could have been exactly the sort of messiah that his followers expected, becoming an earthly king and freeing Israel from Roman rule. His reference to Peter as a "satan" suggests that this was a real temptation for him. But instead he chose another path.

The next passage continues the story:

> Then he called the crowd to him along with his disciples and said: "Whoever wants to be my disciple must deny themselves and take up their cross and follow me. For whoever wants to save their life will lose it, but whoever loses their life for me and for the gospel will save it. What good is it for you to gain the whole world, yet forfeit your soul? Or what can you give in exchange for your soul? If any of you are ashamed of me and my words in this adulterous and sinful generation, the Son of Man will be ashamed of you when he comes in his Father's glory with the holy angels." (Mark 8:34–38)

Yet who would not be ashamed of Jesus if, instead of becoming the successor of King David, he was scorned by all those who really mattered in Jewish life, if he were to die the ignominious, demeaning death of a criminal? The thing that Jesus predicted would happen to him was deeply shameful. His teachings about how God uses power were very difficult for his followers to understand. Even after the crucifixion and resurrection, they continued to expect that Jesus would be an earthly king ("So when they met together, they asked him 'Lord, are you at this time going to restore the kingdom to Israel?'" [Acts 1:6]).

### What does it mean to be "Lord"?

Even more to the point of human need for control are Jesus's many statements and sermons about the Christian use of power and authority. The consequences of the fall meant that both man and woman needed control and power in the hostile world of thorns, but bearing children limited women to their homes and so precluded attaining power in their own right. Finding and raising their place in the power hierarchy was and still is a constant preoccupation of men, however, and the source of much anxiety. Most men find themselves unable to meet other men in any situation without wondering how they rank relative to the other.[22] The obligations of status are constant burdens on men's minds.[23]

Jesus positively denied that Christians should think this way anymore. Consider his statements about the use of power in Mark 10:35–37, 41–45:

> Then James and John, the sons of Zebedee, came to him. "Teacher," they said, "we want you to do for us whatever we ask."
>
> "What do you want me to do for you?" he asked.
>
> They replied, "Let one of us sit at your right and the other at your left in your glory."
>
> . . . .When the ten heard about this, they became indignant with James and John. Jesus called them together and said, "You know that those who are regarded as rulers of the Gentiles lord it over them, and their high officials exercise authority over them. Not so with you. Instead, whoever wants to become great among you must be your servant, and whoever wants to be first must be slave of all. For even the Son of Man did not come to be served, but to serve, and to give his life as a ransom for many."

James and John came to Jesus asking to reign with him when he came to power. They wanted a high place in the chain of command, at the top, right next to Jesus. When the rest of Jesus's companions heard about their request, they were angry, and in terms of the worldly struggle for status, they had a right to be. So Jesus called them all together to explain. No one was going to "lord it over" or even exercise authority over anyone else. If anyone wanted to be great in the kingdom of God, he would have to become a servant, not one who expected to be served.

Bartchy observes,

> These surprising words radically call into question his disciples' view of the kind of power operative in "his glory" by reversing the expecta-

tions commonly associated with the title "Son of Man." According to Daniel 7:13–14, the "one like the son of man," who came to be regarded during the century before Jesus as the one who is to come to judge the world, will be "given dominion and glory and kingdom, that all peoples, nations, and languages should serve him." Jesus identifies himself as that Son of Man and then radically rejects the privileges associated with the role by asserting that he is ready to serve others, even at the cost of his own life.[24]

## This acceptance of servanthood is not just a figure of speech:

It was just before the Passover Festival. Jesus knew that the hour had come for him to leave this world and go to the Father. Having loved his own who were in the world, he loved them to the end.

The evening meal was in progress, and the devil had already prompted Judas, the son of Simon Iscariot, to betray Jesus. Jesus knew that the Father had put all things under his power, and that he had come from God and was returning to God; so he got up from the meal, took off his outer clothing, and wrapped a towel around his waist. After that, he poured water into a basin and began to wash his disciples' feet, drying them with the towel that was wrapped around him.

He came to Simon Peter, who said to him, "Lord, are you going to wash my feet?"

Jesus replied, "You do not realize now what I am doing, but later you will understand."

"No," said Peter, "you shall never wash my feet."

Jesus answered, "Unless I wash you, you have no part with me."

"Then, Lord," Simon Peter replied, "not just my feet but my hands and my head as well!"

Jesus answered, "Those who have had a bath need only to wash their feet; then their whole body is clean. . . ."

When he had finished washing their feet, he put on his clothes and returned to his place. "Do you understand what I have done for you?" he asked them. "You call me 'Teacher' and 'Lord,' and rightly so, for that is what I am. Now that I, your Lord and Teacher, have washed your feet, you also should wash one another's feet. I have set you an example that you should do as I have done for you. Very truly I tell you, servants are not greater than their master, nor are messengers greater than the one who sent them. Now that you know these things, you will be blessed if you do them." (John 13:1–17)

Unlike some ritual washings, the washing of feet had a practical basis. People in this era wore sandals, and their feet got dirty. Jesus said as much in verse 10 ("those who have had a bath need only to wash their feet"). It was an act of both hospitality and hygiene to have a servant at one's door to wash the feet of guests.

Peter reacted strongly to Jesus's assumption of this role precisely because it was a servant's job. Foot washing was considered so degrading a task that Jewish servants were not asked to do it—it was left to Gentile slaves instead[25]—and here was Peter's Lord, who had been given "all things under his power," doing it himself. Jesus's washing of feet was not honorable, and it lowered Peter's own status. But worse than this was the implication: if Jesus could wash feet, would not Peter be expected to do so as well?

So Peter next asked Jesus to wash all of him. Perhaps Peter was trying to "spiritualize" the incident, so that it became an act of ritual significance rather than a mundane task that he too would be expected to perform. But Jesus's assumption of the role of a servant was sincere, not just a motion that he was going through on a special occasion, and it remains truly radical. Bartchy suggests that Peter's reaction in asking to be washed all over is psychologically apt: Peter knew that a man of his day would have to be totally transformed in order to accept this new order of things. Bartchy summarizes Jesus's teachings in John 13:13–17 as follows:

> The earliest Christian confession, that Jesus is Lord, cuts two ways. First of all, you say that *Jesus* is Lord. What this means then is that anybody else is out as lord. That means the emperor can't be lord, that means that my daddy can't be lord, that means that a husband can't be lord. *Jesus* is Lord. That's the first thing to get straight. The second thing to get straight is that Jesus is *Lord*. Now the only way in which lordship can be defined properly . . . within the Christian community is the way in which Jesus carries it out.[26]

The New Testament brims with other occasions in which Jesus showed, by word and example, that worldly notions of authority, honor, and power have no place in the kingdom of God. Jesus made many statements along these lines, saying that one must come to the kingdom of heaven as a little child; that the first will be last and the last will be first; and that it will be difficult for the rich to enter the kingdom. He insisted on receiving women, whom men actively avoided, and little children, with whom men rarely bothered. Jesus never forced anyone to do anything. He did not even heal people against their will (John 5:2–9). He explicitly rejected Satan's offer (and his followers' expectations) of power over the earth (Matt. 4:1–11). He held tremendous authority, able to command spirits and the material world, but mostly his was the power of authenticity—the power of speaking and teaching the true word of God. No doubt, he could have used his personal gifts to command his followers, but he steadfastly refused to do so.

Does this mean that Peter spent the rest of his life as a foot washer, that Christians should literally seek only the work of servants? In the book of Acts, when the apostles found themselves spending their time administering to the physical needs of the congregation in Jerusalem, they correctly stated, "It would not be right for us to neglect the ministry of the word of God in order to wait on tables" (Acts 6:2 TNIV). They appointed others to fill that role and moved on to what they had been called to do. Jesus called them not necessarily to the labor of servants but to the servant's abnegation of privilege. After Jesus washed feet, his followers could no longer treat other people as inferiors. Social status, gender, and political power were to have no bearing in the Christian community. All were called equally to serve each other, not themselves, and all labor was honorable. This abnegation of power and entitlement, while a sacrifice in the world of thorns, freed Christians from a vast burden of shame they might once have felt when they were not on top of the status hierarchy.

## Power and Marriage

While the other aspects of gender roles that Jesus decried affect marital relationships, their impact is often indirect, influencing the individual's personal behavior and anxieties. In attacking the male dominance and status system, however, Jesus addressed an issue of continuing relevance to marriage. "Now the only way lordship can be defined is the way in which Jesus carried it out."

Despite Jesus's call for Christians to forsake the wielding of power over each other, the fallen standards of the status hierarchy have been applied whole hog to Christian marriage, whether in the older ideal of submissive wife/dominant husband, a "chain of command," or the Southern Baptist Convention's softer recasting of husband as "servant-leader" to his graciously submitted wife. True, Jesus never preached against hierarchy in marriage per se, so perhaps those who would preserve it might make a case that marriage is an exception to his forbidding his followers the use of power. They cannot base that case on any of his teachings, however, and in chapter 4 I will show that hierarchy in marriage cannot be based on the teachings of Paul either.

## The Meaning of Jesus's Manhood

Someone once wrote that Jesus had come to earth once before he came as Mary's son, but because the first time he came as a woman, no one paid any attention to her. Certainly no one would have noticed a woman doing the things he advocated. No special meaning would be attached to a woman's renouncing privilege and power—she had no prerogatives to give up. God sent his own Son to buy humankind back from their slavery to the fears and shame of the world of thorns. Only a powerful man filled with authority could effectively model for other men the way to regain a relationship with God.[27] Perhaps Jesus had to suffer a shameful death in order to convince men that he really, really meant it when he said that Christians are not to "lord it over" over people and that refusing to compete for honor and authority over others is not a shame but rather the heart of a redeemed life.

Born of the House of David, a healer of tremendous power, a preacher who could stir multitudes, the Son of God and the Son of Man, Jesus had a lot to give up. He could have been what the crowds wanted him to be. He could have taken what Satan offered. But

> though he was in the form of God, [he] did not count equality with God a thing to be grasped, but emptied himself, taking the form of a servant, being born in the likeness of men. And being found in human

form he humbled himself and became obedient unto death, even death on a cross. Therefore God has highly exalted him and bestowed on him the name which is above every name, that at the name of Jesus every knee should bow, in heaven and on earth and under the earth, and every tongue confess that Jesus Christ is Lord, to the glory of God the Father. (Phil. 2:6–11 RSV)

In Jesus's teachings, no one stands between the individual and God. It is the status hierarchy of the fallen world that makes individuals seek power over each other. If Christ himself would not take on the role of an earthly authority, the church should think twice before encouraging men to grasp it for themselves.

## The New Economics of God's Kingdom

Jesus, then, asked men and women to renounce the first sin and relinquish control back to God, thus gaining their freedom from the onerous burdens and privilege of gender. But still living in the world of thorns, people need reassurance that they can do as he asked and still survive. In reconciling humanity to God, Jesus made possible their return to the fearless state of Eden, teaching:

> Therefore I tell you, do not worry about your life, what you will eat or drink; or about your body, what you will wear. Is not life more important than food, and the body more important than clothes? Look at the birds of the air; they do not sow or reap or store away in barns, and yet your heavenly Father feeds them. Are you not much more valuable than they? Can any one of you by worrying add a single hour to your life?
> And why do you worry about clothes? See how the lilies of the field grow. They do not labor or spin. Yet I tell you that not even Solomon in all his splendor was dressed like one of these. If that is how God clothes the grass of the field, which is here today and tomorrow is thrown into the fire, will he not much more clothe you—you of little faith? So do not worry, saying, "What shall we eat?" or "What shall we drink?" or "What shall we wear?" For the pagans run after all these things, and your heavenly Father knows that you need them. But seek first his kingdom and his righteousness, and all these things will be given to you as well. Therefore do not worry about tomorrow, for tomorrow

will worry about itself. Each day has enough trouble of its own. (Matt. 6:25–34 TNIV)

The first human beings did not trust God's provision for them and ended up in the circumstances predicted in Genesis 3. But Jesus on many occasions assured those who follow him that they have already returned to God's abundance (Matt. 7:7–11; Luke 12:4–7). The descendants of the naked and shame-filled couple of Genesis 3 no longer have to worry: instead of thorns and the rough grass of the field, they can expect God's abundant care in feeding and clothing them.[28] Even more, Jesus tells them to stop worrying about their life, that man no longer needs to eat his bread by the sweat of his brow. God knows what they need, and God will provide for them. With life no longer a zero-sum game, competition, honor, and control are no longer necessary.

Finally, Jesus removes even the fear of death. Innumerable passages in the New Testament assure us of this, including:

For as in Adam all die, so in Christ all will be made alive. . . . The last enemy to be destroyed is death. (1 Cor. 15:22, 26)

For if, by the trespass of the one man, death reigned through that one man, how much more will those who receive God's abundant provision of grace and of the gift of righteousness reign in life through the one man Jesus Christ! (Rom. 5:17)

For God so loved the world that he gave his one and only Son, that whosoever believes in him shall not perish but have eternal life. (John 3:16)

The Revelation explicitly shows Christ setting aside the effects of the curse, especially our alienation from God:

And I heard a loud voice from the throne saying: "Look! God's dwelling place is now among the people, and he will dwell with them. They will be his people, and God himself will be with them and be their God. He will wipe every tear from their eyes. There will be no more death or mourning or crying or pain, for the old order of things has passed away."

On each side of the river stood the tree of life, bearing twelve crops of fruit, yielding its fruit every month. And the leaves of the trees are for the healing of the nations. No longer will there be any curse. (Rev. 21:3–4; 22:2–3)

Although the images of the Revelation usually refer to the second coming, Jesus taught that the kingdom of heaven has been inaugurated here and now, for those who will enter it. In discussing the rich young man, for instance, Jesus didn't necessarily mean that the rich will never go to heaven after they die. He meant that those who will not relinquish control to God are not redeemed from the anxieties and pressures of sin in this life. The kingdom of heaven offers the freedom from fear that comes with a living faith.

And the impact of this redemption on marriage? Accepting Jesus's teachings frees humanity from the scarcity of the world of thorns, from the fears and the imperatives that result in gender restrictions, from the obligations and anxieties that divide man and woman and make love into a matter of economics. Shed of them, man and woman can return to the kind of marriage that Jesus said is the ideal:

"For this reason a man will leave his father and mother and be united to his wife, and the two will become one flesh." So they are no longer two, but one. (Matt. 19:5)

## Jesus and Marriage Today

When life is shaped by the demands of scarcity, the temptation to view other people only as tools of survival is acute. Under conditions of scarcity—conditions that characterized most of human history, and that continue still in much of the world today—the ideal woman's traits, skills, and activities differ greatly from those of the ideal man, so much so that even Jesus's followers had a hard time believing that the divine ideal was of husband and wife as "one flesh." Yet as I will show later, on the basis of Jesus's teachings, Christianity did and does transform marriage and family norms, making the "one flesh" ideal conceivable. Then and now, redemption means turning over the natural order of things in the fallen world.

Many parts of today's world still struggle with the scarcity that marked most of human history. There, Jesus's teachings that women are more than baby-making machines and work horses and that men do not need to be slaves to crippling codes of status and honor remain startling and often revolutionary. Research on the impact of evangelical religion in Brazil, for example, has shown that when men there accept Christian teachings, drinking and womanizing tend to diminish, they give their wives a larger share of family resources, and rates of domestic violence fall.[29] Similarly, missionary Patti Ricotta relates the astonishment with which Ugandans receive the notion that children should be loved and cared for rather than used solely as tools to ease their parents' burdens. There, the Christian teachings of redemption from patriarchy and the material constraints of the fall are desperately needed and often gratefully embraced.

In contrast to these poorer countries and times, the technological progress of the United States, Europe, and other parts of the world has created a heretofore unimaginable level of individual wealth for most of their citizens. As a result, some of the practices Jesus decried—the mistrust of women's sexuality and their consequent isolation, adult men's subordination to their fathers—are no longer issues. For us, those aspects of the curse on the ground have faded. As the endless demand for labor has diminished, women as well as men are freed from manual labor and household production. In our affluence, there is no remaining economic demand for the labor of children. With the primary reason for the sexual division of labor gone, so is much of the subordination of women. In industrialized, modern settings, people enjoy an unparalleled opportunity for marriage of "equal regard": "a relationship between husband and wife characterized by mutual respect, affection, practical assistance and justice—a relationship that values and aids the self and other with equal seriousness."[30]

From a purely material point of view, people in wealthy developed nations can take Jesus at his word that we do not need to worry about what we will eat or what we will put on. But data would suggest that wealth alone, without true reconciliation to God, is not the key to marital happiness. It is in precisely these relatively wealthy countries that many people are not marrying at all, and those who do marry have a hard time staying married.

The problems for sexuality today are not material scarcity. Instead, they are the problems of the rich young man in Matthew

19 and those of the man who wanted to bury his father before following Jesus (Luke 9:59–60). Overcoming the curse on the ground is not the same thing as overcoming our tendency to capital S Sin, our alienation and mistrust of God. Technological progress has given us an affluence that goes beyond God's simple abundance to one that we believe is all our own. Even if we don't have it yet, we feel entitled to it, and we do not want to be beholden to anyone for it—not God, not some man or woman, certainly not a laboring child. It is hard to give up self-controlled wealth and the opportunity to live an independent, rich, self-indulged, self-directed life. And today, women as well as men face the temptations of power.

But what was impossible with human beings became possible with God (Matt. 19:26). As Compassion International, a ministry devoted to helping children in poverty-stricken countries, observes: "We've discovered that changed circumstances rarely change people's lives, while changed people inevitably change their circumstances."[31] It was not the people who sought out Jesus because he fed them, nor those who were already well fed, whose lives were changed. Rather, it was those who believed in his word (John 6:26–29). Jesus taught his followers that when they are no longer alienated from God, they are no longer alienated from the earth or from each other. We can once again look to sex, marriage, and family as blessings of mutual joy, not as self-serving expediencies. The teachings of the apostle Paul, covered in the next chapter, further clarify the new Christian attitude toward family.

# 4

# The Mystery of Marriage
# in Everyday Life

I was startled one morning when my clock-radio came on to the author of a new book on the apostle Paul proclaiming, "Paul never saw a status quo he didn't like." Part of Paul's reputation for supporting the ancient status quo, particularly patriarchy, comes from what some scholars perceive as similarities between his writings on the family and "household codes" of conduct written by philosophers such as Plutarch and Aristotle.[1] These secular writings discussed the duties of slaves, children, and wives but were actually addressed to the family patriarchs, enjoining them on their responsibility to "rule" or "govern" those under their control. Some scholars see Ephesians 5 and 6, in which Paul discusses the relationship between husband and wife, parents and children, and masters and slaves, as his attempt to mirror these codes and thus assure secular authorities of the respectability and conformity of Christian family life.[2] Reading Ephesians 5:22–6:9 (the source of the admonition for a wife's submission to her husband as "head") in the context of Jesus's teachings about the appropriate use of power in Christian relationships, however—or just reading the entire passage at all—makes it apparent that if Paul paralleled any Greco-Roman household code, it was in order to stand it on its head. Far from advocating the status quo of patriarchy, Paul, like Jesus, sought to overturn it.[3]

Jesus defined the ideal of marriage as man and woman joined together by God. In his letter to the Ephesians, Paul presents this same vision of marriage as a one-flesh union. Paul's interests, however, were less in romance for its own sake than in marital unity as a component of, and a metaphor for, the great mystery that will mark the consummation of creation reconciled with its Creator, the union of all believers with Christ. This unity can be attained only when members of the body of Christ—the Christian community—accept their redemption from the constraints of the fall and in turn eliminate all strivings for power and status from their interactions with each other. Hence, in the controversial discussion of submission in Ephesians, "headship," slavery, children's obedience, and the wife's respect for her husband are a misunderstood part of a grand design, the core of which lies in the husband/father/master's emulation of Jesus in giving up his secular privileges.

## Submission and Benefaction

Much of the language Paul uses in his discussion of marriage in Ephesians 5 flows from the first-century custom of patronage. In patronage, powerful, wealthy men provided access to scarce resources (land, money, business connections) to those unable to attain them on their own. In return for their help, the beneficiaries were expected to make known the munificence of their patron, thus contributing to the patron's fame and honor.[4] Roman culture also honored *mediators*, go-betweens who connected people in need of resources to the patrons who could provide them. In *Honor, Patronage, Kinship, and Purity*, New Testament and Greek scholar David deSilva shows how Paul's writings incorporate these notions of benefaction: God, the ultimate patron, provides everything, including life itself, to the human race through the mediation of his Son. Christ Jesus is especially to be honored because "it was considered the height of generosity to give one's life for the good of another (hence the extreme honor showed to those who died in battle to protect a city)."[5] The New Testament language of "grace" and gifts of God refers to this benefaction bestowed by God and Jesus.

DeSilva writes, "A prominent kind of exhortation in the New Testament promotes . . . respond[ing] in accordance with what benefactions one has received, whether pardoning . . . as we have been pardoned . . . or laying down our lives to help one another . . . because Jesus laid down his life to help us (1 John 3:16–18)." To be an ungrateful client was a serious failing, and one that exposed the patron to dishonor. Thus Christians were doubly bound to follow Christ's example, both because he modeled the correct behavior and because this is the correct response to his patronage.

Paul opens the letter to the Ephesians on this theme, praying that "Christians be made mindful of the magnificence of God's generosity (Eph. 1:3; 7–11, 17–19)."[6] Because of Christ's sacrifice for us, we are restored to God's generous provision. The verses immediately preceding the marriage passage demonstrate how our gratitude must be reflected in our treatment of each other:

> Be kind and compassionate to one another, forgiving each other, just as in Christ God forgave you. Follow God's example, therefore, as dearly loved children and walk in the way of love, just as Christ loved us and gave himself up for us, a fragrant offering and sacrifice to God . . . always giving thanks to God the Father for everything, in the name of our Lord Jesus Christ.
>
> Submit to one another out of reverence for Christ. (Eph. 4:32–5:1–2, 20–21)

## Submission

Submission, then, not just to God but to each other, is the fitting response to the gift of our redemption. Unfortunately, the words *submission* and *submissive* have bad connotations in English and so pose a significant stumbling block to our understanding of what Paul wrote about marriage in Ephesians 5:21–33. In common English usage, to be submissive means to be obedient, docile, inferior, meek, quiet, numb, in need of guidance, or childlike. A submissive person is common, a follower, someone without authority, who has given up all hopes of power, even power over her own self. One book on relationships defines submission as giving in to another's control and says, "Submission comes from a position of weakness. . . . Submission means enduring aversive behavior from your partner because you have or believe you have no alternative."[7] The word also has sexual connotations and is linked with the notion of accepting mistreatment—as in to *submit* to a beating. In English usage, a submissive personality is more likely to be regarded as pathological than as desirable.

In Greek, however, the language in which Paul wrote his letters, the word translated "submit" or "be subject to" lacks these connotations. It does not even mean to "obey," and in fact obedience had nothing to do with what Paul asked believers to do. Nor does it mean to agree with someone, to give up one's own preferences, or even to let someone else win at checkers. The root of the word translated "be subject to" (or alternatively, "submit yourself to") is *hypotasso. Hypo* means "under"—like a hypodermic needle, which is used to place medicine under the skin. *Tasso* means to "locate," "put," or "place." Together, they mean "locate or place under." *Hypotasso* is sometimes translated "put under."[8]

In English, we understand *subject* in one of two ways. One way is to read it in the active voice. The active voice of a verb shows the subject of a sentence performing the action in the sentence. For example, *teach* is an active verb—I am teaching you about voices in Greek. The active form of *subject* would be to actively subject someone to one's own will: I put that person under my heel or put the screws on him or her. But in the New Testament, no one is ever instructed to "subject" anyone else. In fact, Jesus expressly forbade it: "You know that those who are regarded as rulers of the Gentiles lord it over them, and their high officials exercise authority over them. Not so with you. Instead, whoever wants to become great among you must be your servant, and whoever wants to be first among you must be slave of all" (Mark 10:42–44).

So in Ephesians 5:21, Paul does not mean "subject" in the active voice—for the whole Christian church to actively "put each other under" might look a lot like a fistfight. Thus, consciously or not, English speakers read it in the passive. In the passive voice the subject of the sentence is acted upon: "I am taught Greek." In the case of submission, in the passive someone else puts me under his thumb and I accept the domination. In the passive, *hypotasso* says, "Submit! Do as you are told! Give up!" In our contemporary English, neither actively subjecting another person nor passively accepting subjugation is regarded as healthy or desirable behavior.

But the word used in Ephesians 5 is not in the passive voice either. Greek has something English does not—a verb form in the middle voice, in which "the subject acts, directly or indirectly, upon itself."[9] "Teach" provides an easy example: "I teach myself Greek."[10] I am being active—teaching—and I am also the recipient of the action. The word translated "be subject or submissive to," *hypotasso*, is in this middle voice, and in this sentence means "place yourselves under one another" or "subject yourself to one another."

In instructing Christians to "submit to one another," Paul is not urging them to exercise power over anyone or to passively yield to the exercise of power over them. Rather, he asks Christians to voluntarily place themselves below other people, in effect to "value others above yourselves" (Phil. 2:3). In asking Christians to subject themselves to one another, Paul asks them to *opt out of the power struggle in which the whole world is engaged*. They do this "out of reverence [or respect] for Christ," because this is what Christ did, continually placing himself below others, taking on the role of a servant, while rising triumphant over the concerns of the world.[11] Due to God's great gift, followers of Christ are no longer subject to the world of thorns. Reconciled to God, they no longer need or desire to hold power and control over other people, especially not among themselves.[12]

## Submission and the Christian Family

### The Roman status quo

In the first century, the Roman Empire ruled the entire known world, and so its mores, values, and household patterns dominated all of society. If there was ever a classic example of a society governed by the imperatives of the curse on the ground, it was Rome. Just as Jesus taught his predominantly Jewish followers how to separate God's will from these imperatives, so Paul did with the ethnically mixed people living in Roman cities. Roman society was organized around a class of wealthy men who controlled large numbers of other people—their wives, children, and slaves. In fact, the word *family* comes from the Latin word that referred to a man's entire household, particularly his slaves. The practice of slavery was a pervasive part of Roman society: in some of the cities around the Mediterranean, a third of the population were slaves, another third were former slaves, and most "free" people lived in unimaginable poverty with few more rights than slaves.[13]

As was and is typical in preindustrial economies, marriages in Rome were arranged in order to further the economic and social interests of the family, often with no regard for the preferences of the prospective spouses.[14] After marriage a bride lived with her husband's family, who were likely to treat her with suspicion. A young wife often had to compete with her mother-in-law for her husband's attention and might rely on sexual attractiveness and manipulation to bend her husband to her will. Her role was to produce a legitimate heir and eventually to assume management of the household. People did not expect to find romance or emotional closeness in marriage. When in need of comfort or counsel, marital partners were more likely to turn to a brother or sister than to each other.[15]

In *The Rise of Christianity*, sociologist Rodney Stark paints an even bleaker picture of Roman family life. Being city dwellers, not farmers, and having abundant labor in the form of slaves, even wealthy Romans were not eager to rear more than two children, and few were willing to rear any girls at all. Exposure or abandonment of unwanted babies, especially females, was a common practice. Between discarding newborns and high death rates among women in general, the sex ratio in Rome was shockingly skewed. One estimate indicates that for every ten males in the population there were only seven females. This imbalance meant that men did not marry until their late twenties or early thirties, while "women" were married by age twelve to fourteen on average and sometimes as young as eight.[16] Divorce was rampant, and because of the age difference between husband and wife at the wife's first marriage, one woman might be widowed or divorced, and remarried several times. Although lack of mutual affection was considered acceptable grounds for divorce and moralists enjoined husbands and wives to love each other,[17] one wonders just what they meant by the term *love*. The fact that no one expected a husband to limit himself sexually to just his wife[18] rules out modern notions of companionate romantic marriage. Certainly there was no question of becoming "one flesh." Greco-Roman marriage was mostly a familial alliance designed to produce legitimate heirs, and concerns about power and family honor pervaded every aspect of it.

### Slaves and masters

To more easily understand how Paul's teachings in Ephesians 5–6 challenged the family structure of the ancient world, I am going to follow Laurence R. Iannaccone's example and start by looking at the most extreme of the power-based relationships that Paul addresses in this passage, that between slave and master.[19] Slavery as it was practiced in the Roman world differed in important ways from its later practice in America. For one thing, Roman slavery was not race based. Although historically slaves had been peoples captured in war, by the time of Christ most slaves had been born into that estate. Further, some had entered slavery more or less voluntarily, selling themselves in order to pay debts or to obtain one of the high-status jobs that could be held only by slaves. Some entered slavery simply to escape the grinding poverty that was the lot of most freeborn people, as it was often better to be a slave in even a moderately wealthy household than to be a poor freeman.[20] Roman slaves could control property, including their own slaves, could form families, and could hold public office. Further, slaves could not necessarily be identified as such on sight, as their owners provided them with clothing that fit their occupation.[21] Many bought themselves out of slavery or were otherwise freed at some point. As Roman law provided that the freed slaves of citizens became citizens themselves, some men sold themselves into slavery in order to eventually gain these valuable civil rights.[22]

Despite the voluntary nature of slavery for some, slavery was a desirable position only when compared to alternatives. Neither male nor female slaves had control over their own bodies, and the sexual use of slaves by masters was taken for granted.[23] Masters also held life-and-death authority over them and could kill one summarily. Slaves could not legally marry, and the families they formed could be broken up at the master's pleasure. But slavery was a fundamental social institution in the ancient world and the basis of business relationships. Instead of employers and employees, the economy was built on masters and slaves—and in fact, Bartchy notes that it was probably the free worker rather than the slave who was most exploited in ancient Rome.[24] A familial bond between slave and master continued to exist after manumission; the freedman might continue to owe service to his former master, and each had an obligation to come to the other's aid in times of illness or destitution.[25]

The Old Testament took slavery for granted, although it regulated it in order to assure fair treatment of slaves. In contrast, Christianity opposed it, although in its early stages it did this not to effect change in Roman law (which was so hopeless an endeavor that it would have been unthinkable) but to better the conditions of its members. Christian congregations used their funds to purchase the freedom of their enslaved members, and some even sold themselves into slavery in order to free others.[26] Christians took Galatians 3:28 seriously ("There is neither Jew nor Gentile, neither slave nor free, neither male nor female, for you are all one in Christ Jesus") and made no social distinctions between slave and free within their congregations or in selecting leaders.[27] However, the Christian movement at this time was a tiny and suspect minority that could effect change only within its own ranks. Only much later in Christian history could it have any impact in eliminating the institution of slavery.

Ironically, the very writings that were later used in the American South to justify slavery make it plain that Paul opposed the practice. In 1 Timothy 1:9–11 he groups slave traders with murderers, liars, and those who kill their parents. In 1 Corinthians 7 Paul acknowledges that many Christians were enslaved, but consoles them by writing:

> Were you a slave when you were called? Don't let it trouble you—although if you can gain your freedom, do so. For those who were slaves when called to faith in the Lord are the Lord's freed people; similarly, those who were free when called are Christ's slaves. You were bought at a price; do not become slaves of human beings. (1 Cor. 7:21–23)

Ephesians 6:5–8, however, really reads as if Paul approved of slavery. Paul urges:

Slaves, obey your masters according to the flesh, with fear and trembling in singleness of heart as to Christ; not in way of eye-service as people-pleasers, but as slaves of Christ doing the will of God from the soul, with good will serving as slaves as to the Lord and not to human beings, knowing that whatever good anyone does, he or she will receive the same again from the Lord, whether slave or free.[28]

Read alone, this passage seems to support the accusation that Paul favored slavery. Slaves are apparently told not only to obey their masters but to serve them wholeheartedly and that God will reward them for their servility. However, before accepting this interpretation, consider Paul's very next words: "And masters, treat your slaves in the same way. Do not threaten them, since you know that he who is both their Master and yours is in heaven, and that there is no favoritism with him" (Eph. 6:9). Paul expected slave owners to "do the same"—to serve their slaves.

Paul's statement that masters must serve and refrain from threatening their slaves signals the deep change that Christianity required in family relationships. Slaveholders held coercive and economic power over all members of their household. Slaves did their master's will not because they were all on the same team, working toward the same goals, but because they had to. Christian slaveholders, however, were to give up their coercive power. Note the language of benefaction here: they must do this because they too have a Master in heaven who does not coerce them. If God does not treat slaveholders as slaves, Christian masters have to treat their slaves with the same respect that they are shown.

Not only did Paul change the orientation of masters toward slaves, he changed the slaves' motivations as well. Slaves were at the very bottom of the hierarchy and its struggle for control. In Christ, however, the world of thorns no longer had a hold over them, and they no longer had to strive against it. Their earthly masters may command their labor, but their "fear and trembling" and "singleness of heart" that Paul enjoined were for the *Lord*. Slaves were no longer to live in fear of their master's coercive power or strive to please men in order to enlarge their own power base. Although legally enslaved and owing obedience to their earthly master, in the spiritual realm they were slaves of Christ and abided in faith that he would take care of them in a way their earthly master could not. The bottom line, Paul told them, is that "he who is both their Master and yours is in heaven," and spiritually the status of "slave or free" makes no real difference.

In no way can Paul's admonitions on slavery be construed as supporting the status quo. They are so radical that those who accuse Paul of complicity with the Roman system must never have read beyond verse 8. Although from a contemporary perspective we might prefer Paul to have simply directed Christians to free their slaves, under first-century circumstances he appears to have believed that it was better to retain these family members in their home and livelihood while transforming them into true brothers and sisters, no longer chattel.[29]

### Children and fathers

At first glance, in Ephesians 6:1–3 Paul also appears to accept the social order regarding children: "Children, obey your parents in the Lord, for this is right. 'Honor your father and mother'—which is the first commandment with a promise— 'so that it may be well with you and that you may enjoy long life on the earth.'" Note that Paul directs that children honor and obey their mothers as well as their fathers. In the next verse, however, Paul addresses just the fathers: "Fathers, do not exasperate your children; instead, bring them up [or nurture them] in the training and instruction of the Lord."

Remember that in a preindustrial economy, a major motivation for having children was so that they could serve their father—work for him, care for him when sick or aged, increase the family honor, run the family business, and so on. Under Roman law, fathers held much of the same coercive authority over children that masters exercised over slaves. Fathers could order the abandonment of an unwanted newborn or kill a disobedient child. Further, sons—at least those who wanted their inheritance—did not become autonomous just by turning twenty-one but remained more or less subservient to their father until he died (daughters usually came under their husband's authority). This meant that fathers had control over their sons as long as they lived.

As with slaves, Paul asks fathers to give up their coercive rights over their children. The patriarch is not to exercise his superior status over his children in order to exploit them ("do not provoke your children to anger" or "do not exasperate your children"). Rather, *fathers* are to serve their *children*, using their children's obedience to "bring them up in the training and instruction of the Lord." Children, like enslaved persons, are not put on earth to serve patricians but to come to a relationship with God in their own right.

As in Paul's instructions to slaves and masters, he asks for a transformation not just in the fathers' motivation but in that of the children as well. "Children, obey your parents in the Lord, for this is right." Obedience and honor are not a matter of doing whatever it takes to keep their parents off their back until they can inherit. Rather, it is a matter of doing right in God's sight—obeying them "in the Lord," not because of Roman civil law.

In its instructions to master and slaves, fathers and children, Ephesians 6:1–9 makes clear that Paul was far from supporting the Roman status quo. It was not so much that Paul subverted the dominant morality as that he transcended it. Its categories were simply not to the point anymore. Masters, fathers, slaves, and children stepped out of the power-laden relationships sanctioned by Roman law and submitted to each other—gave up their struggle for power over each other—out of awe for Christ, who had taken on the same submissive role himself, not out of weakness but because it was "right in God's sight."

### Husbands, Wives, Heads and Bodies

With these admonitions to children and slavery as context, let us return to Paul's words for husbands and wives. Paul's contemporaries would have been somewhat surprised by what he told fathers and alarmed by what he said to slave owners, but they could scarcely imagine what he asked of husbands. In Ephesians 6 Paul asks men to serve those whom society said were subordinate to them—radical enough—but in Ephesians 5 he asks men not only to serve their wives but to become of one will and desire with them.

Paul's well-known (infamous?) injunction that "wives submit to their husbands" is not surprising, since submission characterizes the entire Christian community:

. . . addressing one another in psalms and hymns and spiritual songs, singing and making melody to the Lord with all your heart, always and for everything giving thanks in the name of our Lord Jesus Christ to God the Father. Be subject to one another out of respect for Christ, wives to your own husbands as to the Lord (Eph. 5:19–22).

Seen in context, the injunction "wives to your own husbands" is not a freestanding commandment (as the usual printing of this passage suggests, wrongly placing a paragraph and usually a header between verses 21 and 22) but a qualification of the broader statement that the Christian community should emulate Christ by refusing to seek status and power over each other. Note that verse 22 does not contain a verb, being only a dependent clause to verse 21, "Submit to one another." The admonition that wives, and a few verses later, children and slaves, offer their obedience "as to the Lord" is a further reminder that they submit themselves out of respect for Christ.[30]

The reason Paul gives for wifely submission goes back to the language of benefaction: "For the husband is head of the wife as also Christ is head of the church, himself the savior of the body.[31] But as the church subjects itself to Christ, so also wives, in everything, to their husbands" (Eph. 5:23–24).

Just as the word *hypotasso*, "submit yourself," is a stumbling block in understanding what Paul is saying in this passage, the English meaning of another word—*kephale* (kef-a-LAY), head—throws modern readers completely off track. The problem in understanding what Paul wrote is not the word's translation from Greek into English. *Kephale* is perfectly translated here. It does mean "head," literally, and there is no other way to translate this word into English. Rather, the confusion over its meaning arises because *head* has meanings in English that it did not have in first-century Greek. When an English speaker reads "head" in this passage, he or she automatically understands it to mean "ruler," "leader," or "authority over," as in the head of a corporation. In this reading, the "status quo" interpretation of Paul's writing flows inevitably: "Wives, submit to your husband, because he is your ruler, just as Christ is the ruler of the church."

But *kephale* cannot be translated as "boss" or "ruler" or even as "servant-leader," because while *head* can mean "authority" in English, it did not have that connotation in Greek at the time that Paul wrote the letter to the Ephesians.[32] There was another word for ruler or one who has the right to tell others what to do, *arche* (ar-KAY). This word is used many times in the New Testament when the writers mean one holding authority over other people. If Paul had meant "authority over" or "leader" in his reference to man as head of the woman, he certainly would have used *arche* or perhaps *kyrios* (lord) or *despotis* (the word translated as "lord" in Luke 2:29, Acts 4:24, and Rev. 6:10 or as "head of the household" in Luke 13:25)[33] instead of *kephale*.[34]

Further, "authority over" makes no sense in the context of the rest of the instructions to husbands. In verses 25–33, Paul draws a series of parallels between Christ's expressions of love for the church and a husband's expression of love for his wife. As we will see below, none of these expressions have anything to do with authority or rule.

The Greek and Roman moralists who wrote about household relationships intended the husband/father/master to subject (active voice) or rule his household. The household's obedience to the patrician's rule constituted the best of Roman morality. In contrast, in the New Testament no one is ever directed to actively "subject" (rule) anyone else. The only time "authority" is mentioned in the context of husband-wife relationships is in 1 Corinthians 7:4, and this passage, in which both husband and wife are given authority over each other sexually, is the ultimate exception that proves the rule.

So if Paul did not mean to be making a statement about power or authority relations between men and women here, just what did he mean by *kephale*? Greek scholar Richard Cervin writes, "He [Paul] does not mean 'authority over' as the traditionalists assert, nor does he mean 'source' as the egalitarians assert. I think he is merely employing a head-body metaphor."[35] As it turns out, in his extensive analysis of the use of *kephale* in Greek literature at the time Paul was writing, one of the "traditionalist" scholars to whom Cervin refers, Wayne Grudem, found that its most common usage by far was simply to mean "head," that rounded thing that tops the body.[36] And surprisingly, as we will see, this very basic meaning of the word makes perfect sense in the rest of this passage and in the context of Jesus and the Creator's comments about marriage. Paul was employing a metaphor—head and body, together one flesh.

### The function of the head

The original readers of Ephesians would have understood what Paul meant by his use of the head/body metaphor because he uses it throughout this letter. In the opening sentences of the letter, Paul has told his readers that God's purpose is to unite or bring together all things in heaven and earth in Christ (Eph. 1:10). The word translated "unite" (RSV) or "bring together" (NIV) is literally "head up" or "bring several things together under one head."[37] This sense of the head uniting, integrating, and nurturing the body is explicit in Ephesians 4:15–16: "We are to grow up in every way into him who is the head, into Christ, from whom the whole body, joined and knit together by every joint with which it is supplied, when each part is working properly, makes bodily growth and upbuilds itself in love" (RSV).

Similarly, in his letter to the Colossians, Paul uses *kephale* in the same way:

> He is before all things, and in him *all things hold together*. And he is the head of the body, the church. (Col. 1:17–19)

> [Speaking of anyone who is pursuing "idle notions"]: They have lost connection with the head, from whom the whole *body, supported and held together by its ligaments and sinews, grows* as God causes it to grow. (Col. 2:19)

As we will see shortly, to be head is a truly heroic thing, but it is not a statement of hierarchy. Ephesians 1:23 is particularly useful for understanding Paul's true attitude about power relations between the head and body: "[God] has put all things under his [Christ's] feet and has made him the head over all things for the church, which is his body, the fulness of him who fills all in all" (RSV). This passage makes clear that the relationship between the head and the body is not one of dominance and subordination. The things that are subjected (the word translated "put . . . under" is *hypotasso* in the active voice) are not "put under" the head but under the *feet*, that is, below the entire body. The head does not subject the body but reigns together with it. "All things are yours . . . and you are of Christ, and Christ is of God" (1 Cor. 3:21–23).

Further, in this verse Paul tells us that the body is not the disreputable animal vessel that it was held to be in Greek philosophy. Rather, it is the fullness—the completion or perfection—of the head. This verse presents a beautiful paradox: the church is the fullness of Christ, but Christ is the One who fills the body. How can something fill itself? To insist on knowing which it is, the chicken or the egg, is to miss the point. Paul is saying that head and body, together, are perfected, completed, fulfilled.

Ephesians 5:23 equates Christ's headship with his role as "savior," someone who provides a great benefit in bringing all believers into one. For the husband to be head of his wife in the same sense that Christ is head of the church, then, he does not rule or even lead her but instead is the one who facilitates their unity, growth, and "upbuilding in love."

There is more to say about wifely submission, but because the submission of wife to husband is inextricably linked with the husband's submission to his wife, it will be better understood after we look first at what Paul has to say to husbands.

## Directives to Husbands

In the next verses, Ephesians 5:25–33, Paul addresses husbands, elaborating on their role as head by continuing to draw upon the analogy between Christ's unity with the church and the marriage relationship. Here he asks husbands to do a number of things that sound beautiful but abstract ("make your wife holy," etc.). These directives are not the flowery, meaningless Valentine's-day sentiments they appear to be, but a revamping of the traditional male role as thorough as anything Jesus proposed. Only men who have fully accepted their redemption can do the things for which Paul asked.

### Upbuilding in love

Husbands, love your wives, just as Christ loved the church and gave himself up for her.

First, Paul directs husbands to "love" their wives. Like *head*, this is again a word into which English speakers in the twenty-first century read too much. As you probably know, the Greek language had three words that are translated "love," and none of them meant the complex emotion we call romantic love today. *Eros* was erotic love; *philos* was love for a brother or sister; and *agape*, the word used here, meant caring concern for another person. When Paul told men to "love" their wives, he was not talking as someone at a modern marriage retreat might, instructing couples on how to rekindle *eros*, or romance. Rather, he was telling men to treat their wives with selfless, caring concern. In urging that a man care about his wife as he does himself, Paul seriously challenged patriarchal motives for marriage, in which men took wives chiefly in order to serve their own needs for a legitimate heir and for household management.

Paul challenges contemporary relationships in a similar way. People today fully realize that "I love you" should mean, "I care for you no less than I care about myself." However, our customs increasingly emphasize the notion that each person's most important duty is to his or her own satisfaction and security. The late Ann Landers used to ask those writing to her for advice, "Are you better off with him or without him?" Such a question suggests that no other criteria are more pressing than each individual's own welfare. But finding that one is better off with another person is not the same thing as caring for him or her. Being concerned strictly for one's own welfare has little power to sustain a relationship.

### Giving yourself up

Husbands, love your wives, just as Christ loved the church and gave himself up for her.

What does it mean to be willing to "give yourself up" for someone? Christ, who is given as a model of this kind of love, took giving himself up to the extreme, dying for humanity even "while we were yet sinners" and undeserving.

Dying for each other is a very romantic notion, the stuff of movies and novels, but Paul is not suggesting that husbands should literally die for their wives. He does write elsewhere, however, that Jesus "emptied" himself, that is, gave up his own will, in order to reconcile humankind to God (Phil. 2:7). In the same way, Paul asked husbands to give themselves up—to sacrifice their desire to have their own way and place their own needs first. Part of the way in which husbands are the "heads" of their wives is to esteem their wives' needs and desires to be as important as their own.

No romantic abstraction, the directive to give oneself up goes to the heart of the postfall male imperative to be the one whose will is obeyed, the one served, and the one whose needs and wishes drive all household activities. Literally dying for someone else might well be easier—and certainly more macho—than giving up one's own desires. Today any expression of the masculine need for dominance is soundly rejected by feminist culture, but that doesn't mean that men don't still expect to have their needs given preference in relationship. A book called *Marry Me! Three Professional Men Reveal How to Get Mr. Right to Pop the Question* advises women that in a man's mind, his career is always more important than hers: "You could be president of the United States, and he could be in his first year at a law firm and in his mind, your man's job would still be more important than yours is." Moreover, the authors say, "He wants you to believe his career is more important than yours, too,"[38] and they warn that a professional man's career will always come before his wife and family. But aren't those the anxieties of the world of thorns talking? Isn't saying that "my work is more important than are the people in my life" the same as saying, "I am more important than they are"? Self-centeredness or wanting one's own way is hardly a problem limited to men, but the culture of the fall burdens men with a sense of entitlement to priority status in the family and, harder to bear, shame when they don't get that deference. Paul said that Christian men must set aside those beliefs of entitlement in order to create unity with their wives.

### Does this mean we are supposed to take showers together?

But for what purpose is a husband to "give himself up"? So that the wife can be the one in charge? Not at all. Rather, self-giving fa-cilitates another beautiful paradox in which the lovers become each other's will. The next verse says that Christ gave himself up "in order to sanctify her [the church], cleansing her with the washing of the water by the word, so as to present the church to himself in glory, without a spot or wrinkle or anything of the kind, but in order that she might be holy and unblemished."

The head's self-sacrificing love enables the body to be holy and glorious. In 1 Corinthians 11:7, Paul also writes of man as the head of the woman and then says that "woman is the glory of man."[39] Glory is the thing that magnifies something, that makes it great. Who would not want to be considered the glory of one's family, country, or spouse? So here is another paradox—the head makes the body glorious, and the body's glory in turn brings glory to the head. Love and self-sacrifice for the sake of the other's sanctification result in the reciprocal glorification of both parties. One is the fullness of the one who fills, and together they are magnificent.

Paul makes a telling point here, for while "love does not delight in evil" (1 Cor. 13:6), human beings sometimes do. What if you don't really want the other person to be "holy"? Many people secretly cherish a spouse's weakness. It makes them feel superior, gives them an upper hand, or meets some sick need. Having a weak and dependent spouse can be draining, but it also affords the opportunity to be a hero—or a martyr—if only in one's own eyes. Other times, couples can be competitive with each other, each hating to admit when the other is right. Not long ago it was considered humiliating if a man's wife was more accomplished, held a better job, or made more money than he did. But Paul admonishes couples to allow each other to grow, to help their partners be the best they can be, without fear of being passed up or shamed.

Paul's statement that Christ cleansed the church from every blemish does not mean that couples should criticize each other, but rather mandates forgiveness and acceptance. Marriage therapists are just now discovering the importance of teaching these qualities to troubled couples. While no one can avoid occasional conflict, criticism and demands bring defensiveness and shame into the relationship. Marriage researcher John Gottman found that being angry with one's spouse does not harm a relationship in itself, but how a couple handles that anger makes a big difference in whether or not the marriage will survive.[40] In particular, he found that once defenses are aroused, the hearing of the person being criticized is literally impaired: he or she simply cannot hear you. Under conditions of blame and accusation, it is almost impossible for someone to change. It is not a husband's job to bring his wife to repentance (or vice versa). Marriage does, however, mean providing an accepting, safe environment in which the other person can grow and flourish.

On a different level, letting his wife become holy may require a man to give up the prerogatives and privileges that society tells him are his due. It may require a granting of freedoms that can be frightening. For most of history, women brought worldly "glory" to their husband only in very limited ways. Being a gracious hostess, bearing and rearing accomplished children, knowing how to dress properly, efficiently managing a household, and providing good meals were all skills that brought honor to the husbands of the women who possessed them. People still feel sorry for and contemptuous of men whose wives fail in these areas, regardless of what other accomplishments they may boast. Furthermore, in many societies, including the one to which Paul ministered, women were considered less a source of glory than a potential source of disgrace. In some cultures, women are still expected to behave in ways that preserve a narrowly defined respectability, perhaps by limiting their excursions outside the house or never leaving the house at all (ancient Greek novels sometimes portrayed the Greek man's fantasy of marrying a beautiful "pure virgin" who had never even been seen by another man), [41] by being properly veiled at all times, or by avoiding interactions with men.

Jesus redeemed both women and men from the socially induced prerogatives, anxieties, and obligations of their gender. If wives are to be able to accept this redemption, however, they have to have the approval and active support of their husbands (Paul addresses the support that wives are to give husbands later). They have to be able to "sit at the feet" of Jesus—to take the part of Mary, not Martha—without concern that they will be called to task for failing in their duties as women. They have to be able to interact freely with other Christians, male and female. It can be difficult for a husband to allow his wife these freedoms, for freeing a wife from her traditional obligations might mean that her husband will not meet the expectations placed on him. But this is part of cleansing her from every blemish.

### Love as you love yourself

Paul continues:

> In the same way, husbands should love their wives as they do their own
> bodies. He who loves his wife loves himself. For no one ever hates his
> own body, but he nourishes and tenderly cares for it, just as Christ does
> for the church, because we are members of his body. (NRSV)

Obviously, Paul never had to deal with a culture in which looks are
so important, or people so self-destructive, that one might hate one's
own body. He just assumed that people are naturally motivated to
take care of themselves. Husbands are to treat their wives with the
same respect that they have for themselves. In this kind of love, what
a wife believes, dreams, and feels is as important as what her husband
believes, dreams, and feels. Further, just as a person knows when part
of his body is injured or in need, a husband should be aware of his
wife's needs and treat her pain as urgently as he would his own.

Paul's use of the words "nourish and cherish" continues the head/
body metaphor he is employing throughout this passage. In Ephesians
4:16, he wrote of how Christ as head nourishes the church by upbuilding it in love. In the same way, husbands are to nourish and
cherish their wives—to help them to grow in love. Once again, the
Christian husband wants his wife to be the best she can be, not out
of self-interest but for her sake.

Paul's advice that men cherish their wives takes us back to creation.
The first man rejoiced when he finally found the woman: "This one, at
last! Bone of my bone! Flesh of my flesh!" Day by day we may have a
hard time cherishing our spouse to such an extravagant degree, but at
the very least a husband should affirm his wife, and a wife her husband,
as a child of God and hence worthy of the greatest respect. "Husbands
likewise, dwell together with your wives according to knowledge, as
with a weaker vessel," the apostle Peter writes, recognizing the disadvantages that women bear in the world of thorns. "Giving her honor
as an heir together with you in the grace of life" (1 Peter 3:7).

Nourishing and cherishing have a surprisingly powerful impact
on marriage and on the welfare of the individuals within it. Although
even the most loving spouses cannot solve all, or perhaps not even

any, of the problems their mate encounters in daily life—work, children, traffic, the stock market, aging parents, taxes, cars that break down, roofs that leak—the support of someone who cares can make an enormous improvement in one's ability to deal with these stresses. The authors of *A General Theory of Love* offer evidence that people have a physical need to have someone to stroke them, to look them in the eye, to listen and tell them that everything will be all right. Without this emotional support, they suggest, the regulatory mechanisms of the human body—cardiovascular system, hormone levels, sleep rhythms, immune system—don't function properly.[42] A marriage that provides this support offers a great blessing. Health surveys have found in fact that married people live longer and are healthier than are single people. If a woman's partner does not provide that support, however, the wear and tear of even ordinary life, let alone exceptional traumas, can damage her physically as well as emotionally. And if a man's partner does not cherish him—if she purposefully sets out to hurt him or has a low opinion of his worth—the impact can be devastating.[43]

In her book on successful marriage, therapist and researcher Judith S. Wallerstein identifies a category of marriage in which nurturing and cherishing are the defining components. "Like most people in the mental health field," she says, she once believed that people who come from abusive or neglectful families have a poor chance of sustaining healthy relationships of their own. It is true that many people become stuck in the poor patterns established in their early life. For them, marriage is only a new location in which the old battles are fought again and again. Yet Wallerstein's research showed that for some people coming from troubled backgrounds, marriage is a source of healing. People in these "rescue marriages" credit their spouse's nurturing and perception of them as worthwhile with helping them become the good, healthy people they wanted to be. "With this bounty at the core, a good marriage can promote unselfishness, togetherness, and, to use an old-fashioned word, virtue."[44] She notes that this surprising finding is wonderful news and a great source of hope—"the rescue marriage fulfills a child's fantasy that early miseries will be canceled by the happiness of adult life."[45]

Paul's suggestion that husbands nurture their wives flies in the face of those tough, action-oriented male gender roles that result from the curse on the ground. Living in the world of thorns, boys and men are rewarded for being competitive and aggressive and punished for expressing softer "feminine" needs. Nurturing and cherishing, after all, are "women's work." Little girls grow up well practiced in giving and receiving comfort, while little boys learn that either offering or accepting succor is apt to lead to rejection from other boys. Indeed, men may be so well socialized to feel shame at expression of emotions that they may assume it is kinder not even to acknowledge those of their wife.

However, as difficult as it may be for anyone, male or female, to listen, hear, and offer emotional support, it is an important part of a truly loving relationship. "Nourishing and cherishing" implies compassion and acceptance: acceptance, because sincerely supporting someone else requires taking the other person's side, believing that they are good; and compassion, because *agape* love asks us to truly care. Similarly, people can't receive comfort without letting down their shield and admitting a weakness or injury that requires solace, an admission that invites harm in the world of thorns. Hence the true lover must be truly redeemed.

### Be joined

Paul's next statement is a quote, and significantly, it is the same reference that Jesus gave when the Pharisees asked about grounds for divorce (Matt. 19): "For this reason a man will leave his father and mother and be united to his wife, and the two will become one flesh" (Eph. 5:31).

In patriarchy, women were the ones expected to leave their parents and become part of their husband's family. Many cultures past and present consider girls to be children raised for someone else; hence parents are often reluctant to raise any at all. But this statement, first spoken by the Creator in Genesis 2 and quoted by Jesus and by Paul, denies the spiritually dead world of patriarchy. While even now household finances might require a couple to live with one set of parents, marriage refocuses loyalty from parents to spouse. Although adult children are still to honor their parents "in the Lord," a man's primary allegiance in the household is to his wife.

This attitude represented a dramatic threat to ancient patriarchy, which expected an adult child's loyalty *always* to lie first in his family of origin.[46] In order to establish a Christian marriage, men have to step out of the world in which women exist only to serve them and their family and instead put their focus on unity with their wife.

## The Mystery

> This is a profound mystery, but I am talking about Christ and the church. (TNIV)

The pagan world of Paul's time abounded in mystery cults. These groups featured secret rituals purported to create a "sanctifying union between the suffering deity and the devotees, who in the mysteries acquire a share in the destiny of the god and hence in the divine power of life. . . . In the mystery a heavenly reality breaks into the sphere of the old aeon."[47] Adopting similar language, Paul used the concept of mystery in an eschatological sense, referring to that ultimate end state, the consummation of creation as fulfilled in Christ. Earlier in Ephesians, Paul had referred to the union of the "whole created world in Christ, in whom the totality receives its head and sum" (Eph. 1:9–10) and the "joining of Jews and Gentiles in one body under the head Christ" (Eph. 3:4–6) as a mystery. Now, once again in the context of Christ as head, Paul relates the unity of Christ and the church, the mysterious "consummation of creation," to the "one flesh" relationship intended by God when he created man and woman.

Nowhere in Ephesians does Paul enjoin a hierarchical relationship between husband and wife. The language that has been assumed to prescribe hierarchy, subordination, and the status quo—submission, man as head, and the like—refers instead to a quest for unity within marriage and within the entire Christian community, a unity that will find its fulfillment in the ultimate union of Christ and the church. In this unity, the "heavenly reality" breaks through into the earthly sphere.

## The Response of Wives

Finally, Paul sums up his address to wives and husbands in verse 33:

Each one of you should also love his wife as he loves himself, and the
wife must respect her husband.

In reading Ephesians 5, people often ask why it is that in Paul's
book husbands get to "love," an exciting if not always pleasant emotion, while wives are stuck with "respect," which, while admirable,
is no fun at all. And while we are asking hard questions, why does
Paul designate the husband and not the wife as head?

Perhaps this is because the things that Paul asks husbands to do—to
love as they love their own selves, to help someone else be the best
she can be, to nurture, serve, and cherish—are feminine roles. Service
was expected of wives and mothers. A first-century wife may not have
loved her husband romantically, but "caring concern" was her job. A
wife's self-sacrifice had no particularly Christian meaning, because
even the pagans expected her to devote herself to her husband and
children.

So why should wives respect their husbands? Paul gave husbands
quite a to-do list. He asked men to be Christlike in their most intimate relationship, where people get sloppy about their manners,
and furthermore, in the relationship in which even poverty-stricken
men expected to be served. It would be difficult, if not impossible,
for the husband to make these sacrifices for his wife if she failed to
"respect" him, took advantage of him, or thought less of him because
of his loving behavior.

And certainly a woman might well think less of a man for treating
her in the ways that Paul describes. This kind of behavior represents a
dramatic change from the gender-stereotyped male behavior to which
most couples were accustomed. Remember that marriages in the time
when Paul was writing were arranged matches. The behavior of men
and women in marriage was set by contract. Just as women had a
set of duties and responsibilities, men were expected to act the part
of the patriarch. Women as well as men would consider it shameful
for a powerful man to give up that power, shameful to put someone
else's will ahead of a man's own, shameful to turn down the privilege
to which he was entitled.

In the last fifty years or so, the decline of traditional sex roles has
taken some of this pressure off men in Western culture, but the change
has not been easy. Movies in the first half of the century capture some

of the "working out" of cultural assumptions about modern manhood. Stories and films explored whether a man who was not willing to use violence was a "real man" or not. One such story is a John Wayne movie called *The Quiet Man*. In it, Wayne plays a world champion boxer who returns from the United States to the village in Ireland in which he was born. There he falls in love with and marries a local girl (Maureen O'Hara). His new brother-in-law, however, refuses to hand over the bride's dowry. Wayne's character, wealthy and used to modern American ways, doesn't care about the dowry. His wife will not give it up, however, and wants her husband to fight her brother for it. But Wayne has killed a man in the boxing ring and refuses to ever again strike anyone. Failing to convince him, O'Hara's character ultimately decides that she "loves him too much" to live with what she sees as his shame. One morning Wayne finds her on the train platform, waiting to leave town—and so he has a grand old-fashioned fistfight with the brother, wins the dowry from him, and dumps the hard-won gold at his bride's feet. Together they regather the coins, toss them into a furnace, and go home proudly, her husband finally redeemed. She didn't really care about the money either, just that he be man enough to fight for her. And they live happily ever after.

When I borrowed this 1950s-era film from the library, my 1980s-born children couldn't understand what it was about. Those of us who grew up in the 1960s, however, had seen much of this cultural ambivalence about men and violence in our popular media. During the 1960s, the U.S. government was meeting much resistance in drafting young men to fight in the unpopular war in Vietnam. Television shows, movies, and songs questioned not only whether pacifists could be considered "real men" worthy of women's love but whether it was safe for a woman to love a pacifist. Movies like *Billy Jack* and *Gentle Persuasion* and the television show called *Kung Fu* showed pacifists endangering their women by refusing to use violence (although, of course, being "real men" in Hollywood productions, like John Wayne's character, they ultimately did). There was also a great deal of struggling for power between the sexes in 1950s movies and television shows like *I Love Lucy*. In them, the woman would ultimately give up her struggle and allow her man to take his dominant role. *Thoroughly Modern Millie* (1967), for example, ends with its heretofore feminist heroine proclaiming, "I don't want to be your equal. I want to be a *woman!*"

Men who shared power with their wives were rarely respected in the traditional world, and perhaps still are not today. "Hen-pecked" is the printable version of what such men are called.

So a woman might well lose respect for her husband if he began to treat the servants as brothers and sisters instead of as slaves over whom he held life-and-death authority. She might worry about her financial comfort or even her safety if he stepped too far away from his patriarchal role. She might not like his giving up his prerogatives, and inevitably the respect of his peers, and in turn the respect accorded her. Any slip in his status would have an impact on hers. As mentioned in chapter 2, a woman may not enjoy living with a domineering, aggressive man, but materially she may be better off with him than with a man lower in the pecking order. Selfishly, she might take advantage of his concern for her to establish her own power base in his stead.

A man cannot be truly redeemed, nor can he become one with his wife, if she insists on his retaining the privileges and anxieties of patriarchy. A woman's respect not only made it safe for a man to love her in the way Paul directed, it made it possible for the man to live a redeemed life.

## Respect and Awe

Paul's directive to wives to respect their husbands also explains why it is the husband, not the wife, who is placed parallel with Christ in the head/body metaphor. When Paul asked wives to respect their husbands, he uses the same word he used at the beginning of the passage to refer to the Christian's attitude toward Christ: the word *phobos*, which can be translated "respect," "reverence," "awe," or "fear." Wives, then, were to respect (*phobos*) their husbands, just as Christians are to submit to each other out of respect (*phobos*) for Christ. Historically it was argued that since Christ is superior to the church, the parallel of Christ and husband as head implies that Paul assumed that husbands enjoy superior status over their wives.

This parallel contains both the problem and its solution. Husbands of course enjoyed a dramatically superior status to their wives in all societies up until a relatively few years ago. (Many will argue that they still do.) But it is just this superior status that all Christians are asked to give up. And they are to do this out of their respect or awe for Christ, who "though he was in the form of God, did not count equality with God a thing to be grasped [seized or robbed], but emptied himself, taking on the form of a servant [slave]" (Phil. 2:6 RSV). Christians give up authority and privilege over one another out of respect for Christ, who himself gave up authority and privilege unimaginable.

Husbands and patricians are placed parallel with Christ in Paul's analogy because, when it came to formal authority over subordinates, women had little to renounce. Paul asked husbands to sacrifice everything they had been raised to expect in life, as even poor men expected to be served by women. Just as Jesus warned his disciples that his refusal to accept power would cause them to be ashamed of him, the first-century man who obeyed the strictures of Ephesians 5–6 would have placed himself beyond the pale of cultural respectability. Another metaphorical meaning of the word *kephale* was the "head" of the army—not the general in charge but the soldier in the lead, the first into the battle, the one who took the risks. In creating unity in marriage, the husband takes the dangerous first step. But by giving up his prerogatives, a man can upbuild his wife in love. And in this way, ironically, by rejecting rather than asserting authority over her, by denying rather than following the status quo, the husband is parallel with Christ, and so deserving of his wife's respect and awe.[48]

### Wifely Submission

What then, does "subject yourself" mean for the Christian wife today?

Just as Jesus redefined what it means to be "lord," Paul redefined submission. As my former pastor Don Hammond points out, under patriarchy slaves, children, and wives *had* to obey their masters/fathers/husbands.[49] Unlike slaves and children, in Ephesians 5 women are not asked to obey, but that may be small comfort. Just as it might be easier for the husband to literally die for his wife than to surrender his own will, obedience might be easier for a woman than submission. Obedience requires only behaving in a certain way; submission requires a change of heart. Just as for slaves and children, whose obedience is no longer coerced but given freely as an offering to God, Christianity transforms the wife's attitude. She now "places herself under" her own husband, but no longer out of inferiority or because law, custom, and the marriage contract entitles him to tell her what to do. The apostle Peter, who writes about submission in 1 Peter 3, tells wives that they need no longer obey their husbands out of terror of an unbelieving husband's power over them. Instead, the Christian wife submits in imitation of Christ, whose own submission "even unto death" (Phil. 2:8) has freed her. Submission means opting out of the power struggle, no longer playing by the rules of the fallen world, no longer trying to get one's own way, even by manipulation. Submission means upbuilding in love, allowing a husband to let go of the sword the world of thorns says he must wield, allowing him to accept his own redemption from the anxiety and obligations of worldly manhood. Submission means loving him as she loves herself, giving him her first loyalty, without stopping to consider whether or not she is "better off with him or without him" or whether or not she can get a better deal elsewhere. Submission means nourishing and cherishing, dealing with conflict by soothing each other,[50] becoming in his eyes one who brings peace (Song of Songs 8:10).

As the husband follows the example of Christ in giving himself for his wife—his body and completion, his perfection—the wife responds to him as she responds to Christ's sacrifice: with *phobos*, awe, respect, or reverence. Head and body united in one accord, together both the fullness and the one that fills, the divine peeks through, offering a glimpse into the mysterious union of all believers in Christ.

## The Impact of the Teachings of Jesus and Paul

The teachings of Jesus and Paul and the practices of the early church eventually transformed pagan patriarchy. Christian parents were urged not to marry off their children unless the child desired it.[51] Stark shows that among the early Christians in Rome, the modal age of marriage for Christian girls was eighteen years or older instead of the Roman average of less than fourteen.[52] Early Christianity opposed the abandonment of newborns as well as abortion, a practice that could be ordered by men and often proved fatal to the woman. While Roman law pressured widows to remarry (and thus put control of their resources back into the hands of men), Christian widows were encouraged to retain their independence and, where necessary, given financial support so that they did not have to remarry.[53] Christians were allowed to leave "unpeaceful" marital situations and to give nonbelieving spouses their freedom if they wished, but divorce was discouraged (1 Cor. 7:10–11). Christians bought each other out of slavery.[54] Not recognizing Roman social distinctions, they placed slaves and women in leadership positions within the churches.[55] Christian scriptures assume monogamy, not polygamy.[56] Christianity eliminated the sexual double standard, making men and women equally accountable to each other morally. The Judeo-Christian denial that sex had any spiritual significance was an important move forward in ending the "holy prostitution" of slaves associated with temples of the pagan goddesses.[57] Turn-of-the-twentieth-century theologian Shailer Mathews sums up the impact of Christianity on the natural world by noting that the times and places where people "have come most under the influence of the words and life of Jesus have been those in which institutions at variance with fraternity—branding, polygamy, the exposure of children, slavery, drunkenness and licentiousness—have disappeared."[58]

Later in Christian history, convents and monasteries would provide women and men with an alternative to marriage. The medieval Christian church, continuing efforts to keep marriage from slipping back into being a purely economic institution, discouraged arranged marriages to which the bride or groom did not consent and encouraged relationships that were companionate and sexually exclusive.[59] Similarly, with a few exceptions, Christian churches and societies consistently opposed slavery, and it was certainly Christian abolitionist efforts that resulted in its eventual elimination from the Christian world.

In the 1960s, the "traditional" family of a married couple with a wage-earning, dominant father, a homemaking, nurturing mother, and their obedient children came in for much feminist critique. There was certainly room for improvement in this practice. However, as theologian Rodney Clapp points out, the "traditional" or "patriarchal" family of the late nineteenth and early twentieth

centuries was nowhere near to being either traditional or patriarchal compared to the pre-Christian family.[60] With this distinction
between pagan and Christianized family practices in mind, let us
look at what happened to the family in the teeth of the industrial
revolution.

# 5

# Love in an Age of Wealth

## From the Natural Family to the New Morality

The Christianized version of the family—which I will call "the productive family"—that existed between the time of Christ and the Victorian era eliminated much of the natural family's abuse of the powerless. It is important to note, however, that in structure this family was only the natural family tamed. The work of the various family members was still largely determined by the economic requirements of household production: nearly all of the population worked in agriculture, households produced most of what they consumed, children were still a valuable and necessary commodity, and the sexual division of labor continued to be an important part of the household economy.

The technological developments that changed the way work was allotted between the sexes began to take shape around the turn of the eighteenth century.[1] Shortly after 1780, a man named Oliver Evans designed the world's first partially automated flour mill. Prior to this development, the staple of most American farm households was corn, which individual households grew, ground, and baked into cornbread at home. Although most people preferred wheat bread over corn, wheat is a hard grain that few households were equipped to grind at home. Moreover, whole-grain flour has a short shelf life, as it contains the bran and the germ, which tend to go bad quickly but which are expensive to separate out (white bread was the food of the rich). So although wheat was more desirable, its use as a staple was impractical, as it required frequent and expensive trips to a mill. But Evan's invention of a system to produce fine white flour that kept well and was easily stored and transported soon made it more efficient for families to buy wheat flour (and eventually, ready-made white bread) than to grow and grind their own.

Historian Ruth Schwartz Cowan shows how this and other technological developments, such as canal transportation, efficient stoves both for cooking and for heating, and piped-in water, "industrialized the home" in the United States and Europe, freeing men and children from much of their traditional work (growing and grinding corn; chopping wood for heat; carrying water).[2] Note that these innovations are not "industrial" in our normal understanding of the word. Household heat and water were not produced on an assembly line. But with these developments, more and more of the necessities of life—food, clothing, shelter, education—could be purchased more economically than they could be produced at home. Cowan summarizes:

> Butchering, milling, textile making, and leatherwork had departed from many homes by 1860. Sewing of men's clothing was gone, roughly speaking, by 1880, of women's and children's outerwear by 1900 . . . almost all items of clothing for all members of the family by 1920. Preservation of some foodstuffs . . . had been industrialized by 1900; the preparation of dairy products . . . by about the same date. Factory-made biscuits and quick cereals were appearing on many American kitchen tables by 1910, and factory-made bread had become commonplace by 1930. The preparation of drugs and medications had been turned over to factories or to professional pharmacists by 1900, and a good many other aspects of long-term medical care had been institutionalized in hospitals and sanitariums thirty years later.[3]

As industrialization continued, household production diminished.

> During the nineteenth century, households ceased to manufacture cloth and began to buy it; they similarly ceased to manufacture candles and, instead, purchased kerosene; they ceased to chop wood and, instead, began to purchase coal; they ceased to butcher their own meat and, instead, began to purchase the products of the meat packers in Chicago. There were a variety of reasons for these changes. Some once-rural, now-urban households found that many of these activities were not possible in an urban setting. Other households ceased carrying them on out of economic considerations, since the wages of the young or of parents were able to buy more goods or a higher standard of goods than any of these individuals could have produced by themselves.[4]

This change in the way things were produced had an immediate impact on the daytime composition of the home. Cowan writes, "Virtually all of the stereotypically male household occupations were eliminated by technological and economic innovations during the nineteenth century, and many of those that had previously been allotted to children were gone as well."[5] No longer required at home and needing cash to pay for the newly available conveniences, men increasingly spent most of their waking time away from the household. Although in colonial America fathers had been considered the primary influence in the teaching and rearing of children, as men spent more time away from their children this role was ceded to mothers.[6]

While technological change took men out of the home for much of the day, another member of the household—the servant—disappeared from it entirely. Cowan notes that all the nineteenth-century middle-class households she examined had some kind of paid household help, even if it was only a laundress who came in once or twice a week. Except in wealthy households, paid help greatly decreased and live-in help almost vanished by mid-twentieth century. "Modern technology," Cowan observes, "enabled the American housewife of 1950 to produce singlehandedly what her counterpart of 1850 needed a staff of three or four to produce."[7]

## From "Two Can Live as Cheaply as One" to Feminism

It was probably during the first half of the twentieth century that an old saying, "Two can live as cheaply as one," last made sense. Today that expression exists mostly as the setup for a joke: "Two can live as cheaply as one—for half as long"[8] or ". . . but not if they order room service." The part of the saying that seems most remarkable to us—the idea that two people could live on the same amount of cash as one person—would have been so true as to be hardly worth stating prior to the mid-twentieth century. In the nineteenth century and earlier, the idea that *only* two people could generate a living would have been astonishing. For some time, however, there was a balance between the need for the items and services that could be produced by one person working at home and for the things that could be purchased with the income of one person working outside the home.[9] Marriage continued to make for a more pleasant life than that available to the typical single person of either sex, whose options were often limited to living with parents or in a boarding house, eating expensive or poor-quality meals out, living in a dirty home, sending out laundry or washing it in the sink, having no children, and doing without regular sex.[10] With a husband-"provider," a woman could quit her job (as very many young wives did in this era, even before they had children) and create a comfortable—and thrifty—home for herself and her husband. The "two-living-as-cheaply-as-one" households were no doubt pressed for cash, but because production was still taking place at home, they could get along without much of it. When my mother was a child during the Depression, for example, her entire wardrobe consisted of two dresses, one for school and one for church, because while her mother sewed for her, fabric had to be purchased and the family had no cash. With chickens, cows, and a vegetable garden behind the house, however, the family never went hungry.

By mid-century, however, the two-can-live-as-cheaply-as-one slogan was challenged by an alternate perception, given voice in the 1953 launch of *Playboy* magazine. *Playboy* offered a competing image of the housewife not as the producer of a comfortable home but as a parasite who lounged around the house eating bonbons and living off her husband. *Playboy* urged men to eschew the entrapments of marriage and instead live happily single in a well-equipped apartment where they could entertain the new, single, and sexually available young career woman at their pleasure. Outrageous (and for most men, impossible) as this perspective was at the time, it presented one of the first indications that something serious was happening with the American family. For sometime in the middle of the twentieth century, households passed a tipping point at which the "two-living-as-cheaply-as-one" saying ceased to be meaningful. Increasingly, the efforts of the one at home were reaching what economists call the point of "diminishing marginal returns."

Within a few decades, the technology that made it possible for the 1950s housewife to do without servants was making it possible to consider doing without the housewife as well. Advances had made houses cleaner and even more comfortable, effortlessly maintained living spaces at just the right temperature, offered convenient pre-pared food, and presented a dazzling array of relatively inexpensive clothing and vastly improved methods of cleaning it—all requiring even less time and effort than that put in by one 1950s housewife. Furthermore, with a staggering availability of entertainment and what used to be considered luxury goods offered at enticingly afford-able prices, two could not live as *well* as one, not on one income.

### The Decline in the Value of Children

Of course, even if two might live as cheaply as one, by the mid-twentieth century three, four, or five definitely could not. Just as industrialization had relieved men of most of their household-related chores, it had freed children as well. Moreover, with much of pro-duction now taking place outside the household, children needed different education and skills from those they had been getting at home. Initially, demand for factory workers increased the demand for child labor. The 1870 U.S. census reported that about one in eight children was formally employed. But although working-class fami-lies were still dependent on children's wages, in the U.S. extensive public campaigns in the early part of the twentieth century resulted in the creation of laws outlawing child labor and making education compulsory. By the 1930s even poor children were in school and for the most part out of the productive labor market.[11]

Here a truly significant change began to make itself felt: while children who helped with the farm work or who brought home pay packets were an economic benefit to the family, children who contributed nothing financially and who had to be educated posed significant costs. In response, the industrial revolution triggered a dramatic decline in the birthrates in industrialized countries. In the United States, for example, at the beginning of the nineteenth century more than one-quarter of women aged 15–44 gave birth each year (278 live births out of 1000 women aged 15–44 in the population). By the turn of the twentieth century, that number had dropped by more than half (130/1000), and by 1998 it dropped more than half again (61/1000) to only 21.9 percent of what it had been in 1800.[12] If we look at the numbers in a slightly different way, the average number of children born per American woman dropped exponentially from 7.04 in 1800, to 3.56 in 1900, to slightly under 2 in 2000.[13]

If the traditional sexual division of labor was caused, as Gary Becker suggests, by the compelling need for children along with the equally compelling need to continue to do productive labor, "tradition" was set to blow by midcentury.[14] Except for the increasingly rare family farm, home production of items for sale had ceased in the early part of the century. It is probably misleading even to speak of home production at this point, as by then a good deal of the work that the housewife did was preparation for consumption rather than creating things that could not be obtained otherwise—for example, cooking purchased food to put on the table rather than growing and preserving it herself. Certainly the compelling need for children had disappeared.

Looking at the changes in women's behavior in industrialized society from this perspective turns around a couple of casually held cultural beliefs. The first is that the development of the birth control pill (first available in the United States in 1960) was responsible for the decline in the American birthrate. In fact, fairly effective methods of birth control, and a steadily declining birthrate, existed for decades prior to the Pill. I suggest that cheap, reliable, and socially acceptable birth control was developed because, for the first time, great numbers of people wanted fewer children. The second commonly held belief is that "women's liberation" brought about the observed changes in the status of women in the United States and Western Europe. Actually, when children are not valuable economic assets, the behavior that is optimal for the producers of children—women—changes. With the movement of production out of the home, many of women's and children's traditional functions—home cooking, canning, cleaning house, vegetable gardening, knitting, sewing, brewing beer, keeping a wood fire burning ("tending the hearth"), weaving, preparing medicines, and even, ironically, childbearing—became luxuries or hobbies rather than necessities. Consequently housewives began to experience what Betty Friedan called the "problem that has no name": a sense of restlessness and lack of fulfillment, the feeling that traditional women's work was no longer valued and that they had to find something else to do.[15] To put it less poetically (or politically) than did Friedan, as happened with the tasks performed by men and children, it became more economically efficient for women to earn cash to buy the necessities of life than for them to try to produce them themselves. The women's movement—the undoing of the rational norms of the agriculturally based world—was the response to this massive social change, not its cause. Feminism did not cause the breakdown of the family; rather, the breakdown of the historic functions of the family caused feminism.

### The Household Today

Technological progress, and household change, continues.

A few weeks ago I went to the grocery store looking for fresh spinach—the kind that comes in bunches, with stems bundled together with a rubber band, found in the vegetable coolers. All I could find was prewashed destemmed "baby spinach" packaged in plastic. When I questioned the young man stocking the shelves, he told me that the store didn't carry regular spinach anymore. However, he offered helpfully, they had (even more processed) spinach on the salad bar.

As I was leaving the produce section with my plastic bag of spinach, an odd-looking item caught my eye. It appeared to be a single potato shrink-wrapped in plastic. And that's what it was. The label trumpeted it as a "Handy Potato" and noted that it was prescrubbed and hygienically wrapped and that to enjoy a delicious baked potato all one had to do was purchase it, take it home, and bake it in the microwave for eight minutes.

A few years ago, a young couples group at church asked me to speak at one of their weekly studies. One of the young wives told me that recently another speaker had put the men and the women into separate groups and then asked them to decide on one thing that they really wished their partners would do more often. The women came back asking that their husbands be better listeners, more responsive to their emotional needs. The men thought it would be really nice if their wives would cook dinner once in a while.

It was not that the men were being sexist, my informant hastened to assure me. It was just that, with busy lives and separate careers, the couples rarely ate together, and if they did, it was at a restaurant. The husbands longed for the intimacy of a dinner at home. But unfortunately, she said, all of them worked full time and kept different schedules, so eating together really wasn't practical. Besides, none of them knew how to cook.

The young wife who couldn't cook used to be the staple of many a joke. Then, for a while, it was men's lack of culinary skills that was funny.[16] Today the inability to boil water isn't funny at all—it is a fact of life. As evidenced by the Handy Potato, home cooking today is not essential but fast becoming a luxury, like a hand-knit sweater.

### Women in the household

In biblical times it took two hours a day simply to prepare grain for cooking.[17] Today a quick trip to the corner supermarket and a few minutes at the microwave produce a perfectly edible and nutritious meal. Although housework still requires a nontrivial amount of time, most of it is no longer a matter of survival or even basic comfort, as chopping wood used to be.

Restless at home, women have joined the paid workforce in enormous numbers. In the United States, of all married mothers with children under seventeen, 12.6 percent were in the paid workforce in 1950; in 1994, 69 percent were. In 1994, 58.8 percent of married women with children age one year and under were working outside the home. In 1972, 60 percent of married couples were "traditional," with an employed husband, a housekeeping wife, and children; by 1998, this percentage had dropped to 27 percent. Conversely, in 1972,

33 percent of married couples with children under age eighteen were both employed; in 1998, 67 percent were.[18]

### Singleness

According to economic theory, marriage continues to offer significant economic advantages compared to singleness, including a pooling of risk (if one person becomes unemployed, the other can still provide) and economies of scale (one large apartment costs less than two small apartments). Economists also note that "the long-term horizon implied by marriage gives each of the spouses the ability to neglect some skills and focus on the development of others."[19] Nonetheless, people increasingly find singleness not only possible but preferable. For example, some women will tell you that having a man around the house adds to their workload rather than diminishing it.[20] Social commentators have remarked that even "women who want children do not need or necessarily want a spouse underfoot" because "children are a joy; many men are not."[21] "When I've ended a relationship," said one woman, "I've found myself realizing that although being single is a lonelier life, it's a much easier one. I think that's a secret that the culture tries to keep: If you can pay the rent and afford to go out and have fun, single life is pretty easy."[22]

For men, too, a spouse is a mixed blessing. Married men whose wives are not employed make more money and receive more promotions than single men,[23] but it appears that some men are coming to resent the burden of supporting a family single-handedly. "Imagine volunteering for a lifestyle that forces you to give up nearly half your household income, sell your toys, forgo vacations of the kind your friends enjoy, and work as if three or four lives depended on your next paycheck." This, announces a *Wall Street Journal* article, is the "world of many solo-breadwinner dads."[24] On the other hand, a working wife brings in extra income, but that income may not add enough to her husband's quality of life to make up for the additional domestic burden he will be expected to shoulder. Economically, the variables appear to be increasingly tipping in favor of singleness: the age at marriage has climbed to twenty-five years for women and twenty-seven for men. For those with a college education, the figures are two years higher. More alarmingly, this average "age at marriage" statistic captures only those who actually marry. In 2002, 28 percent of the U.S. population between the ages of thirty and thirty-four were never married, as were 18 percent of those between thirty-five and thirty-nine.[25] Twenty-six percent of the U.S. population lives in a household with only one person in it.[26] In 1947, married couples made up 78 percent of households; in 2002, married-couple households had dropped to 52 percent.[27]

### *Divorce*

When households were centers of production, the things that the husband and wife created required the efforts of them both. The most important product was children, who in turn provided things needed for immediate survival and served as insurance against future need, especially care for parents in old age. Married couples in the past were effectively co-owners of the same business. Few of these businesses were wealthy enough to survive division. Historically, the marriage contract had to be indissoluble so that the legal owner of the property (the husband) would not be tempted to replace his wife when she was no longer productive.[28] This mutual dependence added great stability to marriage. Couples may or may not have been happy, but they stayed together.

Today, couples are likely to have independent careers and produce little together besides children, who have no economic value. Further, their household goods are easily divisible: a divorcing couple can divide up the pension plan funds, draw social security individually, acquire new furnishings, feed and clothe themselves, and so on. A woman no longer needs a man or children to provide her with care in sickness or old age. Whether or not to remain in a marriage has became each individual's choice.

Marriage today depends not on sexual complementarity but almost entirely on the emotions of the two parties to it. Sexual attraction and romantic love, once considered too fragile on their own to sustain marriage, have instead become marriage's sole criteria. Most people today would regard entering into marriage without sexual attraction as foolish or even immoral. The flip side of this is that when love or attraction leaves the relationship, people begin wondering if they "owe it to themselves" to end the marriage. Not surprisingly, for this and many other reasons, divorce rates began to rise in the late 1960s and early 1970s. Of all American adults who had ever been married, the percentage that had also been divorced doubled from 17 percent in 1972 to 33–34 percent in 1996/1998.[29] Although it looked as if the divorce rate had flattened out or decreased slightly in the late 1990s, it picked up again in 2001. In 1972, 73 percent of the children in the United States were being reared by two parents in an uninterrupted marriage; by 1996, this number had dropped to 49 percent. An analysis of 1985 census data showed that among recent first marriages, the divorce rate was 67 percent.[30]

## The Costly Child and the New Morality

Since the Enlightenment at least, philosophers have criticized conventional moral codes that restrict women's sexual expression to marriage,[31] noting the perversity of cultures that punish women who enjoy themselves sexually with a man "who has not promised to support her for the rest of her life." In his book *Sex and Reason*, contemporary legal scholar Richard Posner refers disparagingly throughout to "the cult of virginity," or "chastity," implying that female chastity before marriage is irrationally religious in motivation. A barrage of criticism came from women themselves in the 1960s. The standard feminist critique targets norms of female sexual restraint as designed to protect the property rights of husbands and fathers at the expense of women's right to sexual expression. (Husbands because they consider themselves to "own" a woman's sexuality and want to ensure that no other man could father children on her; fathers because they get greater rewards from marrying off a daughter who is a virgin.)

Many of these thinkers treat female chastity as something that is of no benefit to women but rather as a repressive, self-denying contrivance imposed on them by men, frigid older women, religion, or "society" at large. But engaging in sexual intercourse, even within marriage, is far more costly for women than for men—in fact, more costly for the females of any species than it is for the males. Sex (if I have to remind you) is directly related to reproduction, and females by definition make a greater contribution to reproduction than do males. In the simplest of animals, this greater contribution simply involves supplying the "large, nutrient-rich egg" as opposed to the male's less costly investment of sperm.[32] Birds, for example, build nests, incubate their eggs, feed, and train the hatchlings: males may or may not be involved in these activities; the female always is. The more reproductively sophisticated the animal, the greater is the cost of mating for the female. Female mammals nurture the fetus within their body, give birth to it—a process that sometimes kills or disables the mother—produce milk to feed it, and stay with it and protect it until it has grown enough to survive on its own. The role of the male ranges from mate-and-run, to remaining for one season to help raise the young, to pair bonding with the same female for life, but whatever the case, among mammals, females make a much greater contribution to reproduction than do males.

Not surprisingly, biologists report that in every species it is the female who determines when and with which partner she will mate.[33] From a survival point of view, this only makes sense. The males may be ready to mate anytime they find a receptive partner, but the female that mates at the wrong time of year may lose the resulting young to inopportune conditions. The males of many species are also willing to mate with as many females as possible, because unless the female requires him to stick around, it costs him nothing. For the female, however, mating literally puts all her eggs in one basket. She is investing a whole season's worth of reproductive effort into the offspring of a single male, and so she gets to be fussy about his quality. Several males may court any given female, bringing her bits of food, performing elaborate dances, singing, or sparring. In some species, the male wins a mate by being more beautiful than his competition.[34]

Biologist Richard Dawkins notes that in species that require two parents to successfully raise the young, females require long courtships before mating.[35] Once the female has mated, she has "played her card" and has no more control over the male. If he is the kind to mate and run, the offspring from this mating are doomed. By running up the costs of mating for her suitor, the female assures that she will end up with the sort of male that will stay around to help.[36]

Human women, for whom the need for help in raising their young is acute, certainly fall into the category Dawkins describes. Human beings have a more helpless infancy and longer childhood than any other animal. Further, human mothers are vulnerable pre- and post-partum and face considerable risk of death or disability in childbirth. This being the case, as the libertine philosophers wrote (but not as they meant), in the natural world a woman really was a fool, endangering both herself and her children, if she gave herself sexually to a man "who has not promised to support her for the rest of her life." Correspondingly, Becker observes that virtually all cultures have developed some form of marriage contract to protect women in their domestically specialized role of childbearer.[37]

But how does a female of whatever species induce a male to put in that long courtship and stay around afterward to raise the young or "support her for the rest of her life," whichever the case may be? Males that accept long courtships do so because in those species *all* the females require a long courtship before mating. If they didn't, the suitor would just move from the reluctant female to one more accommodating. But if none of the females are more accommodating, the male has no temptation to desert the one with whom he has already invested his time.[38]

For these animals, humans included, sexual restraint can be thought of as a kind of conspiracy—a monopoly or cartel—practiced by females. Prior to the mid-twentieth-century sexual revolution, women could require men to marry them before they gave them sex because virtually all the other women made the same requirement. Who knows how animals coordinate this control, but among women, it was explicit and often codified in law. Calling these punishments shame-based understates their seriousness: Prior to the twentieth century and still today in some parts of the world, a prostitute, "loose woman," or girl who allowed herself to be seduced by a man who did not marry her might find herself socially ostracized and cast out by her family, insulted publicly, summarily divorced, imprisoned, branded, pilloried, or stoned; she might have her head shaved, have her children taken away or sent to institutions where they could well die, be transported to an Australian penal colony, or otherwise be cut off from the company of respectable people. Ruining one's reputation or having one's virtue compromised had serious ramifications for later chances of a good marriage. Moreover, the family of such a ruined woman or girl would be treated with suspicion as well, and her brothers and sisters might find their own opportunities limited by her disgrace. The legal notion of illegitimacy, which indemnified men and their estates against claims for financial support by children born outside of marriage, also served to protect married women from cheaters on the cartel. As cruel as this seems, female promiscuity and prostitution were not, as advocates for sex workers claim today, victimless crimes. Sex outside the rigid structures of traditional morality made a victim of every woman because it threatened the female control of sex.[39]

One way of looking at legal marriage is as a contract for a woman's exclusive sexual services, those services including not just sexual relations but childbearing, childrearing, and the domestic tasks in which woman specialized. In exchange for her exclusive commitment, a man pledged his complementary services. Female chastity was hence an essential, often explicit, part of the contract. It is likely, though, that the requirements of chastity were most important for the middle class. The rich and aristocratic were sought in marriage for reasons other than their ability to bear children and keep house and were infamous for doing as they pleased sexually. The poor, who could not afford legal marriage, had little to lose or gain either way, so they too were notorious for loose morals.[40] Hence when Western culture embarked on the sexual revolution, the attack on sexual restraint was framed as an attack on middle-class, "bourgeois" values of marriage, family, sexual fidelity, church, and attitudes toward career.

But repressive as they were, the old sexual norms served an important social function. Sexual restraint motivated men to marry, which in turn provided the protection that women needed to bear children, who helped produce the goods needed to live. Man as well as woman's survival, let alone comfort, depended on creating and maintaining family. For in an agriculturally based economy, the family was not only the basic unit of society but also the basic unit of production. In many societies motherhood has been explicitly recognized as an act of patriotism, a service that women provide for the entire society. (The American welfare system was explicitly set up to support widowed mothers in this vital service.) Thus, in the world of thorns, chastity was not just some irrational religious requirement but a necessity of social survival.

## Change in the Value of Children

As the industrial revolution eliminated the economic need for children, many of the *natural* motivations for the sacrifices and commitments that marriage entails vanished. In the past, a man wanted children not because he loved kids but because he needed loyal and obedient workers whose own comfort and survival depended on his own. He needed a sexually complementary partner to produce them and the other goods that women provided. He had to make a legally binding contract with the woman who could produce those children in order to assure her and her family that she would not be discarded or replaced once she had given him those children. Marriage contracts in such societies often spelled out exactly the *financial* recompense due to the person whose spouse sought to break the contract.[41] Women, in turn, accepted their role in the productive, sexually complementary family because, whatever its disadvantages, it remained the only practical way to live.

Today, rearing children poses significant costs, especially in parental time that might otherwise be spent in more pleasurable or income-producing activities. The payback to childrearing, like marriage, is only emotional—and sometime the emotions are not pleasant. Children are no longer items of production but of consumption. Becker notes a shift from the demand for quantity of children to quality of children, a shift that requires even more parental investment in the child. In short, having children today is becoming a luxury.

Further, as much as we love and value our children, few people really find caring for them all day, every day, rewarding. In some European countries, parents express puzzlement at the suggestion that they should want to care for their children themselves.[42] Cowan notes that even when the productive family was strongest, minding small children was considered an arduous, low-status job that didn't require much skill and for which busy housewives had little time. Once past infancy, small children were delegated to the care of a servant[43]—often a child herself—or of slightly older siblings. By the 1950s, of course, all the servants were gone, and once Americans got over the huge burst of pent-up domesticity that followed the end of the Depression and World War II, mothers remembered that minding small children was an arduous, low-status job that didn't require much skill and could be nerve-wracking and boring.

This explains the surprising results of sociologist Arlie Russell Hochschild's study of the conflict between work and home life. Hochschild spent three summers interviewing and observing, at work and at home, the employees of one company. These working parents reported that they were "strained to the limit" in trying to tend to the needs of both their families and their employment.[44] But Hochschild's study found that when you came right down to it, many of the conflicted parents were not yearning for more time at home: they preferred to be at work. After all, at work you get to go out to lunch, wear nice clothes, interact with people who don't whine too much, are allowed to finish entire sentences, and are occasionally rewarded with praise and regularly with money. As one of Hochschild's subjects said after returning to work only six weeks after the birth of her first child:

> People said to me, "You only took six weeks maternity leave?" I answered, "Gee, guys, that was six weeks I didn't have anybody to talk to. My friends are at work. The things that interest me are at work. My stimulation is at work. I am *delighted* to come back."[45]

No wonder, then, that Hochschild found that "programs that allowed parents to work undistracted by family concerns were endlessly in demand, while policies offering shorter hours that allowed workers more free or family time languished."[46] Mothers as well as fathers ignored company policies that allowed them to cut back work hours; fathers rarely took the family leave offered them; and a few purposefully took on overtime assignments to avoid having to go home to change poopy diapers and roll around on the floor with a toddler.[47] She also cites a nationwide survey that showed that people were happy with the amount of time they spent on work, family, and self.[48] "I thought about staying home with the kids," said one mother whose husband earned enough that she had no financial need to work, "but they drove me nuts."[49]

## Why Not?

Men and women today can enjoy perfectly comfortable, secure lives without children or for that matter a spouse. Like home cooking or knitting, children have ceased to be necessities and become expensive luxuries instead. The economic need for children has ceased to motivate marriage. And since marriage no longer plays a role in production, the need for feminine sexual restraint, so profoundly a part of the marriage contract, has also vanished. Marriage no longer has enough economic importance to warrant the extensive policing and restrictions required to enforce the sexual cartel.

In the world of thorns, sexuality, for all the fringe benefits it offers, is just another tool of production. In the new world of wealth, sex is uncoupled from reproduction and has become an item of consumption that can be enjoyed for its own sake. In fact, since one of the things that people most want to consume is sex, restraint appears to be counter-productive to the new cultural order. Norms controlling women's sexual behavior have eroded, eventually resulting in the "if-it-feels-good-do-it" values of the sexual revolution. Popular culture chimed in to extol what was called the New Morality with songs, television shows, movies, and books, from *To Each His Own* (a movie made in 1946 about a young woman who discovers her pregnancy after her heroic fighter-pilot lover is killed and who is forced to give up the child, with tragic consequences), to Joni Mitchell's "My Old Man" ("we don't need no piece of paper from the City Hall, keeping us tight and true"), to *Deep Throat* (a pornographic critique of Freud's male-centered notions of female orgasm), to *Four Weddings and a Funeral* (in which the happy ending involves the hero's asking the heroine *not* to marry him but to live and have children with him instead), to *Sex and the City*'s quartet of beautiful women exercis-ing "sexual prerogatives" once granted only to men. For a long time television shows and movies have portrayed sexual relations as both the key to attaining and a sign that one has attained emotional purity and moral honesty, a coming of age. The sexual cartel—which by definition requires consensus and, however unwilling, the conformity of those it seeks to regulate—has collapsed. Any residual attempts to enforce it are met with name calling and derision.[50]

## The Death of Marriage

The loss of economic value of children in the twentieth century put an end to the old economic motive for marriage. No longer producing anything irreplaceably valuable, households could easily be split up between the two partners. Individuals, male or female, could no longer be legally constrained to honor lifelong contracts, and by the 1980s, most states had revised their laws to allow "no-fault" divorce. Because marriage could not be made binding, it no longer protected domestically specialized women. Since the passage of no-fault divorce, even middle-aged or older women who have never worked outside the home might find themselves divorced with no alimony granted. Stay-at-home mothers of young children find that child-support payments rarely offer enough income to allow them to remain at home. In a legal and societal sense, compared to what it used to be, marriage has ceased to exist.

In turn, other legal concepts related to marriage have also disappeared. Laws against adultery, which was once one of the few bases on which the marriage contract could be nullified, have no legal teeth anymore. The legal notion of illegitimacy, which protected wives and legitimate children from men's indiscretions, has also been overturned. In fact, when women who have never been married to the fathers of their children were granted the right to sue for child support (along with "deadbeat dad" legislation insisting that these men be made to pay), yet another prerogative of the married woman became moot.

With the forces sustaining the sexual cartel gone, young women in the 1960s discovered that they had little restraint on their sexual behavior. Casting away the old morality once inculcated through shame and obligation, young women began asking themselves the same question that importunate young men had been asking forever: *Why not?* Why not enjoy the same "sexual prerogatives" that men enjoyed? Economically dependent on neither man nor child, they armed themselves with reliable birth control, the right to abortion should birth control prove not to be so reliable, and, if all else failed, the knowledge that a good job, welfare, or child support would sustain them. While far from every woman personally embraced the sexual revolution, middle-class women increasingly took it as their right to join the wealthy in behaving as they pleased.

This new attitude spread quickly. Sexually liberated women are no longer ostracized but portrayed in the media as healthy and desirable. Seventy percent of people age eighteen to thirty-four surveyed in 1993 indicated that they saw nothing immoral in bearing children outside of marriage.[51] About 7 percent of American couples living together at any time are not married—and are not arrested, as they might have been early in the twentieth century. Sixty-four percent of women born between 1963 and 1974 have lived with someone outside of marriage.[52] While 5.3 percent of births in 1960 were to unmarried women, in 2002 over one-third were. In 1994, 53 to 54 percent of high school students (grades nine through twelve) reported being sexually experienced.[53] Rates of sexually transmitted disease have soared.

Virgins of either sex are now suspected of somehow not being quite healthy or honest; those who would seek to encourage premarital chastity are regarded as repressive; opponents of abortion are derided as seeking to take away women's basic human rights; and anyone who dares try to enforce old moral standards is called hateful. In the absence of any particularly good reason to refrain, why should it not be so? The New Morality is only, after all, what is natural. Why return to the shame, punishment, ostracism, stigma, gossip, judgment, repression, hypocrisy, and dishonesty of the moral conspiracy?

### "Why Not" Homosexual Marriage?

Another example of the "why not?" attitude brought about by shifts in the economic structures underlying the family can be found in today's growing acceptance of homosexual identity, sexual practices, and demands to legalize same-sex marriage. Not very long ago, the idea of marriage between persons of the same sex would have been considered at best a joke or a futuristic fantasy. Society as a whole condemned homosexual practice, although in fact homosexuality was usually so remote a concept that most people didn't even have a word for it.[54] In a preindustrial economy, it was obvious why men and women married members of the other sex and not each other. A marriage based on the practical need for sexual complementarity left no room for men to marry men or women to marry women. Economic marriage was about household production in a very literal sense, and except for the rich, people chose their spouses more on their ability to build a household than on the basis of sex appeal. Whom one found sexually desirable, whom one loved, and whom one married were entirely different issues. If one found one's spouse sexually attractive, that was very nice, but sex was one of the jobs one did within marriage, not its main motive or purpose. Greek and Jewish cultures even had rules that required men to have sex with their wives on a regular basis, presumably because they might not bother otherwise.

Even the ancient Greeks, who openly recognized that some men "become lovers of boys and are not inclined by nature toward marriage and the procreation of children" and who would have found it sufficient "to live their lives out with one another," did not dream of men marrying each other. Instead, even "lovers of boys . . . are compelled to [marry and have children] by the law or custom."[55] Marriage to a woman was too useful a thing for men's lives to be considered anything but a "must" for all men, even those who loved boys.[56] What possible purpose would marriage between two men (or two women) have served in the preindustrial world?

The need for sexual complementarity in marriage remained constant for thousands of years. As Cowan writes:

> If an eighteenth-century woman had attempted housekeeping without the assistance of a man (or of a good deal of cash with which to purchase the services of men), she would most likely have had markedly to lower her standard of living, to undertake tasks for which she had little training, and to work herself into a state of utter exhaustion—all of which conditions would have seriously endangered her health and probably her life. A similar fate would have befallen a man under the same circumstances had he tried to farm without the help of a woman. Small wonder that most people married and, once widowed, married again. Under the technological and economic conditions that prevailed before industrialization, survival at even a minimally comfortable standard of living required that each household contain adults (or at least grown children) of both sexes.[57]

Further, if marriage developed, as Becker claims, as a legal contract to protect women in their role as child bearers, marriage made no sense for same-sex lovers, who by definition do not bear children and hence do not need this protection.

If the old marriage contract had nothing to offer homosexuals, however, the contemporary version of it does. Legal marriage today offers access to employer-provided benefits such as health and life insurance and survivors' pensions; legal power to make healthcare decisions when one partner is incapacitated; rights to a deceased or disabled spouse's social security benefits; inheritance rights; the right to inherit a deceased spouse's estate tax free; and discounts offered by businesses on items such as mortgages and insurance. Note the pattern here: most of these items, such as support in old age and widowhood, healthcare, insurance, and inheritances, were all things that were once produced in the household. Like more prosaic items such as heat, water, and clothing, today these historic products of the home are being more efficiently produced by government, employers, or businesses.

As these items were "outsourced" from the family, they became divisible. Each member of a couple now has access to them on his or her own, and they do not require any kind of sexual complementarity. Further, these benefits are not distributed by sex but provided equally to men as well as women.

The question then is, if the benefits of marriage no longer depend on sexual complementarity, why should sexual complementarity be required of couples who wish the benefits of marriage? If the basis of marriage today is simply a man and a woman's emotional attachment and sexual attraction to each other, why should marriage be denied to same-sex couples who also feel emotional attachment and sexual attraction to each other? Further, when most of the benefits of legal marriage have been "outsourced" from the family and are being provided by the government, denial of these benefits based on the sex of the individual members of the couple does become, as activists complain, a civil rights issue. So the unthinkable becomes thinkable. Why not homosexual marriage? advocates ask. Conservative refusal to "accept and celebrate" homosexuality seems all of a piece with the old shame and coercion-based traditional morality.[58]

## Christianity and the New Morality

In 1984, wondering why technological advances had removed men and children but stranded Mother in the home, historian Ruth Schwartz Cowan wrote, "Technological systems that might have truly eliminated the labor of housewives could have been built . . . but such systems would have eliminated the home as well—a result that . . . most Americans were consistently and insistently unwilling to accept."[59] Twenty years later, these systems pretty much exist and are willingly accepted. As Cowan predicted, the innovations that utterly transformed the household have, for many people, eliminated the home as well. A majority of twenty-first-century families still look like the productive family (that is, with a mother and father married to each other and children in the home), but only a very slim majority. The diminishing importance of the household as the center of production has led to households that are empty during the day, high rates of divorce, extended or permanent singleness (even with children), and a new set of attitudes toward sexual behavior.

This, then, is why I say that the spiritual problems of families today are the problem of the rich young man (Matt. 19). The astonishing wealth of the developed world in the twentieth and twenty-first centuries has freed most of its people from concerns about survival. Households have been transformed from the locus of production to the locus of consumption. People today sweat not to eat their bread but to consume at a high enough level. In surveys, children today will say that their goal in life is to be rich. Consumer expert Juliet B. Schor writes that nearly two-thirds of parents in her survey agreed that "my child defines his or her self-worth in terms of the things they own and wear more than I did when I was that age." "American children are deeply enmeshed in the culture of getting and spending, and they are getting more so," she writes. "The more they buy into the commercial and materialist messages, the worse they feel about themselves, the more depressed they are, and the more they are beset by anxiety, headaches, stomachaches, and boredom."[60] The thorns that prick us today are gold plated, but they are still thorns.

The near total collapse of traditional structures and morality, and the disparagement that meets Christian attempts to counter them, suggests that the "family values" of the past were not so much values as just the behaviors that were rewarded by the way things worked then. Second-, twelfth-, or eighteenth-century couples did not stay together because they loved each other and their children more than people do today. Nor did they remain chaste before marriage because they were basically more moral people. They stayed married and restricted their sexual behavior because that was what was required of them to survive. For the average person, any other behavior was unthinkable. Christian values appeared to overlap with these requirements, and Christian values helped enforce appropriate behavior, so society supported Christianity. But the requirements were not religious values in themselves.

Now the social and economic forces that used to support Christian values have not only moved out from under them, they have turned on them. These changes have created chaos for families, but they also offer the Christian community an opportunity to factor worldly influences out of our beliefs and practices, to redefine and reintroduce the elements of the Christian message that have been lost. When God created us as sexual beings, he had something different in mind from either the old or the new morality. Marriage was not intended to be a tool of production, nor simply something that could be taken or left as seemed expedient. It was intended to be more than a civil right or the way social benefits are distributed. When God blessed us with children, he did not intend them to be either servants or toys.

Jesus, Paul, and the creation account have told us that the ideal for sexuality is to motivate a "one flesh" unity. The next chapter explores how a small book in the Old Testament, the Song of Songs, dramatically illustrates not only the full meaning and blessings of becoming one, but also the vital steps necessary to achieve this ideal. Although the Song is very old and written during a time when family relations were patriarchal, its message remains relevant for people today regardless of our material circumstances.

# 6

# Reclaiming the Garden in the World of Thorns

The industrial revolution and the end of the need for domestic production give even the average man and woman in the developed world today a freedom unimaginable several decades ago. This freedom opens up possibilities for reclaiming a joyous, one-flesh relationship in a way not available to our ancestors. But ironically, despite the new opportunities, the moral climate that comes with freedom offers very little help or support in actually creating such joy. Popular culture bombards us with the message that "all you need is love," but *love*, like *sex*, is a word difficult to define, and a simple declaration of it is not to be trusted. "I love you" might mean "I care for your well-being more than I care for my own," but it can just as easily mean "I want you sexually," "I am smitten with you," "I get a lot of status being seen with you," "I want to possess you," "I'm in love with the idea of being in love," or "You are nice to have around until you get to be too high maintenance or I meet someone I like better."

"In love" as used popularly in movies and novels seems to refer to a state of irresistible sexual attraction, accompanied by a complete indifference to the possibility that the loved one may possess flaws. Such love, in practice, has little staying power. Witness the movie stars who fall in love with other movie stars, can't keep their hands off each other, have each other's names tattooed in prominent places on their bodies, gush to reporters that the sweet sight of their beloved sleeping keeps them awake at night, et cetera, only to break up a couple of years (or a couple of months) later. Witness your friends who do the same things without benefit of press coverage. Think of the people you loved so madly but thank God you never married—or perhaps did marry and came to regret.

In its initial stages, this kind of love seems to justify anything. The ancient Greeks believed it was hubris to resist it. Such a love makes previous commitments irrelevant—we must act, sexually at least, on the love we feel *now*.[1] For a while, we as a culture even believed that the children of broken marriages were better off when the parents were each properly in love with someone who in turn loved them properly. And certainly, being "in love" is enough to justify, if not compel, sexual relations among single people.

The problem with love as an irresistible romantic feeling lies in that feeling's source. In *Getting the Love You Want*, marriage therapist and best-selling author Harville Hendrix writes that on an unconscious level we fall in love with people who have strengths and abilities that we believe will complete us. Hendrix believes that these qualities are conditioned by our childhood experiences, often by what we did or did not get from our parents/caregivers. "At the very moment of attraction," he writes, "you began fusing your lover with your primary caretakers."[2] People who had an unhappy childhood may *consciously* search for a radically different partner, swearing that they will never marry someone with their father's temper or their mother's shrillness. "But," Hendrix concludes from hundreds of hours of clinical experience, "no matter what their conscious intentions, most people are attracted to mates who have their caretakers' positive *and* negative traits, and, typically, the negative traits are more influential."[3] He suggests that the primitive unconscious portion of our brain, the part that processes emotions and attachment, is trying to re-create the conditions of childhood in order to correct them.[4]

This means that, as compelling as that insistent sexual attraction might be, it may prove to be an unreliable basis on which to build a permanent relationship. When the euphoria of being in love wears off, the couple may find themselves in conflict over the same issues that disturbed their childhoods. Our cultural definition of being in love does not recognize this danger, however. Instead, it insists that people deserve to love and be loved in this way. And if you suddenly find yourself no longer in love with your partner—no longer feel so irresistibly attracted or suddenly become aware of the person's flaws—our culture insists that you "owe it to yourself" to break away. In fact, you can break up and feel righteous about your desertion at the same time, because your partner also deserves to be with someone who *really* loves him or her.

## Love and the Bible

Amazingly, the Bible presents a beautiful and extended definition of love as God intended it to be—the Song of Songs. For over a millennium scholars and casual readers alike have wondered how the Song of Songs, a poem full of playful sexuality but lacking in references to God, "got into" the Bible. Many theologians simply dismissed it out of hand, while others "spiritualized" it, recasting its expressions of longing into metaphors for God's relationship with Israel or Christ's relationship with the church.[5] More recent scholarship has come to recognize the Song as a celebration of human love and thus a biblical affirmation of the sexual element in marriage.[6] Interpreting the Song as simply an erotic poem, however, still does not address the question of why it should be regarded as scripture.

Read in the context of the biblical framework of creation ideal, fall, and redemption, however, the Song of Songs turns out to be far more than an erotic poem. While the Song celebrates (and deeply affirms) sexual love as beginning with irresistible sexual attraction, it also warns against precipitous actions, delivering us safely through that dangerous stage of love-blindness. Then the Song shows us how passion combined with compassion leads to a serene, sustaining love that transcends material wealth in its power and beauty. The Song of Songs describes redeemed marriage and the possibility of living as "one flesh, naked and not ashamed" within the world of thorns. Completing the story of creation, the Song of Songs is a critical part of scripture, showing why God blessed humankind with sexuality, not simply for procreation or for its physical pleasures but for its ability to create a sanctuary for those who love fully.

The title, Song of Songs, means something like "the greatest of songs." It is more commonly known as the Song of Solomon, in part because the first verse reads, "The Song of Songs, which is Solomon's." This ambiguous ascription does not mean that King Solomon actually wrote the poem, however. In fact, evidence suggests that the poem was written well after Solomon's lifetime, perhaps about three hundred years before the birth of Christ.[7] Nor is Solomon the male lover in the poem. Rather, as we will see as the poem progresses, the poet alludes to the legend of Solomon in order to contrast the wealth of Israel's most glorious king with the even greater riches of love.

I created the rendering of the text given here by comparing several different translations of the Song and selecting the wording that made the most sense out of the poem as a whole.[8] There are two characters in the story and a chorus of voices.[9] The two characters, the lovers, are not named; I call them "the Woman" and "the Lover." The Woman is the main narrator. She begins the poem by addressing us directly, drawing us into her circle of intimacy before turning to address her beloved.[10]

*The Woman*
O, that he would kiss me with the kisses of his mouth!
For your love is better than wine,
your anointing oils are fragrant,
your name is oil poured out;
    this is why the maidens love you.
Take me by the hand, let us run together!
Let my king bring me into his chambers. [*King* is a term of
    endearment.]

*The Friends*
We rejoice and delight in you;
we will praise your love more than wine.

*The Woman*

How right they are to adore you!
I am black and comely [the Woman introduces herself],
   O daughters of Jerusalem,
Like the tents of Kedar [a tribe that wove its tents from black wool],
   like the curtains of Solomon.
Do not scorn me because I am dark,
   because the sun has scorched me.
My mother's sons were angry with me;
   they made me keeper of the vineyards.
My own vineyard I have not kept!

This opening introduces one of the main themes of the Song—the priority of love over material wealth. Originally subject to the material concerns of the world of thorns, the Woman tells us she worked for her brothers, who treated her harshly. Now she has put worldly concerns aside and sets about to keep her own "vineyard," the Song's metaphor for the business of love.

*The Woman*

Tell me, you whom my soul loves,
   where do you pasture?
Where do you lie down at noon?
For why should I be like one who is veiled [or, a stranger or vagabond]
   beside the flocks of your friends?

Beginning her new friendship with a forthright request for candor and intimacy, the Woman offers in return the removal of the defenses that separate them. The Lover answers:

*Lover*

If you do not know, most beautiful of women,
   follow the tracks of the sheep
and graze your young goats
   by the tents of the shepherds.

I dreamed of you, my darling, as a mare,
   my very own, among Pharaoh's chariots.[11]
Your cheeks are beautiful with ornaments,
   your neck with strings of jewels.

> We will make you ornaments of gold,
>     with silver filigree.

The Lover's comparison of the Woman to a mare is not as funny as it sounds. Horses are beautiful animals, and in ancient times, when only the wealthy could afford them, they were highly prized. The Woman's strings of necklaces and earrings remind her beloved of the jeweled harnesses of the royal horses of Pharaoh. The Song portrays the Woman as signaling her interest in the man by wearing attractive clothes and ornaments, and he notices them. Although later in the Song these superficial attractions will no longer be important, their inclusion in the beginning acknowledges the fact that love often does begin in that irresistible attraction.

*The Woman*
While my king lay down on his own couch,
    my fragrance wakened the night. [Fragrance is an image of sexual intoxication.][12]
My lover is to me a sachet of myrrh,
    he shall lie all night between my breasts.
My beloved is to me a cluster of henna blossoms
    in the vineyards of Engedi.

*Lover*
Behold, you are beautiful, my love;
Behold, you are beautiful!
    Your eyes are doves. [They are soft, or the lashes flutter.]

*The Woman*
How handsome you are, my lover!
    Oh, how charming!
And our bed is verdant. [lush, green]

*The Lover*
The beams of our house are cedar [perhaps the limbs of trees],
    our rafters are firs.

*The Woman*
I am the rose of Sharon [she says she is just a simple flower],
    a lily of the valley.

*Lover*
Like a lily among brambles
   so is my love among women.

*The Woman*
Like an apricot tree among the trees of the forest
   is my lover among the young men.
In that shade I have often lingered,
   tasting the fruit.[13]
He has taken me to the banquet hall [literally, house of wine;
   throughout the Song, wine is symbolic of sexual love],
   and his emblem over me is love.
Sustain me with raisins,
   refresh me with apricots;
for I am faint with love.

Although the Woman admits from the first that she is no pampered beauty, her lover demurs—compared to her, he says, other women are flowerless brambles. She proclaims him an apricot tree, delicious among the fruitless trees of the forest. They praise each other fiercely and freely, without embarrassment, which is easy enough, as miraculously neither possesses any flaws. Like the first man and woman in the garden, they are unsuspecting of possible hurt that may come from such candor. Nonetheless, this blind attraction is fine, even necessary, the Song assures us. Such mutual enthusiasm will lead to trust and emotional closeness.

Eventually love's eyes will open. The lovers do have weaknesses, and soon enough they will come jarringly home. But love does not yet have to stand up to that test.

*The Woman*
O that his left arm were under my head,
   and his right hand should caress me!
Daughters of Jerusalem, I charge you
   by the gazelles or the wild does:
that you stir not up nor awaken love
   until it is ready!

Although the Song began with the Woman's desire for her beloved's kisses, she now yearns for a more intimate embrace. Her longing has roots in both her admiration for him and his delight in her. Despite blossoming desire, however, the Woman urges restraint. The refrain "Do not stir up or awaken love until it is ready," repeated several times throughout the Song, cautions, "Don't rush love." Physical and emotional intimacy must wait. Here and in Genesis 2, biblical sexuality belongs not to the individual but to the relationship. Longing, which draws lovers together and motivates a deeper love, has a sweetness of its own that we often fail to savor.

The Woman initiated the courtship, but in the next passage, her beloved comes to her:

> *The Woman:*
> The voice of my beloved!
>> Look! Here he comes,
>>> leaping upon the mountains [an image of energy and passion],
>>> bounding over the hills.
> My lover is like a gazelle
>> or a young stag.
> Look, there he stands
>> behind our wall,
> gazing in at the windows,
>> looking through the lattice.
> My beloved speaks and says to me:
>> "Arise, my darling,
>>> my beautiful one, and come with me.
> See! The winter is past,
>> the rain is over and gone.
> Flowers appear on the earth;
>> the time of singing has come,
> and the cooing of doves
>> is heard in our land.
> The fig tree puts forth its figs,
>> and the blossoming vines spread their fragrance.
> Arise, come, my darling;
>> my beautiful one, come with me."
>
> *Lover*
> O my dove, in the clefts of the rock,

> in the hiding places on the mountainside,
> let me see you from every side,
> > let me hear your voice;
> for your voice is sweet,
> > and you are lovely to look at.
> Catch us the foxes,
> > the little foxes,
> > > that ruin the vineyards—
> for our vineyards are in blossom.

The Lover invites the Woman to come tend their love, but the pretty imagery describing the chore—catching little foxes amid the blossoms—belies the significance of the task to which he calls her. The little foxes of hesitation and doubt that impede love's blossoming are not cast out so easily. Commitment will open the door to a whole new world, but once lovers choose one path, they say, "This one and no other." In a single step they sacrifice all other lovers and all other alternative lives. So despite attraction, despite longing, before they plunge they must take time to consider if this is the love they want for a lifetime.

The Woman answers her suitor first in verse and then with a story.

> *The Woman*
> My lover is mine and I am his;
> > he browses among the lilies [and she is a lily].
> Until the day break
> > and the shadows flee,
> turn, lover, be like a gazelle
> > or a young stag on the rugged hills.
>
> All night long on my bed
> > I sought him whom my soul loves; ["I tossed and turned all
> > night"]
> I looked for him but did not find him.
> > "I will rise now and go about the city,
> > in the streets and in the squares;
> I will search for the one my soul loves."
> So I looked for him but did not find him.
> The watchmen found me,

as they made their rounds in the city.
"Have you seen the one my soul loves?"
Scarcely had I passed them,
    when I found him whom my soul loves.
I held him fast and would not let him go
    until I brought him into my mother's house,
and into the chamber of her that
    conceived me.

I adjure you, O daughters of Jerusalem,
    by the gazelles or the wild does:
do not stir up or awaken love
    until it is ready!

Invited by her lover to choose him, in this vignette the Woman finally comes to her decision. Publicly proclaiming this man as the one her soul loves, she searches the city for him and brings him home. The Lover henceforth calls the Woman his spouse or promised bride, something he has not presumed to do before. The next passage, which invokes the presence of King Solomon, also witnesses to the enhanced significance of their relationship:

*The Woman*
Who is this coming up from the wilderness,
    like a column of smoke,
more fragrant with myrrh and incense,
    than all the spices of the merchant!
Look! Here is King Solomon's bed![14]
    Surrounded by sixty warriors, the noblest of Israel,
all equipped with swords
    and expert in war,
each with his sword at his thigh
    prepared for the terrors of the night.
King Solomon made for himself a pavilion
    from the wood of Lebanon.
He made its pillars of silver,
    its back of gold, its seat of purple;
    its interior was inlaid with love.
Daughters of Jerusalem,
    come out.

> Look, O daughters of Zion,
> >  at King Solomon,
> at the crown with which his mother crowned him
> >  on the day of his wedding,
> on the day of the gladness of his heart.

Solomon's glorious presence, linked with marriage and with the bridal chamber, signals the deepened significance of the couple's relationship. The attraction that started with "Let's get acquainted" and "I like how you dress" and grew into besotted love-blindness, has turned serious. The couple's love now befits the attention of Israel's richest and most glorious king—at least in their own eyes. For those passionately in love believe that their love must be as obvious to everyone as a royal procession, and as worthy of public celebration.

In the era when the Song of Songs was written, weddings were not religious ceremonies but private agreements celebrated with a public procession and feasting. If any event in the poem could be considered the equivalent of a modern wedding, it is this passage.

While the poem invokes Solomon's grandeur to solemnize the lovers' union, at the same time it hints that the couple's love will eventually transcend the glory of even Israel's richest king. Solomon's pavilion was set with gold and silver and festooned with beautifully made tapestries. The lovers' outdoorsy bed is merely "green," their beams and rafters the branches of the trees above them (1:16–17). Nonetheless, soldiers, not friends or a lover, attend Solomon's bed. A king, vigilant against usurpers, needs the protection of swords against the terrors of the night.[15] But no one can steal the lovers' treasure, and they know no fear.

With this deepened commitment, the man praises his beloved in more intimate terms than he has used before.

*Lover*
Behold, you are beautiful, my love,
>  behold, you are beautiful!
Your eyes are doves
>  behind your veil.
Your hair is like a flock of goats,
>  flowing down the slopes of Gilead [an image of long, flowing curls].

Your teeth are like a flock of shorn ewes
    that have come up from the washing;
each one has its twin,
      and not one among them is bereaved [remember that the Song
      was written in much poorer times; having all of your teeth was a
      characteristic worthy of note].
Your lips are like a crimson thread,
    and your mouth is lovely.
Your curving cheeks behind your tresses
    are like halves of a pomegranate.
Your neck is like the tower of David,
    built as a fortress;
on it hang a thousand bucklers,
    all of them shields of warriors. [She is wearing necklaces.]
Your two breasts are like two fawns [an image of grace and motion?
    of baby-smooth plumpness?],
      twins of a gazelle,
    that feed among the lilies.
Before the dawn-wind rises
    and the shadows flee,
I will hasten to the mountain of myrrh
    and the hill of incense [a rather explicit sexual image; you figure it
    out].
You are altogether beautiful, my love;
    there is no flaw in you.
Come with me from Lebanon, my bride;
    come with me from Lebanon.

Depart from the peak of Amana,
    from the peak of Senir and Hermon,
    from the dens of lions,
    from the mountains of leopards [places of danger].
You have ravished my heart, my sister [*sister* is a term of affection],
    my promised bride;
you have ravished my heart
    with a glance of your eyes,
    with one jewel of your necklace.
How sweet is your love, my sister, my promised bride!
How delicious is your love, more delicious than wine!
How fragrant your perfumes,
    more fragrant than all other spices!

Your lips, my promised one, distill wild honey.
　　Honey and milk are under your tongue;
and the scent of your garments
　　is like the scent of Lebanon.

A garden locked is my sister, my promised bride,
　　a garden locked, a fountain sealed.
Your branches form an orchard of pomegranate trees,
　　the rarest essences are yours;
nard and saffron, calamus and cinnamon,
　　with all trees of frankincense, myrrh, and aloes,
　　with the subtlest odors—
a garden fountain, a well of living water,
　　streams flowing down from Lebanon.

The Woman, her Lover tells her, has "ravished his heart." But as he details his desire for her, he describes a tantalizing love not yet attained. She remains his "promised one" not yet realized, "a garden locked, a fountain sealed."[16] For although the Woman so yearned for her man that she braved the dark city streets in order to find him, even after her acquiescence she remains veiled. She has not yet surrendered her defenses.

In the poem, the Woman's veil may simply suggest that the lovers have not yet consummated their love. But on another level, the Song teaches that even after marriage lovers can be defended and concealed. Willing to be naked, they still feel shame. Intimacy does not come automatically with the marriage ceremony, but grows. The Song warns, however, that the more time a couple spends together without this opening, the greater the danger posed by holding back. The "little foxes" of doubt grow into dens of lions and mountains of leopards. Come away from your fear, the Lover urges, and the Woman answers yes:

> *The Woman*
> Awake, O north wind,
> 　　and come, O south wind!
> Blow upon my garden
> 　　that its fragrance may be wafted abroad.
> Let my beloved come to his garden,
> 　　and eat its choicest fruits.

*The Lover*
I have come to my garden, my sister, my bride;
    I have gathered my myrrh with my spice,
I have eaten my honeycomb with my honey,
    I have drunk my wine with my milk.
Eat, friends, drink, and be drunk with love.

Flinging herself to wind and sky, the Woman, who is the garden, gives herself to her lover. "Let my beloved come to *his* garden," she cries. He offers himself in return: "I come to *my* garden." Old Testament scholar Phyllis Trible calls this the "language of intercourse," but the Lover describes a desire not only satisfied but fulfilled beyond reason: "I have gathered my myrrh with my spice, I have eaten my honeycomb with my honey, I have drunk my wine with my milk." He invites his listeners to seek the same joy: "Eat, friends, drink, and be drunk with love." Enjoy riches greater than King Solomon's. Exult in the intoxication, not of wine but of love.

## The Second Half of Love

Modern love stories end at about this point, concluding with "And they lived happily ever after" and leaving the reader to trust that the heroes can carry on what they have begun. But the Song of Songs does not end here. In real life, sexual consummation begins rather than ends a marriage, and the Song promises that marriage does not end desire. For physical union takes away the loneliness of longing but not the longing itself, and the continuation of desire accelerates the blossoming of the relationship. The process of becoming more deeply and truly married continues lifelong.

In the Song, sexuality will take the union to profound depths. Another vignette, paralleling the first in which the Woman comes to her initial commitment, tells what this blossoming relationship requires next:

*The Woman*
I was asleep, but my heart was awake.
    I heard my beloved knocking.
"Open to me, my sister, my love,

> my dove, my perfect one;
> for my head is wet with dew,
>> my locks with the drops of the night."
> I had taken off my tunic;
>> am I to put it on again?
> I had washed my feet;
>> am I to dirty them again?

The Woman was dreaming of her lover, but she greets his actual presence with annoyance and shame. She obviously resents the inconvenience of her beloved's late arrival. Her reaction reflects some vanity as well—she complains that she will have to put on her outer garment again. But why, after the intimacy that they have shared, should she feel the need to dress up at all? Further, the poem presents the Lover as less than appealing himself, damp from the night's dew and in search of comfort. Curiously, the Song of Songs is not an epic poem in which the Lover proves his worthiness by undertaking an ordeal for his beloved's favor, nor does she rescue him from some gratifying and thrilling danger. He comes to her in need, but his distress is hardly heroic. He has just gotten his hair wet, and now he rattles the doorknob and pleads to come in out of the dew. The dew? His predicament isn't exciting; it's pathetic. Love's fantasy come crashing down. No wonder she hesitates to open the door.

This midnight visit presents a crisis of candor. Up until now, infatuation has blinded the lovers to each other's flaws, allowing them to indulge in a fantasy of love perfectly groomed. But now everyday life makes itself known. He comes home late and in need of petty comfort; she, rumpled with sleep and without the finery he admires, would rather not be bothered, or perhaps even seen.

The lovers of the Song have testified fervently to each other's beauty and sexual appeal, but their love so far is passionate, sexual love. Such love, called *eros* by the Greeks, concerns itself with the beloved's attractive qualities and nothing else. When *eros* says, "I love you," it means mostly "I want you." *Eros* prefers not to be disturbed at an inopportune time, does not dare be seen with bed hair, and would rather not welcome an untidy lover. So the Song challenges lovers to consider what happens next, as the couple makes the adjustments to the petty annoyances and inconveniences of living with another person. Refusing to open the door, the Woman only seeks to defend them both against disillusionment.

Then she thinks better of it:

*The Woman*
My beloved thrust his hand through the latch opening [the equiva-
    lent of rattling the doorknob],
      and my womb trembled for him.
I arose to open to my beloved.

*Eros* has brought the lovers to this point, but *eros* alone cannot take the relationship further. Everyday life strips passion of its ability to blind, to infatuate. Everyday love—marriage—requires informed acceptance of the loved one as he or she really is. If that first attachment is to endure, it must grow beyond desire and become transfigured into a different kind of love entirely.

And this is what happens in the Song of Songs. Scholars who read it as merely an erotic poem interpret the Woman's trembling womb as an expression of her sexual desire for her lover.[17] But from this point on, we can no longer understand the Song of Songs as "merely" an erotic poem. The Bible uses the image of a trembling womb many times, but nowhere else do translators consider it to mean sexual desire.[18] Rather, "trembling womb" is the Hebrew term expressing compassion: "womb love," the love of mother for child, of God for creation, and now, the grace that lover grants beloved—self-giving, caring concern for the other person, for the other person's sake. This opening of the door lies at the conceptual center of the Song of Songs.

In compassion, the lovers can let go of vanity and pique and give themselves fully. They are finally "naked and not ashamed." But before the Song tells of the beauties of compassionate love, it first warns of its dangers:

*The Woman*
I arose to open to my beloved,
    and my hands dripped with myrrh [an image of yearning and
    yielding],
      my fingers with liquid myrrh,
    upon the handles of the bolt.

I opened for my lover,
   but my lover had left; he was gone.
My soul failed at his flight.
   I sought him, but did not find him;
   I called him, but he did not answer.
The watchmen came upon me as they made
   their rounds in the city.

They beat me, they wounded me,
   they took away my mantle,
   those sentinels of the walls.
I charge you, O daughters of Jerusalem,
   if you find my beloved,
tell him this:
   I am faint with love.

In the first version of the searching story, the Woman passed the city watchmen unscathed. In the second version, however, the watchmen beat her and take away her mantle. This event, so out of keeping with the otherwise benign environment in which the lovers roam, signals the profound change wrought by true caring. Opening her heart and loving devotedly, compassionate love renders the Woman vulnerable in ways that *eros* never could.

The weaknesses of husbands and wives do not often expose people to physical harm, but they do endanger those who love in other ways. Maybe she makes foolish investments. Perhaps he craves a fame he can never have. They hurt; their lover suffers with them. Truly loving requires bearing the burden of each other's imprudent choices, vain ambitions, anxieties, physical pain and ailments, character flaws, and even eventual death. And the Woman's recourse in the face of these dangers? Like Jesus, the Song of Songs says, "Choose the better part, and don't worry about the rest." Choosing to love compassionately, the Woman in the Song can only say, "If you find my beloved, tell him this: I am faint with love."

While caring love exposes the Woman to danger, the Lover himself does not harm his beloved, nor does he wish harm upon her. Willful hurting kills love. Malevolence, perhaps more than anything else, marks the marriage that cannot endure. The Song warns of suffering for the loved one's sake, but it neither condones nor tolerates abuse,

nor does it ask for its passive acceptance. Had the Lover a tendency
to hurt purposefully, the Woman would have done well not to open
the door.

Her defenses cast aside, the Woman has been beaten for the sake
of her beloved. But she remains faithful despite the wounding. As
the Song continues, she now sings her first intimate and extended
praise of the Lover:

> *The Friends*
> What is your beloved more than another beloved,
>     most beautiful of women?
> What is your beloved more than another beloved,
>     that you should have us swear like this?
>
> *The Woman*
> My lover is radiant and ruddy,
>     distinguished among ten thousand.
> His head is golden, purest gold;
>     his locks are palm fronds [wavy],
>     and black as the raven.
> His eyes are doves
>     in a pool of water,
>     washed in milk,
>     mounted like jewels.
> His cheeks are like beds of spices,
>     yielding fragrance.
> His lips are lilies,
>     distilling pure myrrh.
> His arms are golden, rounded,
>     set with jewels.
> His body is like an ivory tusk,[19]
>     encrusted with sapphires.
> His legs are alabaster columns,
>     set upon bases of gold.
> His appearance is like Lebanon,
>     unrivaled as the cedars.
> His conversation is sweetness itself,
>     and he is altogether desirable.
> This is my beloved, this is my friend,
>     O daughters of Jerusalem.

The explicit introduction of compassion has transfigured the lovers' relationship in myriad ways. Perhaps most important, the blind acceptance of infatuation takes on a different character in devoted love. Indeed, compassion may be defined as this: no longer blind to our beloved's flaws, we open the door to him anyway. Love-blind infatuation becomes open-eyed, open-armed acceptance. But as the Woman's song in praise of her beloved demonstrates, only when the Lover is seen as he truly is does she really appreciate him. Then he becomes more than just beloved. He is also a friend.

Acceptance matures the relationship. Love grows mundane without becoming profane. An even greater outflowing of mutual admiration and desire results. Contrary to the woman's fears, honesty does not end romance but makes it ever richer. The lovers are without shame, not now in ignorance but in knowledge. Compassion has given them the strength to be courageous.

The Woman had asked her friends to seek her beloved, but as it turns out, she does not need their help.

> *The Friends*
> Where has your lover gone,
>     most beautiful of women?
> Which way did your beloved turn,
>     so we can help you look for him?
>
> *The Woman*
> My beloved has gone down to his garden,
>     to the beds of spices,
>     to browse in the garden,
>     and to gather lilies.
> I am my beloved's and my beloved is mine;
>     he browses among the lilies.

The Woman hesitated to open her heart fully, and indeed, when she did, she paid a price for her exposure. But her new weakness, her acceptance of the fears and concerns of truly loving, finally flings open the gates of the garden. When the daughters of Jerusalem ask which way they should look for the Lover, she tells them that he had gone down to his garden, to the bed of spices, to browse among the lilies. He goes, however, not away from but to her: as the poem told

us earlier, she is herself the garden, the spices, and the lily. The poem
began with her request to know where this attractive man "pastured."
At its crisis point, she refused him that shelter. But now, at the core
of the Song, she knows the answer to her question—he pastures in
her. "I am my beloved's and my beloved is mine," she sings. Now
begins true union.

While the first half of the Song depicted sexual attraction developing into commitment, the core of the poem tells us that caring
concern and open-eyed acceptance bring about the full realization
of that erotic yearning. The combination of compassion and *eros*
takes the lovers deeper still. In the next song the Lover expresses
his awe at the terrifying force that the Woman's complete love has
become.

> *The Lover*
> You are beautiful as Tirzah, my love,
>     comely as Jerusalem,
>         majestic as an army with banners [awe-inspiring, powerful].
> Turn away your eyes from me,
>     for they take me by storm!
> Your hair is like a flock of goats,
>     flowing down the slopes of Gilead.
> Your teeth are like a flock of shorn ewes
>     that have come up from the washing;
>         each one has its twin,
>         and not one among them is bereaved.
> Your cheeks, behind your veil,
>     are like the halves of a pomegranate.
> There are sixty queens and eighty concubines,
>     and countless maidens.
> My dove, my perfect one, is the only one,
>     the darling of her mother,
>         flawless to her that bore her.
> The maidens saw her and proclaimed her blessed;
>     the queens and concubines also,
>         and they praised her.
> "Who is this arising like the dawn,
>     fair as the moon, bright as the sun,
>         majestic as an army with banners?"

> I went down to the nut orchard,
>> to look at the new growth in the valley,
> to see whether the vines had budded,
>> whether the pomegranates were in bloom.
> Before I was aware, my desire had hurled me
>> into the chariot of my prince.

Solomon's vast harem, shrunken by the poet to only sixty queens and eighty concubines, reflected the great king's lust for material fulfillment, political and economic as well as sexual. The Lover in contrast possesses "only one" beloved, but his exclusive intimacy with her produces a greater wealth than that known by King Solomon. They share only the riches of a simple life, but their love is wealth enough to make him feel equal to a king ("my desire had hurled me into the chariot of my prince").

*The Friends*
Return, return, O Shulammite! [Fully embracing her lover, the
     Woman is now called "One who dwells in peace."]
Return, return, that we may look upon you.

*The Lover*
Why should you look upon the Shulammite,
     dancing as though between two
     rows of dancers?

How beautiful are your steps in sandals,
     O queenly maiden! [In this song, the Lover praises his beloved
     from the feet up.][20]
The curve of your thighs is like
     the curve of a necklace,
     the work of a master hand.
Your navel is a rounded bowl
     that never lacks mixed wine.
Your belly is a heap of wheat [the Lover admires her full figure]
     encircled with lilies.
Your two breasts are like two fawns,
     twins of a gazelle.
Your neck is like an ivory tower.
Your eyes are pools in Heshbon,

by the gate of Bath-rabbim.
Your nose is like a tower of Lebanon,
    overlooking Damascus.
Your head is held high like Carmel [a high mountain in Israel],
    and your flowing locks are like purple [or a tapestry];
    a king is held captive in the tresses.
How beautiful you are, how charming,
    my love, my delight!
In stature like the palm tree [tall],
    and your breasts are like its clusters [of dates].

"I will climb the palm tree," I resolved,
    "I will seize its clusters of dates."
O may your breasts be like clusters of grapes,
    and the scent of your breath like apricots
    and your mouth like the best wine.

The Woman may have feared her lover's response to seeing her without her necklaces and other ornaments, which he has praised in the past. The Lover, however, does not mention her artifacts in the second half of the poem. Now he says instead that her body itself is jewelry, "the work of a master hand" (7:1).

These last images—breasts like clusters of fruit, breath scented like apricots, mouth like the best wine—go beyond the visual and become gustatory. While the Woman's height "like a palm tree" suggests that initially she was unattainable,[21] the Lover now tastes and smells her. Devoted love moves the lovers beyond the titillation of *eros* to a more complete, consuming sexuality.

The Woman responds in terms of fulfillment as well:

*The Woman*
May the wine go straight to my Lover,
    moving gently over lips and teeth.
I am my beloved's,
    and his desire is for me.
Come, my beloved,
    let us go forth to the fields.
We will spend the night in the villages
    and in the morning we will go to the vineyards.
We will see if the vines are budding,

> if their blossoms are opening,
> if the pomegranate trees are in flower.
> There I will give you my love [sexual love].
> The mandrakes give forth fragrance [mandrakes were thought to be
>     an aphrodisiac],
> and at our door is every delicacy,
>     new as well as old.
> I have stored them for you, my beloved.

All the tasting and smelling conveys a frank sensuality, but the lovers' abundance transcends the sexual. They have no concern about any need. The Song names the Woman lover, bride, and daughter of a nobleman, but never housewife. Unlike the hardworking Good Wife in Proverbs 31, she bears no cares or responsibilities. Similarly, the Woman calls the man beloved, bridegroom, and king, but he never acts the part of a husband, with all the attendant worries. He does no work, provides nothing, and unlike King Solomon's warriors, at whom the poet takes a playful stab, he carries no sword. Despite their lack of industry, however, all fruit, spice, wine, and freedom are theirs.

And this is why the poem includes Solomon in the first place. King Solomon, a ruler possessed of great wealth, power, and many wives, relied on men with swords to defend all these from the terrors of the nights. But the lovers need no swordsmen to protect them. Unguarded, they go where they please and sleep in beds of henna blossoms under cedar trees, tasting air floating with exotic spices and intoxicating perfume.[22] A sweet-smelling sachet, the Lover lies all night between the breasts of a woman who knows he neither wants nor needs anyone, anything, but her. She is to him all sweet and tasty things, a lily and a garden, a garden fountain and a well of living water. To her, he is pure gold, his name "oil poured out"—images of voluptuous wealth.[23]

Focused on this superior wealth, the Song not only neglects to mention household cares but also forgoes another topic: nowhere does the poem mention authority, submission, or obedience, nor does it decree who has the right to make a "final decision." In the Song of Songs, man and woman are once again perfect equals, as they were in creation. The true *'ezer kenegdo*, the woman initiates, provides, and shelters as much as the man does. Thus the Song teaches that when people are not wrapped up in material concerns, when they place their priority on love without fear, they have no reason or desire to hold power over each other. They have no need of rules to break an impasse that never comes to be.

Self-giving love takes us back to the garden, free of anxieties and stress. Drives for achievement, possessions, consumption, power, and reputation, psychologists will say, are in the end no more than a yearning for love and acceptance. So, the Song asks, why not cast aside the things that ultimately don't satisfy and strive for love in the first place?

Perhaps this is why Jesus uses some of the same images as the Song of Songs to assure us that his redemption will set aside our concerns about the curse on the ground. In the Sermon on the Mount, Jesus says:

> Do not be anxious about your life, what you shall eat. . . . what you shall put on. . . . Consider the lilies of the field, how they grow; they neither toil nor spin; yet I tell you, even Solomon in all his glory was not arrayed as one of these. If God so clothes the grass of the field, which today is alive, and tomorrow is thrown into the oven, will he not much more clothe you? (Matt. 6:25, 28–30 RSV)

Jesus urges his followers to give up the aftereffects of the fall: striving, anxiety, the need to control. God will provide what you need, he teaches, and part of that provision, that abundance, is sexuality itself, the one-flesh love created in the beginning, the suitable help that human beings need. The Song of Songs, a lyrical love poem seemingly out of place in the Bible, in the end offers a very biblical message: love and relationships, not material strivings, offer a greater wealth than we even know how to crave.

*The Woman*
Ah, why are you not my brother,
   who nursed at my mother's breast!
If I met you outside, I could kiss you,
   and no one would despise me.
I would lead you and bring you
   into the house of my mother,

to the house of she who taught me!
I would give you spiced wine to drink [the verb for "giving drink"
    puns on the Hebrew word for "kissing],[24]
    the juice of my pomegranates.
His left hand is under my head,
    and his right hand caresses me!
I charge you, O daughters of Jerusalem,
    not to stir up love, nor rouse it,
    until it please to awake.

*The Friends*
Who is that coming up from the wilderness,
    leaning upon her beloved?

The first time the friends asked this question, it was King Solomon who came "up from the wilderness" to recognize the lovers' union. The Woman's playful "Ah, why are you not my brother . . . If I met you outside, I could kiss you, and no one would despise me," hints at her desire for further public celebration of their love. But as the friends tell her, a love fully realized needs no outside forces to empower or regulate it. King Solomon's majesty can add nothing to what the lovers now enjoy, and this time it is they, not an army, coming up from the wilderness. Leaning upon each other, they find all that they need.

*The Woman*
Under the apricot tree I awakened you,
    there where your mother conceived you;
    there where she who gave birth to you conceived you.

Earlier, the Woman took her lover to "to the chamber of she that conceived me." Now she says that she finds her love under the apricot tree where his mother conceived him. This talk of conception may have been an ancient way of saying, "We were born to love each other." But this appreciation of their compatibility is not fatalism. God may bring lovers together, but each individual must consciously choose the other, consciously choose commitment and complete self-giving. Only then, "stirred up," do they fully awaken to soul-melding love.

And this ardor, fully realized, becomes a thing of stirring power. Already we have seen how it provides for all of the lovers' needs. The next passage goes deeper still:

> *The Woman*
> Set me like a seal upon your heart,
>    like a seal upon your arm:
> For love is strong as death,
>    jealousy fierce as the grave.
> It burns like a blazing fire,
>    a flame of God himself.
> Love no flood can quench,
>    no torrents drown.
> If one offered for love
>    all the wealth of one's house,
>    it would be utterly scorned.

In ancient times, people use seals—emblems carved of stone or clay—to mark personal property, just as people today put their names on things to mark them as theirs. A seal also functioned like a signature to express one's assent or will. In ancient Hebrew thought, the heart conceived one's will or desire, and the arm carried it out. Savor the beautiful ambiguity in the Woman's profession, "Write my name on your heart." Then I will be your heart, your self. And if I am your heart, does that make your will mine, or my will yours? As a seal on your arm, do I blindly carry out your bidding, or do you ask me to do only what I desire? Like the fullness of that which fills (Eph. 1:23), the Song of Songs presents this complete love as a beautiful paradox. Together, the lovers form an endless circle. There exists no object, no wealth, no power, no acclaim that they desire more than they yearn to be one with each other. Within this circle, even jealousy burns not as a possessive paranoia but as the elemental longing for complete and exclusive allegiance. Intertwined, joined together by God and by their own choice, their own yielding, they become one in flesh, mind, and heart.

Fearless love, which once exposed the lovers to harm, in its fullness renders them immune to all danger:

> For love is strong as death,
>    jealousy fierce as the grave.

It burns like a blazing fire,
    a flame of God himself.
Love no flood can quench,
    no torrents drown.
If one offered for love
    all the wealth of one's house,
    it would be utterly scorned.

The Song of Songs promises that fully developed love can stand up to material threat. God created marriage to provide the safe pasture *ha'adam* must have in order to face down challenges to his peace. And when desiring only unity, lovers defy the curse and its threat of material deprivation and the anxious illusion of safety offered by material wealth, fire from heaven itself melds them together.[25] Now no loss, not even the grave, can leave them bereft.

The next passage at first seems out of place but actually offers another affirmation of the strength of love:

*The Friends*
We have a little sister,
    and she has no breasts. [She is not a woman yet.]

What shall we do for our sister,
    on the day when she is spoken for [to be married]?
If she is a wall,
    we will build upon her a battlement [or tower] of silver;
but if she is a doorway [an open passageway],
    we will enclose her with boards of cedar [build a door for the passageway].

*The Woman*
I am a wall,
    and my breasts are like towers [of protection];
Thus I have become in his eyes
    like one who brings peace [or contentment].

In ancient days, the towers atop the city walls and the boards of a door protected those within. Turning full circle to the beginning, the poem reveals the transformation of an unready girl who has just begun to tend her own vineyard into "one who brings contentment," a woman able to keep in peace those within her walls.[26] The lovers have traversed the long path of surrendering defense and fear, and in their devotion and honesty, they offer each other a profound strength. At the end of their journey, without veil, sword, or golden ornaments, they find safe pasture. Dirty feet and damp hair no longer matter. Love, ready to be awakened, goes beyond transient physical pleasure to complete fulfillment. Peace and contentment subsume satiation.

> *The Woman*
> Solomon had a vineyard at Baal-hamon;
>> he entrusted the vineyard to keepers [he rented it out];
>> each one was to bring for its fruit
>> a thousand pieces of silver [in rent].
> But I look after my vineyard myself;
>> you, O Solomon, may keep the thousand,
>> and those who oversee its produce their two hundred!

"Baal-hamon" means "owner of great wealth" or "husband of a multitude." "A vineyard that brought in one thousand pieces of silver was proverbial for a rich one; . . . thus the one owned by Solomon must have been especially lucrative, since each of the keepers procured that sum."[27] Solomon and the keepers of *his* vineyard—his many wives—were well reimbursed for their marriages, which were mostly political alliances. They shared a vast wealth, but the Song tells us that such earthly relationships are little more than that of landlord and tenant. "But I," the Woman says, "I tend my own vineyard." Rooted in pure love, her vines flourish, and paying neither rent nor wages, the lovers gather the abundant fruit for themselves. Self-giving love, learned over time, chosen daily, provides all.

> *The Lover*
> O you who dwell in the garden,
>> with friends in attendance;
>> let me hear your voice.
>
> *The Woman*
> Make haste, my beloved,
>> and be like a gazelle

or a young stag
on the spice-laden mountains!

What the lovers have by the end of the Song of Songs is a thing of staggering beauty. The Woman came to her lover a young girl, a stranger just past girlhood, veiled and outside the man's circle of friends. By the end of the Song, she has blossomed into a fully realized woman, dwelling in a garden, and the friends wait upon *her* voice. The couple's love has blossomed beyond accounting; at first drawn by a sweet but superficial sexual attraction, the lovers dissolved the barriers between them in mutual surrender. They have no defenses against each other, but this vulnerability, which once exposed them to danger, now keeps them safe. Each wants nothing but what the other wants, and not even death can destroy them. The Song ends with lovers so deep in love and trust with each other that they are each other's will, completely one, richer even than was the glorious King Solomon.

## The Song Today

As a piece of poetry, even an inspired one, the Song of Songs presents an ideal of marriage that is perhaps unattainable for real people who, regardless of their own merit, may never be able to say, "Set me like a seal upon your heart." Nonetheless, the Song provides a beautiful goal for which to strive. It encapsulates many of Jesus's teachings, especially his admonition to forego concerns about material possessions and wealth, social status and honor, controlling other people, and even pride over one's children and excellent household management, and live instead content with God's simple abundance. It is the epitome of Paul's exhortation to treat each other with caring concern, loving each other as we love our own bodies. As such, even an ideal that is not entirely possible to attain can provide significant guidance. Most important, it can prevent us from going in directions that do not lead to joy and fulfillment.

# 7

# Christian Marriage and Family in the Twenty-first Century

In that part of the world that underwent the Industrial Revolution, the economic developments of the twentieth century offer even the average person unprecedented wealth, and with it unimaginable freedom. Individuals can structure their lives to please themselves: marry or stay single; have children or not, married or single; have sex on whatever terms they can negotiate with the object of their desire; work a lot or a little. For the most part, today's spiritual and relational problems no longer cluster around the anxieties of the farmer sweating to earn his daily bread. Instead, they resemble those of the rich man sweating to keep what he already has. Jesus's remark that it is difficult for the rich to enter the kingdom of heaven no longer applies to just a tiny percentage of the population. Having everything already (although still craving more), on their own terms and under their own control, why would another kingdom interest people today? From the perspective of worldly wealth, even the eternal life Jesus offers cannot make up for what Jesus asks them to give away. While the wealth and freedom of this age should make Jesus's teachings come vividly alive for us in ways scarcely possible for our ancestors, they seem to be taking people away from Christ instead. The growing secularization of the developed world today comes less from disbelief in God than from simple disinterest in him.

This is not to detract in any way from the great blessings of wealth and freedom we enjoy. The question is, how will we use them? To build a one-flesh love or to serve our individual pleasures? In many ways, these opportunities, riches, entitlements, and rights are the satans of our era—not Satan as a malevolent red devil with horns and a tail, but the satan who tempted the first couple in Eden and Jesus in the wilderness, the satan who knows the hidden self-centered cravings of our heart and offers them to us. How is it that Christians are supposed to behave in this new world?

## Underlying Principles

As we begin to bring together the biblical message about marriage, sex, and family and apply it to today, the first thing to realize is that all three of these things are completely optional. There is no biblical mandate to marry or have children, and certainly none to suggest that people could not live without sex. The biblical imperatives of sexuality, marriage, and family—"A man will leave his father and mother and be united to his wife, and they will become one flesh," "Be fruitful and increase in number; fill the earth," "Children are a blessing of the LORD"—are not commandments, obligations, or necessities but rather the imperatives of *blessing*. They exult, "Let this wonderful thing happen to you!" rather than demand, "Do this or die."

In fact, the Bible tells us that despite the compelling love depicted in the Song of Songs, the key to a joyful life is found not in our family arrangements but in our relationship with God. Jesus's message of redemption allows us to go back to the Garden of Eden, not just in the next life but in the way we live now. Living by faith in God through Christ releases the curse on the ground. While we still live in a world of thorns, we need no longer be weighed down by anxieties, pain, and tears. Faith in Christ will not necessarily prevent bad things from happening to us, but faith in Christ will always help us triumph over those bad things. Included in these are the gender-linked consequences outlined in chapter 2: sorrowful toil, anxiety, fear, using other people for our own benefit, striving for power and control, and being subjected to the power and control of others.

Christian redemption does not mean becoming a doormat, however, or somehow transcending human needs for recognition, affirmation, and self-control. Rather than becoming passive, Christian surrender is active, an act of bravery and resolve. Creating, achieving, contesting against the odds, and winning are all valid human needs and pleasures. God created enthusiasm, energy, curiosity, and a love of beauty in us, and he does not ask us to surrender these qualities. Rather, problems occur when our eagerness for these joyful things becomes perverted by fear or greed and spins out of control. Then they become giant ego needs that can be gratified only at the expense of other people. Too often our need for affirmation is the flip side of the terrible shame we have learned to feel when we fail to achieve the honor and power that the world of thorns says are due to really worthy people. So faith in God's provision requires us to go a step further and give up not just the desire for power but the shame, anxiety, and fears that underlie the desire. One would not think that it should be hard to give up something as unpleasant as anxiety. But to give up our anxieties means to give up our chance of getting what we want. It means we must stop insisting on having things our own way. Thus the fruits of the Spirit are not shame or guilt but love, joy, peace, patience, kindness, goodness, faithfulness, gentleness, and self-control (Gal. 5:22).

## Careers: Tending the Garden versus Sorrowful Toil

Surrendering to God not only allows but requires us to return to the abundant life for which he created us. The New Testament clearly states that the redeemed no longer have to worry about material concerns, even if their material condition was slavery. There is a greater security, Jesus, Paul, and the writers of Genesis and the Song of Songs tell us, in God's design than in worldly wealth and power.

Yet we don't really live in a garden, and when the bills are due faith does not come easily. We have a practical desire and a responsibility not to live day to day—to have security and enough money already in the bank, to have financial control on our own terms and in our own right. And what about ambition, our desire to achieve? What about the abundance of wealth, power, and prestige newly available to those who are willing to scramble for it? Paul told his readers repeatedly that with God as their patron, there will always be bread. But we aren't happy with just bread. Sometimes we would rather be Solomon, wary of the terrors of the night in a gold-crusted pavillion, than our humble selves safely sharing a bed of lilies with our beloved. And Paul also said that if anyone does not wish to work, neither should he eat (2 Thess. 3:10).

The redeemed attitude toward our need to labor in the world might be found in the contrast between the earth creature's original calling in creation and the work he had to do after the fall. God made the earth creature to have dominion over the earth and to "dress" a garden that gave fruit abundantly, was lushly watered, and bore no weeds or thorns. The earth creature never had to carry water or battle weeds, but worked joyfully with God simply to make paradise ever more beautiful.

After the fall and the curse on the ground, humankind was driven by self-serving ambition and faithless fear. But in Christ, we do not have to sweat it anymore. "So do not worry, saying 'What shall we eat?' Or 'What shall we drink?' Or 'What shall we wear?' For the pagans run after all these things, and your heavenly Father knows that you need them. But seek first his kingdom and his righteousness, and all these things will be given to you as well" (Matt. 6:31–34). Of course, we still live in a world with thorns and we still have to work—often unpleasantly—but when we strive first to honor God, to make his already redeemed creation even more beautiful, our toil is no longer overwhelmed by sorrow. Redemption transforms our urges to create, to produce, to accomplish something, to be surrounded by beauty, into an ambition to make the world a better place. Whether street sweeping or running a major corporation, our efforts can improve the lives of other people and nurture the earth. Productive work becomes an activity that gives value and meaning to life.

Indeed, Paul tells us that God's patronage and provision oblige us to choose the joyful rather than the anxious life. In Ephesians 5–6, he challenges men to give up their ambitions, privilege, and power and use their energies to serve their slaves as brothers, help their wives become glorious, and raise up faithful and redeemed children. This path may lead to less material wealth, less financial security, and certainly less honor and praise among men—but this is the path that leads to righteousness, love, balance, and joy.

Women as well as men crave meaningful work. The need for achievement is, in part, why many women have left the household for paid employment. But children are also a great source of meaning, and most people want both children and careers in their lives. Here is where the conflict comes in: children need a home, and someone to be there with them. This conflict is one of the great family dilemmas today. Resolving it is not a matter of falling back on traditional solutions—there are no traditional solutions that work anymore—but in finding new patterns of approaching our *whole* life as dressing the garden rather than as painful toil.

## Refocusing the Family: Children

The economic model explains that in the past people had children to act as loyal servants and to care for parents in their old age. This theory explains why people do not have as many children as we did in the past, but as my economist friends joke, it can't explain why we have any at all. Yet in the early twentieth century, the emotional value people placed on children rose faster than their financial value dropped.[1] So perhaps economics can explain our persistence in having children after all: children are no longer tools of production but have instead become items of consumption. Although financially costly, children still offer many rewards: affection, companionship, a playmate, an excuse to buy toys and go to Disneyland, and the joy of seeing them grow, develop, and achieve. Children offer parents an opportunity to see the world again with fresh eyes, to relive childhood joys, and perhaps to make up for childhood disappointment, deprivations, and failures.

Our hopes for our children, however, may include aspirations that fulfill the needs of the parents more than those of the children. We all know, were the child of, or have been the parent who signs up a three-year-old for violin lessons; who refuses to speak to the child who muffed a play at baseball; who panics when a child's SAT scores aren't high enough for Stanford; who pushes tutoring centers, extra homework, and endless practice in music, dance, cheerleading, diving, skating, basketball, math, karate or art; who pressures a child to study for a high-status profession; who cajoles, berates, or disciplines the child who doesn't get good grades. It can be hard to tell when these activities are for the child and when they are for the parent. Gary Becker writes that as parents have fewer children, the demand for children shifts from quantity to quality. The richer we are, the more we expect to have high-quality children. From a worldly point of view, high-achieving children are another sign that their parents are high achievers, too.

This is the "sorrowful toil" approach to children, however. In Ephesians 6:1–4, Paul challenges the ancient expectation that children exist to serve their family's needs. Rather than children owing a debt to parents, Paul teaches that parents, as recipients of God's wondrous patronage, have an obligation to their children:

> Children, obey your parents in the Lord, for this is right. "Honor your father and mother" (this is the first commandment with a promise) "that it may be well with you and that you may live long on the earth." Fathers, do not provoke your children to anger, but bring them up [nurture them] in the discipline and instruction [admonition] of the Lord.[2]

Paul asks that rather than use their children to fulfill their own purposes, fathers use their children's obedience to nurture them in the "discipline and instruction of the Lord." Although the definition of high social status differs greatly between the ancient and contemporary worlds, Paul's warning about not using children to increase our own honor and esteem still applies. We rear Christian children to enhance God's creation, not to meet our own anxious needs.

With this as our purpose, we will treat our children differently from the way we would if they were just another token of material success. Recent research into human brain development suggests, for instance, that children who are being nurtured in the Lord cannot be parceled out to the care of strangers at six weeks of age. This research, as well as the condition of thousands of orphans cared for in warehouselike conditions in some former Soviet Bloc countries, shows that human infants require intense physical and emotional interaction with their primary caregivers. Children who do not receive this interaction fail to develop the part of the brain that is involved in emotional connectedness, trust, and the ability to love. When deprivation is extreme, such infants simply die. Those who experience less severe neglect may suffer intellectual as well as emotional problems, which include symptoms that have been referred to as socially induced autism—children who won't look you in the eye, do not respond to affection or warmth, and are unable to trust. Such children function on a primitive survival level, feeling unsafe unless they are in control of themselves and others. They are in a constant state of hyper-arousal in which any perceived threat causes them to flee, freeze, or fight.[3] Although research has not addressed spiritual issues, the attachment disorders that result from neglect or abuse almost certainly cripple a child's ability to form a relationship with God.

Although the extremes of attachment problems come from severe neglect or abuse, child therapists are reporting attachment disorder–like symptoms in children who have been neither neglected nor abused but who simply spend a lot of time away from their parents in infancy. Marriage and family therapist Linda Ikeda speaks for many of her colleagues when she warns that a lack of opportunities to form healthy, reciprocal relationships in early life leaves an individual unable to trust or to develop a conscience. The result of disordered attachment can result in serious adult personality disorders, criminal behavior, or both.[4]

Economist Sylvia Hewlett also "links the 'time deficit' caused by long parental workdays to a series of alarming trends in child development. Compared to the previous generation, Hewlett claims, young people today are more likely to 'underperform at school, commit suicide, need psychiatric help, suffer a severe eating disorder, bear a child out of wedlock, take drugs, be the victim of a violent crime.'"[5]

When women began to leave the home in large numbers in the 1970s, conservative churches and parachurch organizations reacted with alarm and strong pronouncements that mothers belonged at home with their children.[6] I strongly agree that Christians need to seriously challenge the material incentives that encourage them to neglect the developmental needs of children. My own experience taught me that it is very difficult to raise children when both parents hold rigid full-time jobs. We think of a full-time job as a forty-hour week, but when commute time and federally mandated breaks are included, the work week can stretch to fifty hours or more even for employees who are able to leave work exactly at quitting time (and many employees are not). When these hours are combined with those demanded by children, even the best job and the best home become "sorrowful toil" for both parents and child. However, while the conservative reaction to mothers' employment got the potential problems right, their solution—mothers stay home with the children and let men be the "breadwinners"—is too rigid, a political response rather than a biblical one.

The biblical solution takes us back to the basics. We don't have to be caught up in material concerns at the expense of doing what is right. Our relationships to God, to each other, and to our children come first. Eliminating anxiety about material needs allows us to tend the garden rather than painfully battle weeds. Note also that when Paul addressed the parent-child relationship in Ephesians 6, his admonition to nurture was directed to *fathers*, not mothers.[7] Fathers left home first and mothers last because of the material circumstances of the natural family. It does not therefore follow that God prefers that men stay out or that women should always stay in. There is nothing in the Bible to suggest that the traditional sexual division of labor reflects God's will, and there is much to suggest that it does not. Demands that mothers stay at home mask God's higher calling for *both* parents to provide for their children emotionally and spiritually. Enjoining men to nurturing and self-sacrifice in Ephesians 5–6, Paul directs them to join their wives as true partners in childrearing.

Some people are fortunate to have skills that lend themselves to flexible work hours. For others, making joint parenting work will require challenging a lot of assumptions and making material sacrifices. But in achieving balance in our lives, the bigger issue is the willingness to make family a higher priority than our personal needs. Chapter 5 discussed research that found that in the work-family conflict work wins, not because of money issues but because many people find it easier and more relaxing to be at work.[8] Not living under the thumb of conventional work/family practices, however, has many rewards. Studies have shown that "the more conventional a couple's division of labor, the less satisfied they are with themselves, their relationship, and their roles as parents."[9] In her interviews with couples, social commentator Peggy Orenstein found that those most satisfied with the balance in their life had flexibility in their work that freed them to "handle emergencies, stay home with sick kids and, generally, devote more time to family life."[10]

While it is easy to let social and financial pressures convince us otherwise, there are many options for achieving that balance. I won't try to list them all, but here are some ideas.

In my own life, my consulting work combined well with my husband's employment as a university professor. While our work sometimes demanded many hours, we had flexibility in choosing when to work them. Another example of how a couple made joint parenting work is Phil and Cathy Van Loon, both teachers at the community college in Santa Cruz, California. Early in their marriage, the Van Loons each made a commitment to work no more than part time, allowing them to share the responsibilities and pleasure of parenting. They live more modestly than they might if one of them was employed full time and the other stayed home, but they have stuck by this commitment for over twenty years, own a home in one of the nicest places in the world, and rejoice at a decision that allows them to share life together more fully.

Other couples accommodate full-time employment and children by "time shifting" their schedules, with one of them going to work early and the other late, so that one or another is available all or most of the day. For older toddlers and preschoolers, a good nursery school or other childcare arrangements fill in the times when parents' work hours overlap. Nursery schools can be fun for children, offering socialization, activity, and playmates. After all, who else but another two-year-old will jump off the bottom step with yours twenty times in a row? Nursery schools also offer a good alternative to parking children in front of the television. (Ideally a child should not be in out-of-the-home care for more than six or seven hours a day.)[11]

The attachment needs of babies, however, suggest that very young children should not be left to the care of strangers for extended periods of time. The needs of infants involve more than keeping them dry and fed. Ikeda notes that a daycare situation in which there is a high ratio of nurturing adults to infants (no less than one adult for every three babies), and with caregivers highly attuned to each individual baby's personality and needs, is usually sufficient to assure optimal brain development. However, if the infant is in childcare full time, the parents need to understand that their child's primary attachment figure will become that daycare provider. Less than optimal day care, with too many infants per adult or nonnurturing providers not attuned to each infant, can compromise brain development. "As a parent and a professional," writes Ikeda, "I would not take that chance [that infant care might prove less than optimal] with my own child."

Given what has been learned about the importance of attachment, as Christians we must do whatever it takes to be there during this critical period in our children's lives. Settle for a lifestyle that does not require two full-time incomes just to live. Take the family leave offered by your employers, father as well as mother, even if it means that someone else will get your promotion. Negotiate part-time work or flexible hours. If you can't bear to leave your baby when it is time to go back to work, don't. Borrow money if you need it to survive (but don't go into debt just to maintain a self-indulgent pre-baby lifestyle).

Of course, it is exactly this kind of commitment to family that results in the so-called gender gap in wages. The average employed woman does in fact make less money than the average employed man, a difference that is completely accounted for by the fact that women more often than men drop out of the labor force to raise children and on average never make up for that time out. Women with children, even at full-time jobs, also work on average fewer hours per week than do men, a fact that ends up reflected in their income. Orenstein notes that when men take on parenting responsibility, the same thing happens to them: "Men in dual-career marriages receive fewer promotions than their single-earner peers." They also make less money, earning up to 19 percent less for the same job.[12] Despite this very real drawback, switching from a family life structured around "sorrowful toil" to one allowing both husband and wife to do meaningful work makes for happier marriages.

Meeting the needs of your children might mean that you can't make or aren't interested in making any of the flexible options work but want to stick with the "traditional" pattern of mother at home, father at work, especially when your children are infants. After all, although 59 percent of married women with children age one year and under were working outside the home in 1994 (most part time), a sizable number, 41 percent, are at home with their children. It works well practically—men with the support of an at-home wife do better on the job, and one person working full time usually makes more money than two people working part time. Mothers, especially those breastfeeding, often want to spend that time with their little children. The role of sole breadwinner does not, however, absolve men from the responsibility to nurture their children, nor should it be an excuse for self-aggrandizement or claiming preferential status at home (like being the one who always gets to sleep in on Saturdays). In order to afford to stay home full time, a woman may have to scrimp and make do, giving up paid household help, meals out, nice clothes, and the company of adults, in addition to a paycheck and the other rewards of paid employment. Staying home to nurture children can be a considerable sacrifice that should be acknowledged.

Young women may find being at home difficult and frustrating. When my children were young, I used to long just to walk out of the house and around the block without worrying about the kids. The best advice I can give is just to enjoy what you are doing now. If you can keep up some level of professional involvement, that may help, but don't think you can do much work at home with young children around, unless your work does not require more than fifteen minutes at a stretch of uninterrupted thought (and don't count on the fifteen minutes). Husbands should make sure that their stay-at-home wife has some time to herself that she can count on. Knowing you have time later, you will be able to relax and enjoy the children more in the time set apart to be with them, resulting in less of that *they drive me nuts* feeling.

Home schooling may be another way of keeping women fully engaged in meaningful work while meeting the needs of children. While the term *home school* conjures up images of the kids sitting at the kitchen table doing assignments with their mother, the home schooling movement can be more like an educational cooperative. Parents form networks and pool their expertise to offer classes to small or large groups of children. Fathers are usually involved as well. Home schooling also solves the problem of sheltering children from secular influences.[13]

If it is the father who wants to stay home with the children while the wife goes to work, brazen it out. It takes a lot of courage for a man to do this. Employers think little of "holes" in the résumés of women, but when a man has periods of unemployment on his record, they suspect he has been in jail. Unfortunately, learning that you were home with the kids may make them even more doubtful of you. I understand that writing a book is a credible way to cover gaps in employment. (But see the comment above about work that can be done in fifteen-minute increments.)

Whether employed full or part time, mother or father, if you find yourself getting frustrated during your at-home time with children, remember that your responsibility is to care for them and teach them, not to entertain them. A young child will gladly take up all your time and attention. That doesn't mean he or she needs it. You don't have to spend all your time and money in enrichment activities and lessons, either.

The solution to fulfilling our Christian obligations to each other and to our children lies not in rigid prescriptions based on gender but in allowing each partner to "tend the garden" as God calls him or her. Do what makes everyone happy, regardless of how if affects your secular career. You won't regret it later.

### Protecting Children from Secular Values

One of the more important aspects of nurturing children in the discipline of the Lord is monitoring the values to which they are exposed. Children learn a great deal from other children and adults, picking up attitudes and behaviors that you may not even be aware they have. Those parents of your children's friends or teachers who have no or marginal religious commitment may have little interest in protecting their children or yours from worldly influences—they *are* worldly influences. Be concerned about and aware of the values children are learning from their friends, public schools, television, and popular music. One caregiver should be there when children come home from school. "Latchkey" children are prone to get into trouble with alcohol, drugs, and sex.[14] Even high school–aged children should not be left alone too much.

An important part of nurturing children in the discipline and instruction of the Lord is keeping them clean of corrupt worldly values. Choose their environment so they are getting a message with which you agree, even if you must put them in private school or move to another community to find one. Shelter them from social pressures, abusive forces, and the pressures to be popular as much as you can. (Our friends who home school do it specifically to protect their children from "kid culture.") Church should offer such a refuge; if yours doesn't, find one that does. There is nothing wrong with choosing your church on the basis of your children's needs. Be careful, though, of youth programs that stress outreach to unchurched children to the neglect of providing a refuge for believers. The program at the church we attended when our daughter was in middle school was designed solely to attract children who did not otherwise attend church. It was well attended and looked like a thriving and successful operation. The kids who attended, however, had more interest in *Seventeen* magazine, *Friends*, popular music, and getting in on the church retreats at the beach than in anything spiritual. They also regarded themselves as superior to the less sophisticated churchgoing kids and felt free to tease them. Outreach is a necessary part of the Christian mission, but youth programs do no good to anyone if the uncommitted are allowed to set the group's moral climate. A great tool for promoting the discipline and instruction of the Lord is small groups. Family small groups seem to be rare but can have a big impact by providing children with role models of Christian commitment, both among the parents and among the other children.

One of the best things you can do for your children, in terms of both their spiritual growth and their ability to form loving relationships, is to turn off the television. There is very little on television today that is of redeeming moral value, and a great deal that undermines it. The best that children can learn from some of the comedies is that it is funny to be rude. Parents must also avoid the temptation to think that having a child in the room with them as they watch TV is childcare. It is not. Television watching is a terrible time drain. In a culture in which everyone complains that they don't have enough time, there is little reason to watch it. Some churches now caution members about attending R-rated movies. It is surprising that they don't advocate getting rid of television, too.

## Headship, Decision Making, and Conflict

The Song of Songs (8:6) contains the most beautiful passage ever written about handling decision making and conflict in marriage. It reads, simply:

> Place me like a seal upon your heart,
> like a seal upon your arm.

In ancient times, a seal functioned as an official signature. A seal on a document proved that it expressed the will of the seal's owner. The will and desires were conceived in the heart; the arm carried out those desires. To say, "Write my name on your heart, on your arm," means to put the symbol of one's will and ownership on another's desire. Such a statement poses a beautiful paradox: Does this mean that she is his to command? Or is he hers? The Song's answer to how to deal with conflict assures us that true lovers want nothing—no object, no decision, no getting-their-own-way—more than they want to be of one heart and mind with the other.

If a man and a woman have each been redeemed and love each other as Jesus, the Song of Songs and Paul direct, one might imagine that they would experience no conflict or anger. But that is too unrealistic even for a devotee of the Song of Songs like me. Social psychologist John Gottman, in his fascinating studies of married couples, found that the most successful marriages experienced a ratio of one negative interaction for every five positive ones. These negative interactions included anger, which he found has negative effects only if it is expressed with criticism or contempt or is defensive.

> One intriguing question is why negativity is necessary at all for a marriage to survive. Why don't stable marriages have a positive-to-negative ratio that is more like 100 to 1? Wouldn't marriages work best if there were *no* disagreements? Our research suggests that in the short run this may be true. But for a marriage to have real staying power, couples need to air their differences.

In his books with Nan Silver, Gottman reported that couples dislike conflict, but that those who avoided it did less well in the long run than couples who dealt with it early in their relationship. "What may lead to temporary misery in a marriage—disagreement and anger—may be healthy for it in the long run. Rather than being destructive, occasional anger can be a resource that helps the marriage improve over time."[15]

So you can disagree and still have a happy marriage. However, the way a couple deals with disagreements matters a great deal. Here the biblical concept of mutual submission provides the answer. Gottman reports that among the newlywed couples with whom he works, only about 35 percent of the husbands are willing to accept the influence of their wives. Thirty-five is a great deal more than the percentage of husbands who shared power with their wives in the past, but it is a still surprisingly small number in the postfeminist world. "Accepting influence" means listening to their wife's opinion and feelings, treating her with respect, and sharing power and decision making with her.[16] (As wives almost always shared power, this was not an issue for them.) When facing a disagreement with his wife, a man who shares power looks for a mutually satisfactory solution and behaves as if the couple's concordant will is more important than his own. In contrast, men who don't accept influence escalate conflict and insist on having their own way. Whatever the satisfactions of maintaining control, however, they do not make for happy marriages: Gottman found that men who did not share power with their wives had an 81 percent greater chance of divorcing or of having a marriage that just "drones on" unhappily than those who did.

Similarly, sociologists Philip Blumstein and Pepper Schwartz's study of American couples shows that the subordinate status experienced by women in marriage was a major cause of marital unhappiness and breakdown.[17] Based on observations from their counseling practice, marriage therapists Andrew Lester and Judith Lester also found that hierarchy in a relationship makes intimacy impossible. It is difficult, they note, to "experience intimacy with someone who is in a position to make decisions about your life. . . .When the structures allow the other person to control your life, then you normally protect your innermost self from being known by that person. . . . Marriages characterized by mutuality and equality have the most potential for intimacy."[18] Further, they point out that inequality often results in a struggle for power that consumes the relationship:

When one partner does not have equal power he or she often develops some type of problem as a way of expressing anger or trying to equalize power. Problems with sexual avoidance, irresponsible spending, addictions, and depression, for example, can be the result of power imbalance. In marital therapy we find that the spouse who feels powerless finds it difficult to give up behavior that creates conflict. The behavior is a way for the underpowered spouse, usually the woman, to try and establish a sense of power or control that would balance the relationship.

Reminiscent of the disciples' comment on the inexpediency of a "one-flesh" relationship, the Lesters, like Gottman, found that sharing power requires couples to expend more effort on a day-to-day basis and may mean they experience more *open* conflict. In the longer run, however, they found that "couples who are committed to mutuality and equality have a much easier time finding solutions to their problems."[19] If we are to tell good from evil by their fruits, these social scientists make a strong case for eliminating hierarchy in marriage.

The concept of sharing power in marriage might be considered controversial among conservative Christians who adhere strongly to male "headship" in marriage. When we consider what being "head" really means, however, there may in fact be little conflict between the two concepts. In a survey undertaken in 1995, a solid majority of the Christians surveyed said they believed that the husband should be the "head" of the home (90 percent of evangelicals, 70 percent of mainline denomination members, and 59 percent of liberal Protestants). Most are ambivalent as to what this means, however. For those evangelicals who support male headship, 84 percent agree that exercising it means being the "spiritual leader" of the wife, family, or household; 53 percent think exercising headship means being the "final authority" in decision making; and 46 percent think that exercising headship means being the primary breadwinner. These numbers suggest widespread belief in marital hierarchy. Yet the vast majority of evangelicals (87 percent) also claim that "marriage is a partnership of equals," with 78 percent supporting both equality and male "headship." And whereas headship often denotes dominance and authority, many of the interviewees redefined headship in terms of personal sacrifice and responsibility for the family's spiritual welfare:

"The emphasis is not on power but on the burden of responsibility that falls to men."[20]

This is not to say that today's evangelicals reject traditional notions of hierarchy in marriage. Roughly 44 percent of those responding to the survey reported that in their marriage the wife is more likely than the husband to "give in" on contested family decision making. But 21 percent reported that in their marriage it was the husband who was more likely to give in, and over one-third said that the partners were equally likely to yield to their spouse. The fact that over half of the evangelicals surveyed claim *not* to practice hierarchy in their marriage reflects a hitherto unsuspected high level of acceptance of marital equality and mutual submission.

Also relevant from this survey and from work by W. Bradford Wilcox are results that showed that committed evangelical women were employed outside the home at about the same rate as the average American woman but were much less likely to work full time. Evangelical fathers were much more involved in their children's lives, and in mundane household chores, than they were in the past.[21] Despite reports that conservative Christian divorce rates are equal to the rates of divorce among the rest of the U.S. population, this study reported a much lower rate for those defined in the study as "highly committed Christians": 6 percent of the Christians in the survey were currently divorced and not remarried, as opposed to almost 10 percent of the American public as a whole.[22] Also refuting popular perception, Wilcox reports that active conservative Protestant men had the lowest rates of domestic violence in his study.[23]

The public perception of Christian marriage is that it is marked by hierarchy and subordination of women, a perception that some Christian leaders encourage. And among many Christians, it is. But the data above suggest that many others so redefine "head" that it isn't hierarchical in practice.[24] Their lives and relationships bear out the true scriptural admonitions. "Accepting influence," "mutuality and equality," and "sharing power" are all aspects of a redeemed and scripturally correct relationship. Further, when the husband as head is understood not as a metaphor of hierarchy but as the facilitator of one-flesh unity, which I argue is a truer meaning of Paul's designation of husband as head, these beliefs and behavior are quite compatible. Although not always sure what it means, many conservative Christians apparently are living this ideal.

The hierarchical view of gender roles has more to do with the requirements of the world of thorns than with the Genesis account of woman's being created to be like the man and to have dominion over the earth together with him. At the same time, the position of the contemporary secular feminist, who often seems to strive not for equality but for independence, is hardly Christian either. The Christian wife and mother serves husband and children not because of her sex but because of her obligation to the Lord. The Christian husband does the same thing. In Christ, the issue is not their equality or their lack of it. Paul's statement in 1 Corinthians 6:19–20 applies here: "You are not your own. You have been bought with a price. Therefore honor God with your bodies." Both redeemed, neither husband nor wife can demand supremacy over the other, and they help each other do the work that God calls them to do out of their obligation to him.

## Letting Your Spouse Accept Redemption

When Paul asked first-century husbands/fathers/masters to give up their prerogatives as patriarchs in order to live as Christians, he added in the same breath, "And let wives respect their husbands." So wives today—and husbands, too—must allow each other the freedom to live redeemed.

Men and women who put love and family ahead of career and ambition make often considerable material sacrifices. This means that their family can consume less and command less prestige than do those of the more ambitious. Peggy Orenstein observes that while modern women may say they want men who value family over career, they still struggle to respect a man without ambitions: "She adores him." Orenstein quotes such a woman: "He's a 'wonderful guy,' an 'outstanding sweetheart,' and yet when she imagines a husband, she pictures someone who is 'more excellent' than she is. 'I want to be with someone who is always pushing themselves to be better . . . self-improvement, emotionally, physically, and mentally as a full-time job.'" Plus "she's uncomfortable with his limited earning potential."[25] A Christian wife should not put the desire for material things above her husband's commitment to God, including his duty to nurture his children in the Lord.

Today, Paul's instruction to respect those who sacrifice their worldly ambitions for the sake of family applies to husbands as well as to wives. Raised in an era that strongly asserts women's equality with men, young people today take women's careers for granted. Some men see their wife's income as necessary to the achievement of their own materialistic ambitions or need for financial security. The results are dilemmas such as this woman's:

> I am on maternity leave from a good job. I have a six-month-old baby. We could afford to live on his salary, but my husband is pressuring me to return to work. He thinks it is a waste of time for me to stay home because we could afford decent day care and get ahead financially with my income.[26]

The president of Mothers at Home, a support group, writes, "We have received letters from women [at home] who say that their husbands are sometimes mocked at work for 'having a wife that lives off them.' Today it seems that men are congratulated for finding a high- or consistently income-earning wife."[27]

If we can't let each other live without anxiety about material concerns, chances are that we are hoarding up a pile of our own. And if we can't let each other live redeemed from worldly ambitions, we have probably not accepted our own redemption.

## Commitment to Marriage

Our culture tells us that the way to have a good marriage is to "pick the right partner." The Song of Songs and the apostle Paul, along with psychologist Harville Hendrix, tell us that the way to have a good marriage is "to be the right partner. . . . A good marriage requires commitment, discipline, and the courage to grow and change; marriage is hard work."[28] The incredibly difficult instructions that Paul gives husbands in Ephesians 5—love your wife as your own body, sacrifice for her as Christ sacrificed for the church, encourage her growth and development, make her a higher priority than your own self-interest or your parents, strive to be of one mind with her—were directed to people who did not choose one another on the basis of love. This fact challenges the contemporary notion that it is justifiable to break up a marriage or a family when one party is no longer "in love" with the other.

Paul's directives for marriage are as pertinent today as they were when he first gave them. Interestingly, those instructions revolved around doing this "out of reverence for Christ" and in gratitude for God's abundant provision. Once again I propose that the underlying principle of Christian marriage is being reconciled to God through our redemption in Christ. The notion of giving God higher priority than our spouse is not, I admit, a romantic one. Being married to someone who does this has significant benefits, however. When marriage is undertaken and honored as a sacred commitment, the redeemed husband or wife will always be there for you, whether currently "in love" or not.

## Christian Sexual Morality

In chapter 5 I discussed how the material constraints of the world of thorns created a cartel that controlled sexuality by enforcing the chastity of women. Women who cheated on the cartel faced punishment that ranged from being subjected to social shame and gossip, to having their children taken away from them, to death. Although biblical teachings on chastity have a different motivation from the worldly ones, Christian institutions were often used to enforce these norms. As a result, a common secular interpretation of religiously motivated sexual restraint is that religion is itself sexually repressed and hostile. Numerous religious traditions have in fact held that sex is sinful, even within marriage, and justified only when the intent is procreation. Other traditions, religious, philosophical, and sporting, taught that sex saps masculine strength that should be better applied elsewhere. These teachings have led some sociologists and political theorists to interpret religion's regulation of sexuality as simply a repressive attempt to curb the influence of a powerful competing force.

I find none of these repressive attitudes in the Bible itself. Celibacy is not promoted or even considered desirable in the Old Testament, and the Song of Songs is highly sexual. Jesus, whose own celibacy provided a basis for later Christian arguments against sexual expression, points out that God himself created marriage and sex. Further, he states that those who practice celibacy, himself included, are the exceptions rather than the norm (Matt. 19:11–12). Jesus's first recorded miracle took place at a wedding (John 2:1–12).

The writings of Paul are often considered to be antiwoman, antisex, and antimarriage, but Paul acknowledges the importance of sex within marriage. His statements about not marrying may be better understood as giving people permission not to become ensnared in the horrifying institution that family had become in the Roman world. Further, his use of the "one-flesh" marriage relationship as an analogy for the relationship between Christ and the church implies a very high view of marriage and sexuality indeed (Eph. 5:32).

Perhaps a more accurate way of understanding the biblical attitude toward sexuality is to contrast it with the contemporary view. In popular culture, sexuality is seen as a characteristic of the individual. Concepts such as sexual identity, sexual preference, and sexual expression are all located within the individual. Sexuality is also seen as an entitlement and at the same time something that the individual is obliged to express. Thus some groups seem to hold that bisexuals, who presumably can have satisfying heterosexual relationships, not only *may* but *must* act on their homosexual impulses as well. In contrast to the shame-based "traditional" sexual ethic, which was based on societal need to control sexuality, contemporary morality is based solely on an isolated demand for individual gratification.

In contrast, the Bible depicts sexuality as an attribute not of the individual but of the relationship. Before God created woman, the earth creature had no sexuality. It was not 'ish (man) until there was 'ishshah (woman). Only with the creation of another being did sex and sexuality have any meaning whatsoever. Sexuality is thus not something created in the individual for the individual alone. Rather, God created sexuality when he divided one creature into two, in order that they might become one again. The reunited one flesh, however, connoted more than physicality. The biblical addition of "and the man and his wife were both naked, and they felt no shame" (Gen. 2:25) depicts emotional as well as physical intimacy. God created relationship, not just "relations." The apostle Paul reinforces this notion when he praises believers for understanding that marital intimacy should take place "in holiness and honor, not in the passion of lust like heathen who do not know God"

(1 Thess. 4:4–5 KJV Interlinear).[29] From the biblical viewpoint, sexuality exists to draw two people together and to motivate their deeper love.

The Bible's teachings on restraint are intended to protect the individual and his or her ability to create relationship, especially from the emotional crippling that can result from premature sexual activity. As economist Jennifer Roback Morse writes, uncommitted sexual partners, even those who are living together, by definition "practice holding back on one another." By mutual if unspoken agreement, their lack of commitment acknowledges that they will not be there in the long run and so cannot trust or be trusted. Those who violate that tacit agreement, who give themselves fully to a premature caring, "feel scared a lot of the time, wondering whether their partner will somehow take advantage of their vulnerability." Even if their mutual attraction leads beyond "just fun" to something deeper, unlearning the habit of holding back, of being afraid to love, can be difficult.[30] Sex without commitment is sex without loyalty, trust, or honesty. Twenty-eight percent of people who are cohabiting with, but not married to, their partners have cheated on them in the past year.[31]

Morse also points out that oxytocin, a chemical released in breast-feeding that creates the bond that mothers feel with their babies, is also released when women climax during sex. Oxytocin may also cause women to bond with their lovers. Men don't produce oxytocin, but sex is an important part of bonding for them too. Learning to break those biological and emotional bonds and enjoy sex "just for fun" cannot help but damage the capacity for future relationships, relationships that are "for keeps." Precipitous, casual, or even "joyful, loveless"[32] sex works against everything the Bible offers as a truer understanding of love.

In keeping with its protective function, New Testament morality, unlike the old coercive social morality, does not describe punishments for sexual sin but warns of its negative consequences. Among these are loss of self-control and sexual addiction:

> Do not let sin reign in your mortal body so that you obey its evil desires. Do not offer any part of yourself to sin as an instrument of wickedness. (Rom. 6:12–13)

> Beloved, I beseech you as aliens and exiles to abstain from the passions of the flesh that wage war against your soul. (1 Peter 2:11 RSV)

> [When] I am carnal, sold under sin, I do not understand my own ac-
> tions. For I do not do what I want, but I do the very thing I hate. Now
> if I do what I do not want . . . it is no longer I that do it, but sin which
> dwells within me. I can will what is right, but I cannot do it. For I do
> not do the good I want, but the evil I do not want is what I do. (Rom.
> 7:14–19 RSV)

Once we yield ourselves to sin, we can become caught up by it and
end up doing things we don't want to do. An example of this can be
seen in a 2004 newspaper article about the sexual behavior of U.S.
college women. The article pictures several young, attractive, well-
dressed, obviously upper-middle-class women, who talked with pride
and shame about their "number," the count they kept of the lovers
they had had. One young woman reported that when they first arrived
at college, "two friends told her they planned not to have sex with
more than 10 guys, but if they did, number 11 would become their
husbands. . . . Then number 11 came along. . . . They've now moved
beyond that number and are still searching."[33] With no potential
husband in sight, these women didn't know how to stop themselves
from letting their number grow even larger.

The writings of both Paul and Peter (1 Peter 4:2–4) equate sexual license with idolatry. Immorality sets people at odds with God, and contributes to more loss of control. In consequence of their rebellion:

> Therefore God gave them up in the lusts of their hearts to impurity,
> to the dishonoring of their bodies among themselves, because they
> exchanged the truth about God for a lie and worshiped and served the
> creature rather than the Creator, who is blessed for ever. Amen.
>
> For this reason God gave them up to dishonorable passions. Their
> women exchanged natural relations for unnatural, and the men likewise
> gave up natural relations with women and were consumed (burned)
> with passion for one another, men committing shameless acts with
> men and receiving in their own persons the due penalty for their error.
> (Rom. 1:24–27)[34]

God created sexuality, but the immoral worship and serve the creation rather than its Creator. Just as he did after the fall, God does
not punish the rebellious but steps back from those who refuse his
truth, allowing them to have their own way and suffer the natural

consequences (they dishonor their bodies/God gives them up to their desires/they receive in their bodies the due penalties for their error). This pattern seems to be a particular problem with homosexuality, which Paul addresses specifically in this passage. According to therapists, homosexual men often suffer disproportionately from sexual compulsion and addiction. They suggest that most people who become sexual compulsives, whether male, female, heterosexual, or gay, experience some kind of tension which they seek to relieve through sexual activity. Sex is an effective tension reliever, but because sex does not address the underlying source of the problem, the relief is short lived. So the individual seeks another sexual encounter, then another. Eventually, the brain sets up pathways that demand this kind and level of activity, no matter how destructive it proves to be in other aspects of the person's life. Sexual acting out (dishonoring their bodies) sets up an irresistible pattern of behavior (receiving in their bodies the due penalty for their error).[35]

Unlike the coercive norms regulating the sexual cartel prior to the sexual revolution, the restrictions imposed on sexuality in the New Testament are not intended as punishments. Rather, they are intended to protect individuals from the natural consequences of uncommitted sex. In the Song of Songs, sexual longing, appropriately restrained, motivates commitment and trust, which leads eventually to a mature, all-fulfilling sexuality, "one flesh, naked and unashamed," and all that goes with it. Christianity urges self-restraint before marriage because indulging in sex outside of a committed relationship has too much potential to cripple the individual's ability to achieve that emotional maturity.[36]

## Living Redeemed

A letter to a columnist who specializes in advice to people under the age of 30 asked,

> I have found a wonderful girl and we're in a wonderful relationship. . . .
> We've both experienced pain and hurt in our previous relationships. . . .
> It's become apparent both of us are afraid of the other person's leaving.
> I consider both of us level-headed and realists, but we are crazy in love

and both feel like it's too good to be true. Do you think it's healthy to have a small amount of fear not tied to anything particular that either has done to the other, but perhaps due to the past?

If he had asked me, my answer would have been "Well, if it is lack of commitment you fear, make a commitment. Promise you will never leave. Get married. If being crazy in love and having a wonderful relationship isn't enough to motivate marriage, what is?" The nationally syndicated advice columnist, however, replied, "I believe . . . that anticipation of loss is the mark of the level-headed realist. I've said it before, and I believe it even when I'm not feeling cranky: Most relationships end. . . . Which means a little fear is not only healthy but also smart . . . in the take-nothing-for-granted sense."[37] The most optimistic advice she had to offer was "carpe diem" (seize the day). In today's secular world, there is no such thing as commitment. Even marriage is not really a binding commitment, not in a forever sense. Neither of these two can credibly promise never to leave; they could always fall out of love and so change their mind. Because today's attitudes toward relationships lack a moral absolute, people can never trust each other enough to find the kind of love celebrated in the Song of Songs.

So the answer for Christian relationships is to seize not just the day but that moral absolute. The biblical message about marriage is romantic, poetic, and by worldly standards, complete nonsense. Jesus and Paul see all our obligations to each other, whether in marriage or family, in terms of our redemption and the release from material obligations this redemption brings. We don't need to be anxious about food, drink, or clothing because God will take care of us; career and ambition are less important than reconciliation with God; family members should give up notions of holding authority over each other in awe of Christ; parents should nurture their children because they belong to God; children should obey their parents to honor God; immorality should be avoided because rebellion against God causes deep hurt to ourselves.

Following these admonitions takes us spiritually out of this world and into one in which the smallest family action is tinged with implications of the divine. But in honoring the divine in everyday life, we are freed to trust each other as well. Here is what the divine makes possible:

we love without fear; seize more than just a day; safely relinquish our grip on power, control, and fear; and slip the grip that power, control, and fear have on us.

As the disciples complained when Jesus taught that the marital ideal was to become one flesh, this way of living is neither practical nor expedient. Expedient or not, however, living redeemed has worldly pay-offs. As already noted, couples who put family first are more satisfied with their relationships and their lives than couples who are career focused. Highly committed Christians have a lower rate of divorce. Couples who share power, who take each other's concerns into account in decision making, have much happier marriages than those who do not. Other research has shown that marriage (as opposed to staying single) leads to greater overall happiness and physical and mental health. Children who are raised by both parents, who do not spend long periods of time in the care of nonfamily members, whose family is religiously involved, or who are religiously active themselves do much better on measures of mental and physical health, have fewer problems with substance abuse and depression, do better in school and complete more years of schooling, are less likely to have a child as an unmarried teen, and are more likely to delay their "sexual debut." Surprisingly for the contemporary cultural image of the happy, sexually active single, surveys also show that married, religious people are actually the most "sexually active" and have the highest levels of emotional and physical satisfaction from their sex lives. The more one attends church, the higher one's level of satisfaction with sex![38]

The attitudes and behaviors encouraged by the Bible are not encouraged by contemporary economic and social trends, and certainly not by popular culture. Living as Christians definitely makes us "fools" in more worldly eyes. But "the foolishness of God is wiser than human wisdom, and the weakness of God is stronger than human strength" (1 Cor. 1:25). If happy marriages, happy children, and happy lives are the goal, following biblical norms leads to great success.

# 8

# The Christian Family and the Limits of Politics

"I know we are living in a morally and spiritually corrupt society when someone can go up and down my street with a leaf blower."

Caller, National Public Radio
San Francisco, California
January 31, 1997

Christianity arose within and ultimately triumphed over the world's most successful patriarchy, the Roman Empire. Despite its monumental achievements in raising the status of women and children and in eliminating slavery, however, many people today equate Christian belief with sexual repression, patriarchy and the subordination of women, hypocrisy, racism, homophobia, disregard for the poor, and exploitation of the environment. The very secular values and attitudes of the new moral order are probably not as unitary or as widely held as they seem: the use of leaf blowers (see the quote at the beginning of the chapter) may or may not be included in the average person's list of contemporary spiritual depredations. But what is considered immoral has changed dramatically in the past several decades. Evangelist Mardi Keyes, for example, has observed that the prevailing attitude on college campuses calls for not merely tolerating all forms of sexual behavior but celebrating them.[1] Those who disapprove of promiscuous sex are more likely to be labeled immoral than those who engage in it.

I began this book by stating that Christianity is struggling to find solutions to contemporary problems with marriage and the family because we do not understand what the problem is. I propose at least one of the real problems is this huge disjunction between the sexual motives of the world and those of believers. As a problem definition, it is overly broad. But it is here, in sexual behavior, that not only Christianity but marriage and family as well are being slowly but surely corrupted by the world.

## Christianity and the Old Morality

Before we as Christians can take our message on sexual morality, marriage, and family back into the changed secular world, however, we must take the rap for not maintaining it in the first place. Understanding the hostility with which religion is now viewed requires us to admit the extent to which Christian morality was co-opted to serve the purposes of the material world. In the absence of *continuing*, determined, and clear-visioned moral suasion, sexual mores and family structure (or the lack of them) are shaped by economic incentives and constraints. These practices may be disastrous for both the individual and society in the long run, but people don't live in the long run. In a kind of vicious circle, somewhere in the past two thousand years, Christianity allowed its institutions to be taken over by the demands of the world of thorns. It succeeded in maintaining and propagating its values mostly where they coincided with material incentives. It is in these intersections, however, that those values are also most likely to be corrupted.

Christian teachings on and practice of slavery offer a good example. The early Christian church opposed the practice of slavery, although as a tiny and suspect minority within the Roman Empire, Christians could do little about it.[2] As time passed and the church acquired more influence, it did offer strong prohibitions against slavery. But while the church itself was faithful, its teachings (including papal bulls threatening slavers with excommunication) were ignored whenever the practice of slavery offered an opportunity to fulfill what Pope Gregory XVI called the "desire for sordid gain."[3] Rodney Stark concludes that "organized opposition to slavery arose only when and where . . . [it] was not counteracted by perceived self-interest." This "explains why abolition movements did *not* prosper in the American South."[4] In contrast, slavery failed to prosper in the American North, where it simply was not profitable enough to make defying religious teachings against it worthwhile.

Like the issue of slavery, how successful Christianity is in promulgating its teachings on sexual morality varies depending on how they interact with economic incentives. In the agrarian world, before and after the time of Christ, men need children for economic reasons and make contracts with women to provide those children. In consequence, these cultures prize the chastity of women but are pretty much indifferent to male sexual behavior as long as it does not interfere with other men's rights.[5] As Christianity spread, its teachings on the importance of chastity for men as well as women achieved moral salience and a fair degree of compliance, but even then these teachings were most successful in keeping middle-class girls virgin until marriage. They were less successful in restraining the sexual behavior of boys and men. If a young man came to his marriage bed with a little "experience," the attitude was, well, what could you expect? If the bride was not a virgin, however, a scandal might ensue.

This relative success of encouraging the chastity of women, however, came not from greater feminine religious devotion but from extensive social constraints. Historically, the marriage contract protected women in the less powerful role in which childbearing placed them.[6] These contracts would not have been accepted, however, if men could have gotten women's products for free. In order to regulate sexuality, society developed codes of conduct that enforced a sexual cartel, which, like any cartel, punished cheaters—women who gave men sex without first obtaining a promise of marriage. Even into the twentieth century, ruining one's reputation, becoming the subject of gossip, or having one's virtue "compromised"—let alone bearing a child out of wedlock—had serious ramifications for a young woman's chances of a good marriage. The degree of coercion applied to ensure the chastity of women (but rarely anything as severe for men) provides strong evidence that its motives were more than spiritual.

Brutal as these measures were, the old sexual norms served an important social function. Sexual restraint motivated marriage, which in turn provided the protection that women needed to bear children, who in turn helped produce the goods needed for life. Man's as well as woman's survival, let alone comfort, depended on creating and maintaining family. Thus, in the world of thorns, a moral code that enforced the chastity of women was necessary for the survival not just of individuals but of the society itself.

That the old sexual norms intersected with biblical teachings about sex and family was only coincidental. The New Testament, with its stories of Jesus preventing the stoning of an adulterous woman and forgiving other sinful women, set aside the coercive chastity of the Old Testament. Sexual restraint in the Bible had an entirely different purpose. Christian *churches*, however, have less clean hands. Religiously motivated teachings were co-opted to support economic imperatives, and churches used socially sanctioned coercion to keep their members in line. How many novels, starting with *The Scarlet Letter*, have been written about individuals' struggles with guilt and shame and the punishments imposed by churches not just for committing sexual sins but even for experiencing desire? How many people do you know who have rejected religion because of the shame-based morality to which they were subjected as children and young adults? No wonder that many people today reject Christianity and consider it hateful, the enemy of love. In their minds, religion is inseparably linked with the old tyranny of shame and repression.

## Culture Wars

By mid-twentieth century, the changing household had drastically reduced the economic need for children. Except for a few farming households (the percentage of the American labor force employed in agriculture fell from 47 percent in 1870 to 4 percent in 1970 and to little more than 2 percent in 2002),[7] the only real role that the family now plays economically is in consumption. The shift from children as tools of production to expensive luxuries caused an avalanche of changes. Sexual restraint and the protections it afforded were no longer necessary, at least not in their former role of producing the necessities of life. Neither men nor women have a material incentive to sustain marriage either as a precursor to sexual involvement or as a lifetime commitment. Women have little reason to remain in the home and much reason to seek paid employment. Most significantly, women have no need to enforce the sexual cartel and its abuses. Norms controlling women's sexual behavior (and by extension men's) eroded quickly. The sexual cartel, which requires consensus and, however unwilling, the conformity of those it seeks to regulate, collapsed.

A significant segment of society actively resists going back to the shame-based and economically based enforcement of traditional sexual morality. And really, who can blame them? A morality that exists only through coercion is not a morality at all. In fact, absent the material needs that generated it, the old morality, with its judgments, gossip, ostracism, and punishments, begins to look extremely *immoral*. The old morality existed not to protect and promote love but to repress and restrain individuals in order to protect the material welfare of the society.

As cruel as the sexual cartel was, however, its repudiation left a moral hole into which a not inconsiderable proportion of the population has dropped. For while the educated middle-class youths who kicked off the sexual revolution may have been perfectly happy as sexual "free agents," their abandonment of the moral cartel proved not to be a victimless crime.

Studies of intelligence have shown that highly intelligent people are virtually immune to a wide array of social ills. They are less likely to divorce, to have unplanned pregnancies, to live in poverty, or to have problems with their children. Add a secular orientation, and these smart, well-educated, affluent people become the ones we call the "cultural elite." And while these individuals care about romance, sex, weddings, fidelity, and children as much as their more conservative counterparts, they are usually well satisfied on those scores. Their privileged status leaves them independent, with no personal need for traditional sexual morality or for the family as an institution. From their vantage point, the old morality offers only shame and repression. Why bother with it?

Indeed, following the conservative "values" win in the 2004 presidential election, *Los Angeles Times* columnist Michael Kinsley wrote that by contesting the secular goal of "liv[ing] in a society where women are free to choose abortion and where gay relationships have full civil equality with straight ones," conservative, religious Americans oppressed liberal, secular Americans.[8] From the secular perspective, these restrictions seem unkind, unloving, immoral, and even hateful. Why shouldn't everyone enjoy the same freedom of expression that the elite enjoy? Isn't it truly cruel, a kind of bondage, to force women to suffer through an unwanted pregnancy? Why shouldn't teenagers be allowed an outlet for their natural sexual urges? Why stigmatize the innocent children of unwed mothers? Why withhold full civil rights (including government benefits) from people whose only crime is that they happen to love a member of their own sex? And why distract the nation's moral attention from other, more worthy issues that require social consensus, like poverty, income inequality, environmental degradation (including outlawing leaf blowers), and war?

I don't want to accuse these opinion leaders, who I do not doubt are compassionate people, of a "let them eat cake" attitude. But in not only abandoning but actively working against norms of sexual restraint, and offering no other to take their place, they have abandoned those who need the protection that traditional morality offered. Once a culture has discarded the strong moral voice of sexual restriction and with it painted-with-the-same-brush religion, the amoral "natural" impulses spring back up. The circumstances of the contemporary natural family of course differ in many ways from those of the pagan family. In the ancient world, the only ones who enjoyed any kind of freedom were the few men on top, and everyone else existed only to serve them. In our wealthy contemporary Western world, the number of people with the means to enjoy individual sexual expression without suffering for it materially—who are smart enough, educated enough, or wealthy enough to work their way out of what few problems they encounter—is much larger now than at any other time in history. The elite now include women and those who prefer to have relations with members of the same sex. But frighteningly, this freedom still comes at the expense of those who cannot afford to cope with negative consequences: the poor, the uneducated, the young, increasing numbers of fatherless children, and the unborn.

## The Cost of Sex

The maintenance of sexual morality matters to the poor, the young, the less-well educated, and members of disadvantaged minority groups because sex today is nonproductive and thus has become in a sense costly, a luxury good. Sexual activity carries with it potentially serious consequences from which people lacking in means find it difficult to recover. But the New Morality leaves these individuals to struggle on their own with how, and why, to turn down sexual activity. In the 1980s and 90s, as the number of teenagers having intercourse at younger and younger ages soared, so did teen pregnancies, abortions, and the number of children who were born fatherless and poor. Chlamydia, a sexually transmitted disease that can cause fertility problems, infected large numbers of young women. Even more serious is the emergence of AIDS in the 1980s. Also in the eighties, another previously unknown problem, date or acquaintance rape, became prevalent on college campuses and among single adults. By the early 1990s, two-thirds of African-American births were out of wedlock, as were eighteen percent of births to Caucasians. Increasing numbers of women and children lived in poverty, and in some poor neighborhoods, fatherless boys ran rampant in neighborhoods that housed no married men.

Studies have found that girls who begin sexual activity in their early teens are less likely to have stable marriages in their thirties[9] and are more likely to have an unmarried pregnancy, multiple sexual partners, and to contract a sexually transmitted disease.[10] Between out-of-wedlock childbearing and the dramatic increases in divorce, by 1990 36.3 percent of American children lived apart from their fathers.[11] As children grow up without fathers to protect them but exposed to maternal boyfriends or stepfathers, sexual abuse of children becomes more common. Ironically, we no longer stigmatize innocent babies with the label "illegitimate," but the social dysfunction of growing up without a father is almost too great to be chronicled. Just one evidence of this dysfunction is the following: "Among white families, one study finds that 'daughters of single parents are 53 percent more likely to marry as teenagers, 111 percent more likely to have children as teenagers, 164 percent more likely to have a premarital birth, and 92 percent more likely to dissolve their own marriage.'"[12]

A fourteen-year-old girl obviously has far fewer resources to deal with an importunate boy and the aftermath of sexual relations than she would have when faced with the same young man ten years later. At twenty-four, a woman can make meaningful decisions about whether or not she wants sex, whether she wants it with this man, and whether his motives for having it match hers. Compared to a teenager, a twenty-four-year-old is mature enough to use birth control and to protect herself from disease. How can a teenager barely old enough to stay home alone carry out the complicated planning required by "safe sex"? But in today's inhibition-free environment, how does she counter her would-be lover's cajoling? If she really loved him she would, he argues; if she won't she must be frigid; she won't get pregnant because . . . ; it's no fun with a condom. Many a young girl today gives in to such wheedling simply because she doesn't know a good reason not to, and because if she won't, he threatens that he will drop her and find another girl who will. And he probably can find a more willing (or more pliable) girl. The sexual cartel is gone, remember.

Ironically, its disappearance means that the twenty-four-year-old, who may be better prepared when she says yes, may also have even fewer excuses to say no. For all the talk of women's controlling their own sexuality today, in many ways single women have less control than ever. Before the sexual revolution, the average man looked forward to marriage and the more comfortable life and regular sex it offered. Compare that state of affairs with the one implicit in a book of advice for women who want to marry a professional man. Noting men's fear of commitment, the three male authors say, "True love gives men the first glimpse of a time when there will be no more sex with other women. This change is scary for a man."[13] Women today are competing for a man's commitment not only against an indefinite number of other, sexually willing women but against male fantasies of those women. Moreover, today "when a man moves in with a woman, he sacrifices a lot. He has to change his comfortable routine. He essentially gives up any chance of dating other women. . . .When a man makes the decision to move in with a woman, he gives up a huge chunk of his independence *just for her*."[14] The "three professional men" also advise, "It should not take a man more than three years to figure out if he wants to marry you. That's two years dating and one year living together. . . . Thankfully for women, even men slow to commit don't take longer than five years from the first date to the walk down the aisle with Ms. Right (Marriage = two years dating + one year living together + two years of engagement)."[15] But even then, it isn't a matter of just waiting out the time: the authors also warn of a list of things that a woman can do or say that will make a man decide not to marry her after all. And of course, with so much time passing, much of that dating involves sleeping together.

The staple of the traditional family, a chaste courtship followed not by sleepovers and cohabitation but by a wedding, has no place in this scenario. Our successful, attractive, professional authors would no doubt advise that expectations such as these are the new fantasy. And these are the guys who are actually willing to marry! "Players" have even less patience for chastity. If they don't get what they want soon enough, they just move on to someone else.

For every step down the ladder of privilege and desirability a woman finds herself, the fewer her options and protections. Just as the fourteen-year-old is more likely than the twenty-four-year-old to make a damaging mistake, poorer, less educated, less intelligent, less ethnically privileged, or less attractive women have less room to protect themselves or recover from any negative consequences that might follow sexual activity. While many college campuses have become sexual free-for-alls, young people who don't go to college are even more likely to engage in unsafe sex, to contract diseases, to have an unwanted pregnancy, or to become stuck in a cohabitation arrangement with a partner who refuses to marry them. This doesn't begin to count the many broken hearts and damaged individuals, male as well as female, eager to love and be loved forever, who have no idea of how to accomplish their goals.

## Politics and Religion

The early Christian movement was reviled and persecuted in the Roman world. In encouraging believers to free themselves from Rome's patriarchal, honor-driven family structure and in treating women, children, and slaves as "coheirs" with men in God's kingdom (1 Peter 3:7), Christianity offended Rome's most basic standards of morality. In its beginnings, Christianity consisted only of small bands of believers, geographically separated and communicating only with difficulty. The fledgling movement could have been easily swallowed up again in the Roman material imperative. But it was not. Armed only with the Holy Spirit and the message of redemption, Christianity eventually conquered Rome.

In the same way, contemporary Western culture finds Christianity offensive. Secular culture views Christians as simple-minded, sexually repressed, hypocritical, dangerous zealots who seek to take away rights and freedoms. This time, Christians (in name at least) are the majority rather than the tiny minority they were in the beginning, but that majority is being eaten away by the enticing offerings of the new economic and material order: a comfortable, sexually active, and secure life in which marriage, family, and religion are completely optional. A life in which each individual is in total control, able to devote himself or herself to whatever career, sport, computer game, form of sexual expression, or other pastime suits his or her fancy. What's wrong with that? Nothing, except that ultimately this is narcissism and idolatry. Nothing, except that this freedom, satisfaction, and control come at the expense of other people. Nothing, except that these ideas of a natural and free sexuality work against a biblical love, the "one flesh" union described by the creation accounts, Jesus, Paul, and the Song of Songs.

The real problem with the "family optional" lifestyle is that, despite the certainty with which the worldly voices speak, the social history of the years since the 1960s reveals them to be confused. The developed world embarked on this great social experiment, only to discover a few years later the great dysfunction that it caused. Oddly enough, secular society's solution to these problems—yet more sexual freedom—is another dose of the same medicine that caused the problems in the first place.

In *The Rise of Christianity*, Rodney Stark outlines the patterns and reasons for Christianity's growth from a small group of Jews devoted to the teachings of a man who endured shameful execution by the Romans to the religion that dominated the Western world. To oversimplify Stark's analysis, Christianity became a world religion because it had a great deal to offer a confused and miserable natural world. No longer subject to worldly anxieties, the early Christians did not hoard their resources but gave freely to help each other out of slavery and poverty. When their pagan neighbors fled the plagues that struck the crowded Roman cities, abandoning loved ones to die, Christians stayed to nurse the sick. Ironically for today, when Christianity is publicly equated with the oppression of women, Stark contends that a major factor in its growth was that it treated women so well.[16] Defying the social contempt it brought, Christianity elevated women and slaves to positions of leadership and respect. Christianity and Christian morality thrived because they made a real difference in people's lives.

## No Fear

A lesson we can learn from this history is that whatever actions Christians take in our present moral crisis should not be based on fear or anxiety. Although the loss of social and moral institutions makes it more difficult for Christians to maintain their own marriages and to raise godly children, our commitment to each other is based in Christ, not in politics. We do not have to control other people's behavior or attitudes to be safe. As Peter wrote, "Do right and let nothing terrify you. Now who is there to harm you if you are zealous for what is right? But even if you do suffer for righteousness' sake, you will be blessed. Have no fear of them, nor be troubled . . . and keep your conscience clear, so that, when you are abused, those who revile your good behavior in Christ may be put to shame" (1 Peter 3:6, 13–14, 16 RSV).

Further, fear is a political weapon, not a tool of moral reform. When people are afraid, they are easily manipulated and politicians raise money.[17] There will always be someone out there trying to stir up fear. It should not be Christians.

Nor should Christians use fear to motivate repentance in nonbelievers. The early Christians did not go around telling their pagan neighbors that they were going to hell for their immoral practices. Early Christianity did not offer its world fear or shame. Rather, the message the early Christians carried was the joy and peace of the risen Christ, the living God, and how Christ's redemption reconciles us to God.

Paul defines the Christian attitude toward the immoral behavior of others:

> I wrote to you in my letter not to associate intimately with immoral people, but I did not mean the immoral people of this world, or the covetous and rapacious or idolaters, since then you would need to go out of the world. But rather I wrote to you not to associate intimately with anyone who bears the name of brother if he is a fornicator or a covetous man or an idolater or a railer or a drunkard or rapacious—do not eat with such a one. For what have I to do with judging outsiders? Is it not those inside the church whom you are to judge? God judges those outside. (1 Cor. 5:9–13)[18]

Modern Christians are often charged with being judgmental and intolerant, but Paul let us off the hook as moral police. Not only does God not expect us to attempt to discipline nonbelievers, Paul tells us we are not to do so. Indeed, for Christians to attempt to impose their standards on non-Christians resembles too much the coercion employed by traditional morality. Similarly, Peter instructs Christians not to get involved in name-calling debates with those who disagree with us:

> Christ suffered for you, leaving you an example, that you should follow in his steps. "He committed no sin, and no deceit was found in his mouth." When they hurled their insults at him, he did not retaliate; when he suffered, he made no threats. Instead, he entrusted himself to him who judges justly. . . .

> Do not repay evil with evil or insult with insult. On the contrary, repay evil with blessing, for to this you have been called so that you may inherit a blessing. (1 Peter 2:21–23; 3:9)

## Futility of Politics

The experience of Cal Thomas, minister, newspaper columnist, and former adviser to the Moral Majority, offers important insights about what we can expect from Christian interactions with politics. Thomas recounts the elation with which the Moral Majority, a conservative group formed in the 1970s to influence the political process for Christ, greeted Ronald Reagan's election as president in 1980.[19] They believed that "we had the power to right every wrong and cure every ill and end every frustration that God-fearing people had been forced to submit to by our 'oppressors.'"[20] But he gradually came to realize that this cure would not happen. After the twelve years of Moral Majority access to the Reagan and then the Bush administrations, Thomas says,

> the impotence and near-irrelevance of the Religious Right were demonstrated on the day William Jefferson Clinton was inaugurated. Clinton's first two official acts as president were to sign executive orders liberalizing rules against homosexuals in the military and repealing the few abortion restrictions applied under presidents Reagan and Bush.
>
> With a few pen strokes, Bill Clinton erased the little that the Moral Majority had been able to achieve during its brief existence.[21]

Thomas noted that the failed campaigns of Christian conservatives Gary Bauer and Alan Keyes in 2000 "ratify our conclusion that any restoration of the moral underpinnings of this nation will not take place either mainly or mostly in and through the political structures."[22] Thomas concluded that their political efforts failed to reform society because "politics and government cannot reach into the soul. That is something God reserves for himself."[23]

The Religious Right's failure to forge a partnership with government is just as well. As the history of Christianity's transformation into a state church by the Roman Emperor Constantine in 306 shows, becoming co-opted by a government inevitably corrupts the church. Christians can only offer their values, not impose them on others. The problems of family, marriage, and sexuality in the twenty-first century are not political ones. Politically, the old morality has already lost: economic factors continue to push the average person in the opposite direction. Laws are not the answer anyway. As abortion rights advocates point out, short of a police state, making abortions illegal will not stop women from getting them. Similarly, even the best divorce laws cannot make good marriages. Laws cannot make parents love their children. Christian love is not a legal institution but a moral one.

## False Friends

Christians also need to be "as wise as serpents" when it comes to political movements that appear to be family friendly but may be just the opposite, or can be flipped to work against family interests. For instance, in the late 1990s Democrats, led by President Clinton, suddenly got behind the Republican demands for welfare reform and helped them pass it. Conservatives and liberals alike were concerned that welfare was creating a permanent underclass of poor children and their mothers. The liberal turnabout, however, may not have been based on these concerns about fatherless families. Rather, welfare reform seems to have become suddenly acceptable because so many middle-class women were themselves working outside of the home. If paid employment was good for them, what possible justification was there for poor women to stay home with their children?[24] The terms of welfare reform also allowed states to put the money saved from welfare cuts into government-sponsored childcare—another priority on the secular feminist agenda. Only after the reform was passed did childcare experts ponder the wisdom of depriving fatherless children of their mothers as well.

## Growth of Government

Many other social programs replace functions that were previously filled by the family. Support in old age and widowhood, healthcare, insurance, and inheritances were all once products of the household but are now being produced by government, employers, and other businesses.

Like heat, water, and clothing, it is certainly more efficient for services like insurance and pensions, which benefit from a pooling of risks, to be offered by entities larger than the family. Some people, however, cannot afford or choose not to purchase these services that the rest of society feels they must have. This creates an impetus for government to step in to provide them. Social security, public education, the welfare system, public health clinics, Head Start and subsidized childcare programs, school-based programs that provide breakfast and lunch, and in some areas medical and dental care, are only the most obvious examples.

When government steps in to provide a service, however, it usually requires that everyone participate in the program. People can refuse to accept the services provided, but they cannot opt out of paying for them (social security and public education, for example). In highly socialized countries the tax burden to provide these services is often so great that people have little control over issues such as how much time to devote to work versus to caring for their children. While those countries often offer private alternatives to publicly provided goods, such as medical care, the high tax burden makes the private alternatives even less affordable than when there was no "free" alternative at all. Thus the more programs a government provides, the more it controls matters that were once considered private family concerns.

Because *everything* was once produced in the household, "family values" thus appear to be at the heart of many conflicts over whether and how government will provide a service. As marriage continues to fail and more people live and have children alone or in uncommitted pairs, activists will call for more government provision of the joint products that the singletons cannot produce. Legal scholar Richard Posner has pointed out that welfare programs in the United States and Scandinavian countries are attempts to use the government to replace, at least financially, the fathers who are rapidly vanishing from their children's lives.[25] As the outsourcing of household services gets closer and closer to the spiritual core of the family, however, it becomes apparent that there is a great deal that the government cannot replace. Welfare payments, food stamps, and court-ordered child support may allow a child's physical survival, but they fall far short of actually replacing the emotional, social, and spiritual resources provided by fathers. Government sponsored day care keeps children safe and dry, but it cannot replace mothers. Public schools may give a child an education, but they cannot replace the values taught by a Christian family, and the values they do teach are often not Christian. Domestic partner laws and legal marriage, gay or straight, may provide affordable insurance and inheritance rights, but they cannot guarantee a real lifetime commitment. Too often, however, providing for people's minimal physical needs encourages them not to seek fulfillment of the deeper spiritual ones.

This is not to say that Christians should refuse government services or stay out of politics. By all means, when you are given the opportunity, vote your moral conscience. Organize or support campaigns on moral issues. Argue against the expansion of government. Run for public office. But don't be surprised if political mandates in themselves are not enough to reverse ongoing moral degradation. Jesus said that God made marriage to last forever, but Moses had to allow divorce because our hearts were hard. What our world needs is not a return to the law. We need changes of heart, and those are not created through government mandate. If the prospect of not aggressively fighting immorality depresses you, examine your motives. The problem with giving up our anxieties is that it means giving up our chances of getting what we want, the way we want it. "Fear not, little flock," Jesus said, "for it is your Father's good pleasure to give you the kingdom" (Luke 12:32 RSV). Mostly, what we need to do as the church is to keep our "eyes on the prize," to maintain biblical values and standards against that which is "natural."

## An Irresistible Love

Wonderfully for us, the Bible does not use negativity, fear, or punishment to motivate us to good behavior. Instead, the Bible offers us an irresistible positive—a love that is soul-stirring, deep, and passionate—and tells us that God had this in mind for us from the beginning. Christianity offers guidance in sexual issues not because Christianity is against sex but because it is so very much for it. Biblical standards of sexual morality protect us from too-easy and too-early exposure to sexual pleasure in order that our longings will motivate a lasting and joy-filled relationship.

The Bible tells us that God created sexuality, marriage, and family when he divided his first lonely creation into two beings, male and female, in such a way that they would long to become one again. The creation accounts, Jesus, Paul, and the Song of Songs all portray man and woman coming together, united, one flesh, a seal upon each other's heart, a paradox of joint wills, the fullness of the other's longings. "For this reason a man will leave his father and mother and cleave unto his wife, and the two will become one flesh." "And they were both naked, the man and his wife, and were not ashamed."

Ultimately, this positive message of what God intended us to be to each other when he made us male and female is the only effective weapon we have in the battle to save marriage and the family. Fortunately, it is more than enough. Our duty as Christians is not to pass laws to prevent the spread of immorality. Our duty is to let our redemption, our joy, our peace, and our love for each other permeate our lives to such an extent that we become the light of the world, a city on a hill that cannot be hidden (Matt. 5:14).

The Bible offers a single, simple ideal for marriage: a union of two souls that is romantic, poetic, and by worldly standards completely impractical. But God did not create sexuality and marriage to be practical. Practicality is for those who live outside the garden. Redeemed as Christians and as lovers, we keep the fruit of our own vineyards.

# Acknowledgments

Many thanks, first, to Linda Ikeda, who helped me in so many ways that I am sure I will miss acknowledging some of them. Linda got me working in this area again after I had lost interest in it; encouraged, supported, and pushed me through the process of finding a publisher; read and proofread many drafts; promoted and distributed endless copies of our previous work, *Male and Female in Christ*; and shared with me her own expertise in attachment. She is a dear friend worth her weight in rubies. Thanks to my daughter, Nicole, who also proofread, edited, provided endless encouragement, and has presold a million copies of this book to her friends. Thanks to my son, Andrew, who listened to my biblical analysis one night on a long car trip. Thanks to New Testament historian S. Scott Bartchy for his critical insights, which came along at a critical time. Thanks to Medad Birungi, Anne Mikkola, and especially Patti Ricotta, none of whom I knew but whose interest in my work (and requests to have me come teach in Uganda) gave me much-needed encouragement. Thanks to David Zimmerman for his encouragement to finish the book and for referring me to editor Rodney Clapp; and many thanks to Rodney Clapp for his encouragement, enthusiasm, and direction on this project. Thanks to Ruth Goring for her insightful copyediting.

And more thanks than I can express to my husband, Larry Iannaccone. A stalwart champion of the apostle Paul, Larry pushed me past the common misperception of Paul as "male chauvinist pig" to a fuller appreciation of the wealth of Paul's writings. I am grateful to him for encouraging me to read the economic literature on the family that provides much of the basis for my analysis; for the idea of looking at what the Bible says about marriage through the window of Jesus's statement in Matthew 19; and for his framework of understanding Paul's statements about the submission of women in the context of what he says to slaves. I also thank him not only for his emotional (and financial) support and belief in me but also for demonstrating throughout our marriage his deep and abiding belief in the equality and worth of all persons, male or female, in Christ.

# Notes

## Introduction

1. Rodney Clapp, *Families at the Crossroads* (Downers Grove, IL: InterVarsity Press, 1993), 13, 35.

2. William J. Bennett, Empower America website; quoted in David W. Machacek, "Same-Sex Culture War," *Religion in the News* 7, no. 1 (Spring 2004): 6.

3. Peter Spring, Family Research Council website; quoted in Machacek, "Same-Sex Culture War," 5.

4. A not uncommon example of how poorly conceived solutions make matters worse is found in the story of a young woman in the first Sunday school class my husband and I taught on this subject. While dating and engaged, this woman and her fiancé had an "equal-regard" relationship. As conservative Christians, however, they decided that once married they should adhere to the so-called biblical model of male dominance and female subordination. So they did—and these artificial constraints destroyed their marriage. Couples speaking at Christians for Biblical Equality's marriage conference in 2000 recounted similar stories. Although these marriages survived, the young wives in particular experienced debilitating emotional distress in their submissive role. This distress is not atypical. Social scientists have found that the exercise of power in marriage is a major cause of unhappiness and marital breakdown. See John Gottman and Nan Silver, *The Seven Principles for Making Marriage Work* (New York: Three Rivers, 1999), 66; Philip Blumstein and Pepper Schwartz, *American Couples* (New York: William Morrow, 1983); Andrew D. Lester and Judith L. Lester, *It Takes Two: The Joy of Intimate Marriage* (Louisville: Westminster John Knox, 1998), 120–121.

5. Medad Birungi, President of WorldShine Ministries, Uganda, personal observation. Edward C. Greene, *Rethinking AIDS Prevention* (Westport, CT: Preager, 2003), 12.

6. Douglas J. Brower, *Beyond "I Do": What Christians Believe about Marriage* (Grand Rapids: Eerdmans, 2001), 10.

## Chapter 1  Love and Sex as God Created Them

1. Richard Posner, *Sex and Reason* (Cambridge: Harvard University Press, 1992), 50.

2. S. Scott Bartchy, "Undermining Ancient Patriarchy: The Apostle Paul's Vision of a Society of Siblings," *Biblical Theology Bulletin* 29 (1999): 69–78. Also in S. Scott Bartchy, *Call No Man Father* (Peabody, MA: Hendrickson, forthcoming).

3. George Ricker Berry, *The Interlinear Literal Translation of the Greek New Testament* (Grand Rapids: Zondervan, 1976), 53.

4. Because the next sentence, Matthew 19:12, lists the various ways that some become "eunuchs," Jesus's statement "Not everyone can accept this word" may be taken to be his agreement that it is better not to marry. It seems unlikely, however, that Jesus would quote scripture, defend it against the Pharisees, and then agree with his disciples' objection to it, nor does it seem reasonable that he would refer to their objection rather than scripture as "this word." Further, Jesus's use of the word *eunuch* rather than *virgin* or *unmarried* suggests that those who cannot receive marriage are not simply celibate but somehow asexual, that is, neither male nor female, and therefore not an exception to God's intent in creation.

5. I am indebted to Laurence R. Iannaccone's manuscript "Women and the Word of God" for this understanding of the significance of Jesus's reference to creation.

6. Feminists dislike this version of creation, which was often used to support hierarchy in marriage, and indeed biblical scholars of the twentieth century proposed that Genesis 1 and 2 are actually contradictory accounts, written by different people at different times and coming out of opposing traditions.

7. Phyllis Trible, *God and the Rhetoric of Sexuality* (Philadelphia: Fortress, 1978), 80.

8. Thomas Lewis, Fari Amini, and Richard Lannon, *A General Theory of Love* (New York: Random House, 2000), 69–70.

9. Gilbert Bilezikian, *Beyond Sex Roles* (Grand Rapids: Baker, 1985), 255.

10. Joy Elasky Fleming, *Man and Woman in Biblical Unity* (Minneapolis: Christians for Biblical Equality, 1993), 8–9. That we don't use "help" in this sense any more is verified by the grammar checker on my computer, which flags it as ungrammatical.

11. Ibid., 8.

12. Ibid., 9.

13. David Freedman, "Woman, a Power Equal to Man," *Biblical Archaeology Review* 9, no. 1 (January-February 1983): 58.

14. Trible, *God and the Rhetoric*, 90.

15. Annie Wickstrom in "Lynn Minton Reports, Fresh Voices: Do You Expect Fidelity When You Marry?" *Parade*, July 4, 1999.

16. Martin Luther, *Lectures on Genesis*, in *Luther's Works*, vol. 1, ed. Jaroslav Pelikan (St. Louis: Concordia Publishing House, 1958).

17. The interweaving of the two texts is also seen in the separation of the waters and the dry land (Gen. 1) but not their integration in rain because there was as yet no one to cultivate the land (Gen. 2).

18. Thanks to Patti Ricotta for pointing this out.

19. Plato, *The Symposium*.

## Chapter 2 The Economics of the Fall and the Subordination of Women

1. Martin Luther, *Lectures on Genesis*, in *Luther's Works*, vol. 1, ed. Jaroslav Pelikan (St. Louis: Concordia Publishing House, 1958).

2. For example, when Fanny Longfellow, wife of the poet, took chloroform during the birth of one of her children, her sister scolded her for eluding God's will. Queen Victoria's use of chloroform in childbirth apparently ended religious objections to it. Bhavani-Shankar Modali, "Pain Relief Options during Childbirth," www.painfreebirthing.com/evolution.htm.

3. Joy Elasky Fleming, *Man and Woman in Biblical Unity* (Minneapolis: Christians for Biblical Equality, 1993), 28–29. Phyllis Trible, *God and the Rhetoric of Sexuality* (Philadelphia: Fortress, 1978), 129–30.

4. My treatment here provides an explanatory foundation for many similar conclusions reached by Mary Stewart Van Leeuwen in *Gender and Grace: Love, Work, and Parenting in a Changing World* (Downers Grove, IL: InterVarsity Press, 1990).

5. Ruth Schwartz Cowan, *More Work for Mother: The Ironies of Household Technology from the Open Hearth to the Microwave* (New York: Basic Books, 1983), 32.

6. Olwen Hufton, *The Prospect before Her* (New York: Vintage, 1998), 64.

7. Adam Smith, *An Inquiry into the Nature and Causes of the Wealth of Nations* (New York: Modern Library, 1937), 70–71.

8. Thomas Laqueur, *Making Sex: Body and Gender from the Greeks to Freud* (Cambridge: Harvard University Press, 1990), 101.

9. Fleming, *Man and Woman*, 32.

10. Gary S. Becker, *A Treatise on the Family*, enlarged ed. (Cambridge: Harvard University Press, 1993), 38 and generally all of chap. 2, "Division of Labor in Households and Families."

11. That is, until looms became heavy and dangerous pieces of equipment that were rented for limited periods; then men did the weaving.

12. Ruth Bleier, *Science and Gender: A Critique of Biology and Its Theories on Women* (New York: Pergamon, 1984); Becker, *Treatise on the Family*, 43n.

13. Young women today are probably less cheered by Proverbs 31 than were we. What woman can read "Her lamp does not go out at night" today and not feel tired?

14. Karen Sacks, *Sisters and Wives: The Past and Future of Sexual Equality* (Westport, CT: Greenwood, 1979), 93.

15. Jill Ker Conway, *True North* (New York: Borzoi, 1994), 234.

16. Cowan, *More Work for Mother*, 207.

17. Ibid.

18. Ibid., 165, 170.

19. Even sexual dimorphism, the tendency for the males of many species to be bigger than the females, makes more sense when seen in terms of feminine rather than masculine needs. Men are not larger than women are because they need to be stronger to protect them; women are smaller than men in order to preserve scarce calories for the requirements of pregnancy and nursing (rather than to support body mass).

20. Becker, *Treatise on the Family*, 43.

21. Ibid., 33.

22. While it is undeniably true that men on average are stronger than women are, greater male upper-body strength does not make much sense of women's historic subordination to men. Strength is a relative dimension, and some women are stronger than some men. More telling, however, is the observation that the male status hierarchy does not depend on physical strength. Weak but rich old men have more status and power than strong poor men do. There is no reason that possessing greater strength should make men dominant over women when it does not make them dominant over other men.

23. Becker, *Treatise on the Family*, 30–31.

24. Ibid., 40.

25. Margaret F. Brinig and Douglas W. Allen, "'These Boots Are Made for Walking': Why Most Divorce Filers Are Women," *American Law and Economics Association*, 2000, 126–69. This line of reasoning is analogous to economic analyses of "firm-specific" versus general human capital.

26. S. Scott Bartchy, "Undermining Ancient Patriarchy," *Biblical Theology Bulletin* 29 (1999): 68–78, quotation on 68.

27. Becker, *Treatise on the Family*, 88, 90, 90n.

28. Evolutionary psychologists such as David Buss (*The Evolution of Desire*) argue that the characteristics we find attractive signal health and fertility (clear skin and eyes, symmetry of features, wide hips, and full breasts). Fads and fashions in what people find sexually attractive, however, suggest that such a claim cannot be made so simply. For example, although throughout history men have liked women with wide hips, a recent survey found that young American men said they found "wide hips" on women unattractive.

29. Becker points out that men's great variability in productive capacity also explains the prevalence of polygamy (or more accurately, polygyny, in which one man is simultaneously married to more than one wife). A woman (or her family) may find it more to her advantage to be the twelfth wife of a wealthy man than to be the only wife of a pauper. Eighty-five percent of all human cultures have practiced polygyny. Becker, *Treatise on the Family*, 88, 90, 90n.

30. Melford E. Spiro, *Gender and Culture: Kibbutz Women Revisited* (1979; reprint New Brunswick, NJ: Transaction, 1996).

31. The fact that men have a greater propensity to violence than do women is often used as evidence of just how different men and women really are—and to suggest that manhood (and testosterone) is dangerous. Much of this difference in expressions of violence, however, can be explained by the different pressures placed on men. For example, in her book *Men, Women, and Aggression* (New York: BasicBooks, 1993), Anne Campbell concludes that men and even little boys use aggression instrumentally, that is, in order to get something they want. She reports that mothers and teachers insist that they disapprove of and punish aggressive behavior in little boys. But, she notes, despite the punishment, the aggressive boy is still most likely to end up with the toy. And often what boys are really fighting for is not the toy but social dominance and the respect of other children. Aggression readily provides that to boys, despite punishment from adults. In contrast, Campbell observes that women's use of physical violence tends to be expressive, that is, occurring when they have lost control of their emotions. My own analysis suggests that girls and women use violence less often than men because there is little they want that can be gained by physical aggression (although in *Odd Girl Out* [New York: Harvest/Harcourt, 2003, chap. 7], Rachel Simmons observes that physical violence among girls is more common in some nonwhite ethnic groups). The material pressures on girls and women lead them to want to be admired—and no one will think a girl pretty because she slugs someone. Similarly, women are less likely than men to engage in violent crime because it is easier and safer for a female to extract money by using her sexuality than by using her fists or a weapon. Simmons finds that girls' aggression tends to be social and emotional rather than physical.

32. Deirdre McCloskey, personal conversation.

33. An example of the fears and confusion that continue to permeate contemporary male-female interactions may be found in a Valentine's Day column expressing alarm at the "decline of courtship" among today's young singles (William Raspberry, "Love's Dying Ritual," *Washington Post*, February 14, 2005). The columnist, William Raspberry, quotes from a paper written by a young woman student about a sorority event she attended with a boy she had invited because she "needed a date" and thought he was cute. After the party, she wrote, she went back to his room with him "'to talk,' but obviously talking turned into making out." Afterward, "I walked home late at night by myself. He offered for me to stay at his place, but I said that I would just walk home. He responded with false concern, asking if I would be OK going back by myself. I promised him I would be fine. This dialogue is standard. The boy cannot appear too apathetic, the girl cannot act too needy and dependent. We are afraid to forfeit the independence that took so many years to acquire in return for an escort back to the dorm. . . . He and I could have a future together, but we will never know. There will never be a next date. If he were to ask me out next weekend, he would appear weak. I could not ask him out again for fear of appearing obsessed." Raspberry concludes,

"What a dysfunctional, ego-destructive and profoundly sad 'equality' the young folk have fashioned.

"Do you suppose any of them send—or receive—Valentine's Day cards?"

## Chapter 3   Jesus, Power, and Marriage

1. This chapter owes a great deal to two talks by S. Scott Bartchy: "Jesus, Women, and Power," presented at Sunstone Symposium, Salt Lake City, 1997, and "Undermining Ancient Patriarchy," at Sunstone West Symposium, Los Angeles, 2000. Gilbert Bilezikian also makes many of these same points in *Beyond Sex Roles: What the Bible Says about a Woman's Place in Church and Family*, 2nd ed. (Grand Rapids: Baker, 1985).

2. Plutarch, a prominent Greek moralist, wrote that wives should feel honored if their husbands looked to other women for satisfaction of their baser lusts. Plutarch, "Advice on Marriage," quoted in David deSilva, *Honor, Patronage, Kinship, and Purity* (Downers Grove, IL: InterVarsity Press, 2000), 178.

3. In all of these statements, Jesus makes the exception that divorce is allowable for the innocent party. It becomes apparent in the writings of Paul that it was remarriage that was the problem for Christians; separation in the interest of "peace" was acceptable (1 Cor. 7).

4. Couples could not marry without some accumulation of resources. The girl's share of those resources was normally called a dowry, and it was basically her share of her father's estate. Those girls whose families were too poor to provide them with a dowry often worked as servants in someone else's household until they had saved up enough money to provide their own marriage fund.

5. Bilezikian, *Beyond Sex Roles*, 94.

6. Ibid., 95.

7. See deSilva's excellent chapters on purity in *Honor, Patronage* for a more detailed explanation of this practice.

8. Everett Ferguson, *Background of Early Christianity* (Grand Rapids: Eerdmans, 1993), 71.

9. Leonard Swidler, *Biblical Affirmations of Woman* (Philadelphia: Westminster Press, 1979), 276. As Anita Diamant's novel *The Red Tent* (New York: Picador, 1998) points out, women's regular periods of "uncleanliness" provided a time of rest and freedom from mundane labor. Similarly, periods of ritual uncleanliness after childbirth may have served to give new mothers a much needed break. Feminists have criticized the longer period of impurity following the birth of a girl as implying that the female is inferior and polluting. In economies that value boys over girls, however, girl babies generally receive less care than do boys, even to being given less time to breastfeed. Infant girls benefited rather than suffered from an extended period in which their mothers were restricted from doing much besides care for them. By the time of Jesus, however, laws such as these that were originally intended to protect were being used to harm. This public healing may have been intended to serve as a reminder that the law was made for people, not people for the law.

10. Carolyn Osiek and David L. Balch, *Families in the New Testament World: Households and House Churches* (Louisville: Westminster John Knox, 1997), 38.

11. Lesly F. Massey, *Women and the New Testament: An Analysis of Scripture in Light of New Testament Era Culture* (Jefferson, NC: McFarland, 1989), 14.

12. Osiek and Balch, *Families in the New Testament World*, 38.

13. Naomi Wolf, *Fire with Fire* (New York: Random House, 1993), 21.

14. S. Scott Bartchy, "Who Should Be Called Father? Paul of Tarsus between the Jesus Tradition and *Patria Potestas*," *Biblical Theology Bulletin* 33 (2003): 135–47.

15. DeSilva, *Honor, Patronage*, 75.

16. S. Scott Bartchy, "The Holy Spirit as Patron of the Christian Community," audiotape, Sunstone Symposium, Salt Lake City, 1997.

17. Bartchy, "Jesus, Women, and Power."

18. See John 12:6.

19. DeSilva, *Honor, Patronage*, 23 and the entire book.

20. Ibid., 71; Bartchy, "Jesus, Women, and Power."

21. Brent Walters, "Lectures on Women in the New Testament," Ante-Nicene Archives, San Jose, California, 1996.

22. Private observation from Laurence R. Iannaccone.

23. Observation by Linda M. Ikeda, a licensed marriage and family counselor. Marriage counselors Andrew and Judith Lester write: "As a male you may have internalized to some degree the tradition that as a man you should have more power than women, specifically power *over* women. You have been raised to function in hierarchical structures, seeking status in over/under relationships, and you will have to guard against bringing that same worldview into your marriage. Husbands are particularly vulnerable when the relationship is under stress, and these deeply ingrained constructions of reality insert themselves into their interactions. Suddenly, a couple is in a power struggle" (Andrew D. Lester and Judith L. Lester, *It Takes Two: The Joy of Intimate Marriage* [Louisville: Westminster John Knox, 1998]).

24. Bartchy, "Jesus, Women, and Power."

25. Bilezikian, *Beyond Sex Roles*, 116.

26. Bartchy, "Jesus, Women, and Power." Jesus's redefinition of what it means to be "lord" shows that attempts to update the Bible by eliminating "lordship" language miss the point.

27. Sara Butler, quoted in Stanley J. Grenz with Denise Muir Kjesbo, *Women and the Church: A Biblical Theology of Women in Ministry* (Downers Grove, IL: InterVarsity Press, 1995), 209.

28. Interestingly, the images of abundance that Jesus used—lilies and the comparison with Solomon's glory—are also used in the Song of Songs.

29. Andrew Chestnut, *Born Again in Brazil: The Pentecostal Boom and the Pathogens of Poverty* (Rutgers, NJ: Rutgers University Press, 1997).

30. Don Browning, "The Problem of Men," in *Does Christianity Teach Male Headship? The Equal-Regard Marriage and Its Critics*, ed. David Blankenhorn, Don Browning, and Mary Stewart Van Leeuwen (Grand Rapids: Eerdmans, 2004), 3.

31. Compassion International website, www.compassion.com/about/compassionfaq/default.htm#aboutusfaq6.

## Chapter 4  The Mystery of Marriage in Everyday Life

1. Craig S. Keener, *Paul, Women, and Wives: Marriage and Women's Ministry in the Letters of Paul* (Peabody, MA: Hendrickson, 1992), 167–68; David L. Balch, "Household Codes," in *Greco-Roman Literature and the New Testament*, ed. David E. Aune, SBLSBS 21 (Atlanta: Scholars Press, 1988), 25.

2. Balch, "Household Codes," 26–29. Some twentieth-century theologians in fact used Ephesians 5–6 to support their notion of the "chain of command," with God over man, man over his wife, and the couple together over their children, an idea with which the Greeks and Romans would have been comfortable.

3. S. Scott Bartchy, "Undermining Ancient Patriarchy," *Biblical Theology Bulletin* 29 (1999): 68–78.

4. David deSilva, *Honor, Patronage, Kinship, and Purity* (Downers Grove, IL: InterVarsity Press, 2000), 107–119.

5. Ibid., 136–37.

6. Ibid., 155.

7. Andrew Christensen and Neil S. Jacobson, *Reconcilable Differences* (New York: Guilford, 2000), 124.

8. For example, see the Revised Standard Version translation of Ephesians 1:22: ". . . and he has put all things under his feet."

9. F. Kinchin Smith and T. W. Melluish, *Greek* (Warwick Lane, London: Teach Yourself Books, St. Paul's House, 1972), 128.

10. However, while the middle voice occurs in the reflexive, as in this example, it can also be an indirect reflexive, intransitive, causative, possessive, reciprocal reflexive, have a "developed meaning," and be something called a deponent verb. The ending of the word indicates which voice a verb is in. Smith and Melluish admit that "it is all a little frightening at first" (*Greek*, 130). I confess that I stuck with Greek through tense, gender, number, and cases—all of which change the word ending—but when I hit voices, I gave up trying to learn to read Greek on sight. All of this means that it can be very difficult for an English speaker to translate a verb in the middle voice.

11. S. Scott Bartchy, private conversation.

12. The New Testament is full of directives for Christians to submit themselves to others: Christians to their leaders (Heb. 13:17, "Have confidence in your leaders, and submit to their authority") and to worldly authority (1 Peter 2:13, "Submit yourselves for the Lord's sake to every human authority"; Titus 3:1, "Remind the people to be subject to rulers and authorities"; Rom. 13:1, "Everyone must submit himself to the governing authorities"); younger people to their elders (1 Peter 5:5, "Young men, in the same way be submissive to those who are older. All of you, clothe yourselves with humility toward one another"); slaves to masters (1 Peter 2:18, "Slaves, in reverent fear of God submit yourselves to your masters"); Christians to God (James 4:7, "Submit yourselves, then, to God"); and the church to Christ (Eph. 5:24, "Now as the church submits to Christ").

13. Carolyn Osiek and David L. Balch, *Families in the New Testament World: Households and House Churches* (Louisville: Westminster John Knox, 1997), 76; S. Scott Bartchy, *First Century Slavery and 1 Corinthians 7:21* (Eugene, OR: Wipf and Stock, 2003), 58; Rodney Stark, *The Rise of Christianity* (Princeton, NJ: Princeton University Press, 1996), 151–56.

14. Bartchy, "Undermining Ancient Patriarchy"; Osiek and Balch, *Families in the New Testament World*, 53.

15. Bartchy, "Undermining Ancient Patriarchy," 68.

16. Stark, *Rise of Christianity*, 105. Stark notes that while scholars once believed these marriages to young girls were not immediately consummated, his evidence suggests they were.

17. Osiek and Balch, *Families in the New Testament World*, 61.

18. Plutarch, quoted in ibid., 63; Stark, *Rise of Christianity*, 117.

19. I draw heavily on Laurence R. Iannaccone's manuscript "Women and the Word of God" for insights gained in his analysis of slave-master, child-father, wife-husband relationships.

20. Bartchy, *First Century Slavery*, 47.

21. Ibid., 72–73; Osiek and Balch, *Families in the New Testament World*, 77.

22. Bartchy, *First Century Slavery*, 47.

23. A common pagan practice was to "expose" or abandon unwanted infants. Many of these children died, but some were picked up by slave traders and raised as slaves (Osiek and Balch, *Families in the New Testament World*, 65; Bartchy *First Century Slavery*, 45). Prostitution was a common fate of these children.

24. Bartchy, *First Century Slavery*, 70.

25. Ibid., 79–82.

26. Keener, *Paul, Women, and Wives*, 204; Bartchy, *First Century Slavery*, 48.

27. Keener, *Paul, Women, and Wives*, 204.

28. All citations of Ephesians 5:21–6:9 in this chapter are my own translation, based on Alfred Marshall, *The RSV Interlinear Greek-English New Testament* (Grand Rapids: Zondervan, 1975). For this passage see also Bartchy's exegesis in *First Century Slavery*.

29. This is the course Paul recommends in his letter to Philemon. Philemon's slave Onesimus apparently sought shelter with Paul in the midst of a dispute with his master. Acknowledging Philemon's legal rights, Paul sent Onesimus home, but without making overt demands, he clearly asked Philemon to free Onesimus and accept him back as a brother in Christ (Philem. 8–21).

30. This ambiguous phrase has been interpreted a number of ways. Osiek and Balch, for example, believe that Paul is telling wives and slaves to submit to their master as if he were the Lord (*Families in the New Testament World*, 184). Finding this directive unacceptable and inconsistent with Paul's other writings, they therefore dismiss the letter to the Ephesians as the work of a "deutero-Paul," i.e., a false Paul who wrote in imitation of the original.

31. DeSilva writes, "The tendency of New Testament authors to speak of Jesus as 'Savior' is also in keeping with his role as benefactor, for the term was applied as an honorary term to great and powerful figures who brought a city deliverance

from an enemy, provided famine relief and removed other threats to the well-being and stability of a group of people" (*Honor, Patronage*, 140–41).

32. Richard Cervin, "Does *kephale* (Head) Mean 'Source' or 'Authority Over' in Greek Literature? A Rebuttal" (St. Paul: Christians for Biblical Equality, n.d.). *Kephale* appears to have acquired the metaphorical meaning of "ruler" later, but Cervin notes that while a modern Greek speaker agreed that *kephale* could mean "top authority" in modern Greek, he thought it sounded "a little funny" (19n).

33. Brian Neuschwander, "Women as 'Master of the House,'" www.beachcitygas .com/writing/despotis2.htm.

34. As in English, the Hebrew word *r'osh* has the literal meaning of head, the body part, and the metaphorical meaning of leader. When the Old Testament was translated from Hebrew into Greek, the translators were careful to distinguish when *r'osh* designated "leader" and when it meant the body part (Cervin). Paul, who knew both languages, would not have used *kephale* when he meant *arche*.

35. Cervin, "Does *kephale* (Head) Mean 'Source,'" 19.

36. This is not, incidentally, what Grudem thought he had proved. He was trying to prove that *kephale* meant "authority over" and not "source" as egalitarians argue. In 2,336 cases of the use of *kephale* in Greek literature, Grudem found no cases where it was used to mean "source," 49 where it means a "person of superior authority or rank, or 'ruler,' 'ruling part'" (although Gilbert Bilezikian, claiming Grudem's categorization was methodologically flawed, discounts both of these numbers), but 2,034 instances of *kephale* referring to the physical head of a human being or an animal. Summary by Wayne Grudem, in the appendix to *The Role Relationship of Men and Women* by George W. Knight III (Chicago: Moody Press, 1977, 1985). Cited in Gilbert Bilezikian, *Beyond Sex Roles: What the Bible Says about a Woman's Place in Church and Family*, 2nd ed. (Grand Rapids: Baker, 1985), 216.

37. Heinrich Schlier, "anakephalaiomai," in *Theological Dictionary of the New Testament*, ed. Gerhard Kittel (Grand Rapids: Eerdmans, 1964), 3:681–82.

38. Bradley Gerstman, Christopher Pizzo, and Rich Seldes, *Marry Me! Three Professional Men Reveal How to Get Mr. Right to Pop the Question* (New York: Cliff Street, 2000), 250.

39. Because of gross misunderstanding of 1 Corinthians 11, Paul's calling woman the "glory" of the man ends up being used to argue that she should be subordinate.

40. John Gottman and Nan Silver, *The Seven Principles for Making Marriage Work* (New York: Three Rivers, 1999).

41. DeSilva, *Honor, Patronage*.

42. Thomas Lewis, Fari Amini, and Richard Lannon, *A General Theory of Love* (New York: Random House, 2000), 85 and throughout the book.

43. Ibid., 142–144.

44. Judith S. Wallerstein and Sandra Blakeslee, *The Good Marriage: How and Why Love Lasts* (New York: Time Warner, 1995), 92 and pt. 3.

45. Ibid., 93.

46. Bartchy, "Undermining Ancient Patriarchy."

47. G. Bornkamm, "Mysterion," *Theological Dictionary of the New Testament*, ed Gerhard Kittel (Grand Rapids: Eerdmans, 1964), 4:805, 820, 822.

48. S. Scott Bartchy, "Power, Submission and Sexual Identity Among the Early Christians," *Essays on New Testament Christianity*, ed. C. Robert Wetzel (Cincinnati: Standard Publishing, 1978): 50–80.

49. Don Hammond, sermon, Church of the Chimes, San Jose, California, 2002.

50. Gottman and Silver, *Seven Principles*, 234.

51. In contrast to Roman custom, Paul taught that parents were not bound by the social obligation to marry off their children at young ages and could keep them at home unmarried: "But if anyone thinks that this is a bad thing [unbecoming] for his unmarried child [to remain unmarried], if he or she [the virgin] is of betrothal age ['past the bloom of youth'], and it [the match] is appropriate, let him do as he wishes. He doesn't sin; let them marry. But one who stands firm in heart, who is not under necessity, but has authority concerning his own will and has decided in heart to keep his child unmarried, he does well. So both the one giving his unmarried child in marriage does well, and the one not giving in marriage does better" (1 Cor. 7:36–38).

He specifies that if the boy or girl is be given in marriage, they should be past puberty ("the bloom of youth") and the match should be fitting. Paul's caveats about the parent's being "firm in the heart" and "having authority concerning his own will," however, suggest that parents themselves may not always have had complete control of keeping a child at home indefinitely. Preexisting betrothal contracts could have been very difficult to get out of, and the children themselves may have had strong feelings in the matter—hence Paul's statement about behaving in a becoming manner toward the child (my own translation, based on Brent Walters, "Lectures on Women in the New Testament," Ante-Nicene Archives, San Jose, California, 1996). The possible interpretation of this passage as referring to parents and children rather than a man and his fiancée (the usual understanding) is noted in the New English Bible, The American Standard Version, and the New American Bible. The word usually translated "fiancée" (in the NIV/TNIV) or "betrothed" (RSV) is actually "virgin" and is gender-neutral (that is, can refer to a male or a female).

52. Stark, *Rise of Christianity*, 107.

53. Ibid., 104.

54. Some even entered slavery themselves in exchange for the manumission of a fellow Christian (1 Clement 55:2, cited in Bartchy, *First Century Slavery*, 48).

55. S. Scott Bartchy, "The Holy Spirit as Patron of the Christian Community," audiotape, Sunstone Symposium, Salt Lake City, 1997; Galatians 3:28.

56. In fairness to the Romans, this was one "natural" family practice of which they, being so short of women, were not guilty.

57. Eric Fuchs, *Sexual Desire and Love: Origins and History of the Christian Ethic of Sexuality and Marriage* (New York: Seabury, 1983), 46; Robert A. J. Gagnon, *The Bible and Homosexual Practice* (Nashville: Abingdon, 2001), 100–110.

58. Shailer Matthews, *The Social Teachings of Jesus: An Essay in Christian Sociology* (New York: Macmillan, 1897), 191–97.

59. Richard Posner, *Sex and Reason* (Cambridge: Harvard University Press, 1994), 45.

60. Rodney Clapp, *Families at the Crossroads* (Downers Grove, IL: InterVarsity Press, 1993), 13, 35.

## Chapter 5  Love in an Age of Wealth

1. Ruth Schwartz Cowan, *More Work for Mother: The Ironies of Household Technology from the Open Hearth to the Microwave* (New York: Basic Books, 1983).

2. Ibid., 49.

3. Ibid., 78.

4. Ibid., 41–42.

5. Ibid., 64.

6. David Blankenhorn, *Fatherless America: Confronting Our Most Urgent Social Problem* (New York: BasicBooks, 1995), 13. Blankenhorn notes that eighteenth-century childrearing manuals were directed to fathers, but in the next century they gradually changed to address mothers.

7. Cowan, *More Work for Mother*, 100.

8. Howard Kandel, comedy routine.

9. Cowan, *More Work for Mother*, 100.

10. Ibid., 67.

11. Viviana A. Zelizer, *Pricing the Priceless Child* (Princeton, NJ: Princeton University Press, 1985), 6.

12. For the first two figures, U.S. Department of Commerce, Bureau of the Census, "Birth Rate—Total and for Women 15–44 Years Old," in *Historical Statistics of the United States: Colonial Times to 1970* (Washington, DC: U.S. Government Printing Office, 1975), 49. For the last, table 93, "Characteristics of Women Who Have Had a Child in the Last Year, 1995–1998," in *Statistical Abstract of the United States*, Internet version, www.census.gov/prod/2001pubs/statab/sec02.pdf.

13. Cowan, *More Work for Mother*, 43, and U.S. Census Bureau, "Population Profile of the United States: 2000," Internet version, www.census.gov/ population/ pop-profile/2000/chap04.pdf. Historian Ruth Schwartz Cowan's fascinating history of the impact of the industrial revolution makes much of the fact that the tasks performed by men and children were the first to leave the economically productive household. Why, she asks, was it not women's work that left the home? Why do we not find instead neighborhood communal kitchens and men at home doing smithy work in the backyard? Her book *More Work for Mother* was published in 1983, without the benefit of economist Gary S. Becker's explanation for the sexual division of labor. Without Becker's model, Cowan can only guess that women's traditional work was the last to be "industrialized" because that pattern fit with nineteenth-century social conventions (*More Work for Mother*, 150). Within the framework of Becker's model, however, we see that the "women's work" that stayed in the home—cooking, cleaning, infant care, caring for sick children—and tasks that left the home and came back again, such as laundry, remained women's work

because whether in the first, nineteenth, or twentieth century, these were and still are the tasks that are compatible with childbearing. Granted, late-twentieth-century couples were having far fewer children, but as long as they were having any at all, and as long as women were the ones who bore them, the physical demands of pregnancy, recovery from childbirth, and breastfeeding (not to mention the strong physical bond that most women feel with their newborns) continued to dictate that women be the ones at home with their children. And as long as you are at home, it is probably easier and certainly less expensive to do the laundry, cleaning, and cooking yourself rather than "outsource" them. I myself found that housekeeping was just about the only work I could do with young children at home. Combining childcare with work requiring extended concentration (in my case, writing, scholarly research, class preparation) or quiet (making phone calls) can be very difficult.

14. The social and moral upheavals of the 1960s should not be considered as discrete events but rather as a continuation of trends in family life and sexuality that had been well under way for decades but were interrupted by the Great Depression, World War II, and the reactive, but temporary, return to domesticity that followed them in the 1950s.

15. Betty Friedan, *The Feminine Mystique* (London: Penguin, 1963).

16. Another staple of the twentieth-century gender wars was the inept father (or child) who couldn't operate the washing machine and ended up with a room full of suds. I always thought this too unrealistic to be funny until it happened to me in Italy. I read enough Italian to recognize the word for soap, but not enough to distinguish dish soap from dishwasher detergent. Using the wrong soap really does result in those "Mr. Mom" mountains of bubbles (but it still isn't funny).

17. Carol A. Newson and Sharon H. Ringe, eds., *The Women's Bible Commentary* (Louisville: Westminster John Knox, 1992), 247.

18. Tom Smith, "The Emerging 21st Century American Family," National Opinion Research Center, University of Chicago, November 24, 1999, 31, table 8.

19. Linda J. Waite and Evelyn L. Lehrer, "The Benefits from Marriage and Religion in the United States: A Comparative Analysis," *Population and Development Review* 29, no. 2 (June 2003): 255–75.

20. Sylvia Hewlett, *Creating a Life: Professional Women and the Quest for Children* (New York: Talk Miramax Books, 2002), 143.

21. Caryn James, "A Baby Boom on TV as Biological Clocks Cruelly Tick Away," *New York Times*, October 16, 1991, C15, and Katha Pollitt, "Bothered and Bewildered," *New York Times*, July 22, 1993; quoted in Blankenhorn, *Fatherless America*, 76, 77.

22. Peggy Orenstein, *Flux: Women on Sex, Work, Love, Kids, and Life in a Half-Changed World* (New York: Doubleday, 2000), 99.

Another effect of women's growing financial independence is that for the first time, women share the hitherto male prerogatives of choosing partners based on their physical attractiveness (see my discussion of this in chapter 2). "No pecs, no sex," warned one advertisement for a gym. Heterosexual men have, in response, become more concerned with and spend more time and money on clothing, hair, and fitness than before. The phenomenon of the "Metrosexual"—straight men whose emphasis on their appearance seems more typical of gay men—is less about acceptance of gay culture than about being physically attractive to women.

23. Waite and Lehrer, "Benefits from Marriage and Religion," 258.

24. Sue Shellenbarger, "The Sole Breadwinner's Lament: Having Mom at Home Isn't as Great as It Sounds," *Wall Street Journal*, October 10, 2003, D1.

25. U.S. Census Bureau, *Statistical Abstract of the United States: 2003*, table 63.

26. U.S. Census Bureau, *USA Statistics in Brief: Population and Vital Statistics* (Washington, DC: U.S. Government Printing Office, 2004).

27. U.S. Census Bureau, "Households by Type and Size, 1900–2002," no. HS-12, in *Statistical Abstract of the U.S.: 2003*.

28. Gary S. Becker, *A Treatise on the Family* (Cambridge: Harvard University Press, 1993), 30–31.

29. Smith, "Emerging 21st Century American Family," 1–2. Smith noted, "The 33–34% level is lower than the commonly cited figure that 'half of all marriages end in divorce.' The latter is a projection of how many married people will *eventually* divorce."

30. A 1989 study of U.S. Census records and researchers at the University of Wisconsin, cited (without further reference) in John Gottman, *Why Marriages Succeed or Fail . . . and How You Can Make Yours Last* (New York: Simon and Schuster, 1994).

31. For example, Voltaire wrote, "It is an infantile superstition of the human spirit that virginity would be thought a virtue and not the barrier that separates ignorance from knowledge" (www.famousquotes.ws/dp/2–36.htm).

32. Richard Dawkins, *The Selfish Gene* (New York: Oxford University Press, 1990).

33. From an item in the *San Francisco Chronicle*. The writer could not tell me the source.

34. In an animal species in which the males and females look markedly different, it is the male, not the female, that is the beautiful one—maybe he is more colorful, has a long, extravagant tail or a fancy topknot, or is much bigger.

35. Dawkins, *Selfish Gene*, 150.

36. Ibid.

37. Becker, *Treatise on the Family*, 30–31.

38. Dawkins, *Selfish Gene*, 150.

39. Feminists complain that men controlled women's sexuality under patriarchy, but the proof that they didn't lies in the fact that men didn't usually get what they wanted. If male biology controlled sexuality, old-fashioned morality would have looked a lot more like that of the present day.

40. Richard Posner notes cases in which middle- and upper-class women would complain when poor women presumed to marry.

41. In the 1980s, Gary Becker raised the ire of feminists, who were strongly advocating the adoption of no-fault divorce laws, by warning that such laws

would prove detrimental to women. Earlier marital dissolution laws required the consent of both parties, which if not given voluntarily had to be won through a lawsuit. In Becker's understanding, this meant that the partner who wanted out of the marriage had to pay off the other party, whether through a generous property settlement, alimony, child support, or child custody agreement. Today the divorce itself can be granted quickly, with the property settlement taking place afterward, a situation that can put the less financially well-off partner at a severe disadvantage.

42. Laurence R. Iannaccone, personal conversation.

43. Cowan, *More Work for Mother*, 29–30.

44. Arlie Russell Hochschild, *The Time Bind: When Work Becomes Home and Home Becomes Work* (New York: Metropolitan Books, Henry Holt, 1997), 25.

45. Ibid., 75.

46. Ibid., 25.

47. Ibid. Interestingly, despite her findings that few people were interested in spending less time at work, Hochschild concludes by calling for more "family-friendly" policies and regulations.

48. Ellen Galinsky, James T. Bond, and Dana E. Friedman, *The Changing Workforce: Highlights of the National Study* (New York: Families and Work Institute, 1993), 98; cited in Hochschild, *Time Bind*, 34.

49. Hochschild, *Time Bind*, 185.

50. The female sexual cartel is not entirely dead, however. Consider an item in a newspaper column written during the sex scandal involving President Bill Clinton: "My friend Riva is very upset. 'Monica Lewinsky crossed a line,' she says. 'This oral sex thing—everyone knows Jewish girls don't do that. Now she's ruined it for the rest of us'" (Anne Beatts, "What Jews Don't Do Besides, Well, That," *San Francisco Chronicle*, February 8, 1998, E8).

51. William A. Galston, "Beyond the Murphy Brown Debate: Ideas for Family Policy" (New York: Institute for American Values, 1993), 8.

52. Smith, "Emerging 21st Century American Family," 2.

53. Survey conducted in 1994, reported in www.ncbi.nlm.nih.gov/entrez/query .fcgi?cmd=Retrieve&db=PubMed&list_uids=9711454&dopt=Abstract. The numbers have dropped since then, but whether due to abstinence education programs or a switch to oral sex is not clear.

54. Thomas Schmidt, *Straight and Narrow?* (Downers Grove, IL: InterVarsity Press, 1995). In 1 Corinthians 6:9–10 Paul had to coin a word to refer to homosexuals. *Arsenokoitai* is a direct Greek translation of the Hebrew "men-bedders" condemned in Leviticus 18:22 and 20:13. The *malakoi* also criticized in these verses, "the soft ones," probably were effeminate men or cross-dressers. The term *homosexual* comes from Germany and originally referred to a disease state (Schmidt, *Straight and Narrow?* 23). Homosexuals themselves coined the term *gay* in the middle of the twentieth century to offset the public perception of homosexuals as depressed and isolated.

55. Plato, *The Symposium;* quoted in Robert A. J. Gagnon, *The Bible and Homosexual Practice* (Nashville: Abingdon, 2001), 357.

56. Pseudo-Lucian, *Affairs of the Heart*, c. 300 C.E.; quoted in Gagnon, *Bible and Homosexual Practice*, 357.

57. Cowan, *More Work for Mother*, 25.

58. These things seemed to be linked to marriage now only because these were things produced in marriage in the past. Indeed, Allan C. Carlson objects that "a series of recommendations from the American Law Institute . . . would strip traditional marriage of most of its distinctive legal status—not by direct repeal, but rather by extending the protections afforded by marriage to other relationships," such as "cohabitating domestic partners, both heterosexual and homosexual," in David Machachek, "Same-Sex Culture War," *Religion in the News* 7, no. 1 (spring 2004).

59. Cowan, *More Work for Mother*, 101.

60. Juliet B. Schor, *Born to Buy: The Commercialized Child and the New Consumer Culture* (New York: Scribner, 2004); quoted in Michelle Singletary, "The Color of Money," *Washington Post*, November 14, 2004, F1.

## Chapter 6   Reclaiming the Garden in the World of Thorns

1. In 1992, a rather badly written novel featuring this theme became a huge bestseller. Robert Waller's *Bridges of Madison County* featured a married woman falling "in love" with an itinerant photographer. Concerned about her children's welfare and her husband's reputation, she stays in her marriage, but any moral scruple the character might suffer over her adultery is more than justified by the strength of her emotions.

2. Harville Hendrix, *Getting the Love You Want* (New York: Henry Holt, 1988), 88.

3. Ibid., 30.

4. Ibid., 35. Hendrix's clinical work focuses on moving our expectations about what love should provide from the childish unconscious to a mature consciousness.

5. For example, see Watchman Nee, *Song of Songs* (Fort Washington, PA: Christian Literature Crusade, 1965; first published in China, 1945).

6. Tim and Beverly LaHaye even find instruction in sexual techniques in the Song of Songs (*The Act of Marriage: The Beauty of Sexual Love* [Grand Rapids: Zondervan, 1976]). One of the more beautifully rendered of the "erotic love" translations is *The Song of Songs: A New Translation*, by Ariel Bloch and Chana Bloch (Berkeley: University of California Press, 1995).

7. Hebrew, like any living tongue, changed throughout the years as its speakers were exposed to other languages and cultures. The Hebrew usage in the Song of Songs indicates that the poem was written in roughly the third century B.C.E., perhaps seven hundred years after King Solomon lived (Bloch and Bloch, *Song of Songs*, 25).

8. These sources include the New Revised Standard Version, the Revised Standard Version, the New International Version, the Jerusalem Bible, James Moffatt's translation, and Bloch and Bloch, *Song of Songs*.

9. In Hebrew, the original language of the Song of Songs, the gender and number of the pronouns used indicates when it is the Lover, the Woman, or the friends who are speaking in any particular passage. Unfortunately, this is not obvious in English translations, and so labels are needed. I follow the New International Version of the Bible in allocating the speeches.

10. Phyllis Trible, *God and the Rhetoric of Sexuality* (Philadelphia: Fortress, 1978), 146.

11. Bloch and Bloch, *Song of Songs*, 51.

12. Robert Alter, "Afterword," in ibid., 120.

13. Bloch and Bloch, *Song of Songs*, 55.

14. Ibid., 160–61.

15. Ibid., 163.

16. Trible, *God and the Rhetoric*, 153–55.

17. For example, see ibid., 162, or Bloch and Bloch, *Song of Songs*, 17. In a response to an earlier version of this chapter, Molly Bennion argues that the Woman complains about the Lover's late night visit because she does not want sex just then (i.e., the tunic she does not want to put on again is a provocative undergarment; "dirtying" her feet refers to intercourse). Molly McLellan Bennion, "Temporal Love: Singing the Song of Songs," *Dialogue* 36 (fall 2003): 153–58.

18. Trible, *God and the Rhetoric*, 33, 45. Trible actually understands this particular passage as indicating the Woman's sexual feelings for her Lover, but in another chapter of the same book she points out that every other biblical instance of this image indicates compassion.

19. Marvin Pope, *The Song of Songs*, Anchor Bible (New York: Doubleday, 1977).

20. Bloch and Bloch, *Song of Songs*, 200.

21. Ibid., 205, citing Michael V. Fox, *The Song of Songs and the Ancient Egyptian Love Songs* (Madison: University of Wisconsin Press, 1985).

22. The lovers' out-of-the-way trysting places suggest to some interpreters that the couple's relationship is furtive and illicit. I suggest instead that the Song's depiction of the lovers sleeping comfortably outdoors amid blossoms is another image of the wealth, safety, and honesty of true love.

23. Some scholars have proposed that the Song of Songs is not a single, integrated poem but a collection of songs sung at weddings (see, for example, the introduction to the Song of Songs in the Jerusalem Bible). The overall flow of illusions and development of themes like this one, however, argue for the Song's integrity as a single work of art.

24. Alter, "Afterword," 125.

25. Thanks to Kim McCall for pointing out the divine origin of the flash of fire (as noted in the Jerusalem Bible).

26. This chiastic structure, in which verses at the end of the poem explain passages in the beginning, is typical of Hebrew poetry. Previously established images shed light on the meaning of their latter usage, just as the latter image helps interpret the earlier ones. Once again, this alternated repetition and the

overall progression of the themes of love argue for the integrity of the Song as a single piece of literature.

27. Bloch and Bloch, *Song of Songs*, 219–20.

## Chapter 7 Christian Marriage and Family in the Twenty-first Century

1. Court judgments to parents against parties who had accidentally caused the death of their children were vastly higher for the "economically worthless" child of the 1940s and later than they had been for the wage-earning child of the previous period. Viviana A. Zelizer, *Pricing the Priceless Child: The Changing Social Value of Children* (Princeton, NJ: Princeton University Press, 1985), 5.

2. Alfred Marshall, *The R.S.V. Interlinear Greek-English New Testament* (London: Samuel Bagster and Sons, 1958), 773.

3. Thomas Lewis, Fari Amini, and Richard Lannon, *A General Theory of Love* (New York: Random House, 2000); Daniel J. Siegel, *The Developing Mind: How Relationships and the Brain Interact to Shape Who We Are* (New York: Guilford, 1999); Jennifer Roback Morse, *Love and Economics: Why the Laissez-Faire Family Doesn't Work* (Dallas: Spence, 2001). Economist and social critic Morse points out that the unattached child is exactly the kind of individual posited by classic economic theory, who always behaves in such a way as to maximize his utility.

4. Linda M. Ikeda, personal correspondence.

5. Sylvia Hewlett, *When the Bough Breaks: The Cost of Neglecting Our Children* (New York: BasicBooks, 1991), 81; quoted in Arlie Russell Hochschild, *The Time Bind: When Work Becomes Home and Home Becomes Work* (New York: Metropolitan, 1997), 10.

6. Carrie A. Miles, "Saints and Society: The Effect of Social Change on the Mormon Church," Ph.D. diss., University of Chicago, 1982; Laurence R. Iannaccone and Carrie A. Miles, "Dealing with Social Change: The Mormon Church's Response to Change in Women's Roles," *Social Forces* 68, no. 4 (June 1990): 1231–50; Sally K. Gallagher, *Evangelical Identity and Gendered Family Life* (New Brunswick, NJ: Rutgers University Press, 2003).

7. This is not to say that Paul did not expect mothers to nurture their children. Nurturing was what women did, and it did not need to be commanded.

8. Hochschild, *Time Bind*; also Peggy Orenstein., *Flux: Women on Sex, Work, Love, Kids, and Life in a Half-Changed World* (New York: Doubleday, 2000).

9. Orenstein, *Flux*, 109, citing Philip Cowan and Carolyn Pape Cowan, "New Families: Modern Couples as New Pioneers," in *All Our Families: New Policies for a New Century*, ed. Mary Ann Mason, Arlene Skolnick, and Stephen D. Sugarman (New York: Oxford University Press, 1998), 169–92.

10. Orenstein, *Flux*, 285.

11. Hochschild, *Time Bind*, 10.

12. Orenstein, *Flux*, 285.

13. Interestingly, my husband and I have observed a tendency for home schoolers to have larger than average families. Organizational theory teaches that a successful organization will expand until its least reducible component is fully

engaged. That is, if a business has a machine that works at a certain capacity, the business will seek to grow until that machine is busy all the time. Families in which the mother stays at home with children are in an analogous circumstance to a business with such a machine. The parents will continue to expand their family, or what is produced in the family, until the mother is fully occupied.

14. Hochschild, *Time Bind*, 10.

15. John Gottman and Nan Silver, *The Seven Principles for Making Marriage Work* (New York: Three Rivers, 1999), 66.

16. Ibid., 101.

17. Philip Blumstein and Pepper Schwartz, *American Couples* (New York: William Morrow, 1983).

18. Andrew D. Lester and Judith L. Lester, *It Takes Two: The Joy of Intimate Marriage* (Louiville: Westminster John Knox, 1998), 120–21.

19. Ibid., 122.

20. Gallagher, *Evangelical Identity*, 72.

21. Ibid., chap. 6; W. Bradford Wilcox, *Soft Patriarchs, New Men: How Christianity Shapes Fathers and Husbands* (Chicago: University of Chicago Press, 2004). W. Bradford Wilcox, "The Cultural Contradictions of Mainline Family Ideology and Practice," forthcoming from Columbia University Press in a book edited by Don Browning.

22. Gallagher, *Evangelical Identity*, 191, compared with figures from U.S. Census Bureau, *Statistical Abstract of the United States: 2003*. Wilcox reports similarly low rates of divorce for Christians who attend church regularly.

23. Wilcox, *Soft Patriarchs*, 182.

24. Iannaccone and Miles, "Dealing with Social Change"; Gallagher, *Evangelical Identity*; Sally K. Gallagher, "The Marginalization of Evangelical Feminism," *Sociology of Religion* 64, no. 3 (fall 2004): 215–37.

25. Orenstein, *Flux*, 71–72.

26. Heidi Brennen, summarizing letters she receives from members of her support group, Mothers at Home; quoted in David Blankenhorn, *Fatherless America: Confronting Our Most Urgent Social Problem* (New York: BasicBooks, 1995), 115.

27. Brennen, quoted in Blankenhorn, *Fatherless America*, 116.

28. Harville Hendrix, *Getting the Love You Want* (New York: Henry Holt, 1988), 90.

29. George Ricker Berry, *The Interlinear Literal Translation of the Greek New Testament* (Grand Rapids: Zondervan, 1976), 808.

30. Jennifer Roback Morse, "Why Not Take Her for a Test Drive?' *Boundless Webzine*, October 2001. See also *About Last Night . . .* This movie version of David Mamet's *Sexual Perversity in Chicago* indicts contemporary culture's failure to give young people the tools to cope with real love.

31. Philip Blumstein and Pepper Schwartz, "Intimate Relationships and the Creation of Sexuality," in *Homosexuality/Heterosexuality: Concepts of Sexual Orientation*, ed. D. P. McWhirter, S. A. Sander, and J. M. Reinisch, Kinsey Institute Series 2 (New York: Oxford University Press, 1990), 317, table 18.2; cited in

Thomas E. Schmidt, *Straight and Narrow?* (Downers Grove, IL: InterVarsity Press, 1995).

32. Katie Roiphe, *Last Night in Paradise: Sex and Morals at the Century's End* (New York: Vintage, 1997).

33. Laura Sessions Stepp, "Score Card: For Some Young Women, Love Is a Numbers Game." *Washington Post*, May 22, 2004, F1, 4.

34. *RSV Interlinear*, 605.

35. Thomas Gregory, "The Power of Peer Rejection: Interview with Richard Fitzgibbons, M.D.," NARTH website, www.narth.com/docs/peer.html; Jeffrey Satinover, *Homosexuality and the Politics of Truth* (Grand Rapids: Baker, 1996), 140–43.

36. Advocates of sexual freedom applaud early sexual activity as a means to facilitate interpersonal honesty and to promote the individuals' "comfort with their bodies," i.e., lack of shame. But consider again the story told earlier about the "decline of courtship" among today's young singles (William Raspberry, "Love's Dying Ritual," *Washington Post*, February 14, 2005; quoted in notes to chapter 2). After a sexual encounter in the dorm room of a boy she barely knew, a woman college student wrote, "I walked home late at night by myself. He offered for me to stay at his place, but I said that I would just walk home. He responded with false concern, asking if I would be OK going back by myself. I promised him I would be fine. This dialogue is standard. The boy cannot appear too apathetic, the girl cannot act too needy and dependent. We are afraid to forfeit the independence that took so many years to acquire in return for an escort back to the dorm. . . . He and I could have a future together, but we will never know. There will never be a next date. If he were to ask me out next weekend, he would appear weak. I could not ask him out again for fear of appearing obsessed." It is hard to see how such customs make for any sort of honesty, self-respect, or trust.

37. Carolyn Hax, "Tell Me about It," *Washington Post*, November 26, 2004, C4.

38. These findings and others are summarized in Linda J. Waite and Evelyn L. Lehrer, "The Benefits from Marriage and Religion in the United States: A Comparative Analysis," *Population and Development Review* 29, no. 2 (June 2003): 255–75.

## Chapter 8  The Christian Family and the Limits of Politics

1. Mardi Keyes, "The Challenge of Homosexuality: Speaking the Truth in Love," audiotape distributed by Christians for Biblical Equality, Minneapolis.

2. S. Scott Bartchy, *First Century Slavery and 1 Corinthians 7:21* (Eugene, OR: Wipf and Stock, 2003), 62.

3. Pope Gregory XVI, Apostolic Letter, 1839; quoted in Rodney Stark, *For the Glory of God* (Princeton, NJ: Princeton University Press, 2003), 344.

4. Rodney Stark, *Glory*, 339.

5. As part of that indifference, many of these cultures tolerated or ignored sexual relations between grown men and adolescent boys, although the modern

notion of "homosexual identity," gay marriage, or even sexual relations between two grown men would have been inconceivable to them.

6. Gary S. Becker, *A Treatise on the Family* (Cambridge: Harvard University Press, 1993), 30–31.

7. U.S. Department of Commerce, Bureau of the Census, *Historical Statistics of the United States: Colonial Times to 1970* (Washington, DC: U. S. Government Printing Office, 1975), 126.

8. Michael Kinsley, "Am I Blue? I Apologize for Everything I Believe In. May I Go Now?" *Washington Post*, November 7, 2004, B7.

9. Robert E. Rector, Kirk A. Johnson, Lauren R. Noyes, and Shannan Martin, *The Harmful Effects of Early Sexual Activity and Multiple Sexual Partners among Women: A Book of Charts* (Washington, DC: Heritage Foundation, 2003).

10. Robert Rector, Kirk A. Johnson, and Jennifer A. Marshall, "Teens Who Make Virginity Pledges Have Substantially Improved Life Outcomes," Heritage Foundation, Washington, DC, September 21, 2004.

11. David Blankenhorn, *Fatherless America* (New York: BasicBooks, 1995), 19.

12. Irwin Garfinkel and Sara S. McLanahan, *Single Mothers and Their Children* (Washington DC: Urban Institute, 1986), 30–31; quoted in Blankenhorn, *Fatherless America*, 26.

13. Bradley Gerstman, Christopher Pizzo, and Rich Seldes, *Marry Me! Three Professionals Men Reveal How to Get Mr. Right to Pop the Question* (New York: Cliff Street, 2000), 10.

14. Ibid., 205.

15. Ibid., 191.

16. Stark, *Rise of Christianity*, 95.

17. Cal Thomas and Ed Dobson, *Blinded by Might: Why the Religious Right Can't Save America* (Grand Rapids: Zondervan, 1999), 58; David W. Machacek, "Same-Sex Culture War," *Religion in the News* 7, no. 1 (spring 2004): 6.

18. My translation, based on Alfred Marshall, *The RSV Interlinear Greek-English New Testament* (Grand Rapids: Zondervan, 1970), 668. Immorality within the church is another matter. Here Paul warns us of the "leavening" effect of sin, enabling it to spread throughout the community. In 1 Corinthians 5:1–2, 5–7 Paul writes: "It is actually reported that there is immorality among you, and such immorality as is not found even among pagans; so that a man has his father's wife. And you are puffed up (defensive?) rather than mourning. Remove this man from among you. . . . Deliver him to Satan for the destruction of the flesh, in order that the spirit may be saved in the day of the Lord. Your boasting is not good. Do you not know that a little leaven leavens the whole lump of dough? Purge out the old leaven, that you may be renewed" (my translation, based on Marshall, 667). While church communities are freed from the obligation to judge nonbelievers, they must still guard against immorality among those called brother or sister. Otherwise the tolerated sin will spread to the entire community.

One can imagine the drama that was playing out in the Corinthian church. A man loves his father's young widow, who is forbidden him by laws against incest.

He tells everyone at church of his dilemma. What should he do? They sympathize with and defend him. Paul tells them to stop. In turning the man who was sleeping with his stepmother over to Satan (satan as tempter and tester, not tormentor), they will be withdrawing their support of him in order that he may suffer the full impact of his sins and turn away from them. Paul later refers to this incident (2 Corinthians 7:8–13) and expresses his joy that his rebuke led to repentance, although it isn't clear whether the penitent was the man who committed the sin or the church that supported him.

Of course, this is not to say that sinners should be barred from attending church. If that were so, not only could no one come to repentance, no one would be able to come at all. Rather, Paul would have us send away those who wish to be justified and accepted in their immoral behavior.

19. Thomas and Dobson, *Blinded by Might*. Describing their jubilation at Reagan's election, Thomas gives one of my favorite lines of all time: "Had we not been Baptists we would have danced in the streets" (21).

20. Ibid., 26.

21. Ibid., 30–31.

22. Ibid., "Preface to the Second Edition," 7.

23. Ibid., 13.

24. "Work Urged for Welfare Mothers," *San Jose Mercury News*, June 4, 1993, 6A—a report on statements made by Health and Human Services Secretary Donna Shalala. See also Jason DeParle, *American Dream* (New York: Viking, 2004), 96–98, 134.

25. Richard Posner, *Sex and Reason* (Cambridge: Harvard University Press, 1994), 166.

# Index